AMONG STRANGERS

A Family Story

Marietta Pritchard

IMPRESS

NORTHAMPTON, MASSACHUSETTS

*for Howie —
Time passes, friendships
stay —
Marietta*

For my mother,
Eva Fürth Perl,
who both understood and exercised
the power of memory

I felt the same astonishment as in reading a fairy-tale where
turrets and a terrace come to life and turn into men and women.
In this sense of the words, we may say that history, even mere
family history, restores old stones to life.

—Marcel Proust,
Remembrance of Things Past: The Guermantes Way

Contents

Acknowledgments

M Y GREATEST DEBT is owed to my mother, who gave me her father's letters as well as an incredibly generous measure of her time and expertise. Before her death in 2003, she had read one of this book's earlier drafts and, I'm happy to say, with considerable pleasure. She would have surely been delighted with the final volume beautifully crafted by James McDonald of Impress.

Others whose practical assistance and encouragement have kept me moving include Mel Heath, who published versions of two sections in the *Massachusetts Review*; Chris Jerome and Dick Tedeschi, severe and excellent readers and editors; Cathy Portuges, whose own Austro-Hungarian experience provided a crucial and sympathetic sounding board; Caz Phillips, who gave me hope; a writing group consisting of Mickey Rathbun, Terry Allen and Susan Rieger, who suffered through some of my early efforts; my son Will and daughter-in-law Mo Healy, as well as Warner and Ann Berthoff, all of whom stayed interested; and my husband, Bill, who would really have preferred to have me reading Wordsworth the whole time.

AMONG STRANGERS

A Family Story

This portrait of my grandmother Elza Fürth by Clemens von Pausinger was made in 1917, when she was 40.

1

Moving Beyond Endings

I DON'T KNOW MUCH GEOLOGY, but I'm always picking up stones. A dozen stones from the Massachusetts coast make a decorative pile on our side porch. Three stones from Cornwall sit atop a bookshelf on our staircase. The smooth-surfaced North American stones are rounded, apple sized; the Cornish ones, flattened, grooved as if by organic decay, fit easily in a closed hand. Stones from the same beach tend to look alike. Stories from the same family do too.

In recent years I've been collecting family stories, stories I'd probably heard but not listened to when I was younger. (It's hard to be interested in other people's stories when you're working so hard to get away from those people.) Family stories are like the stones on a beach. The action of the waves, the presence of certain minerals combine to produce similar effects, something like the way people who've been married a long time tend to look alike. They rub against each other in the stream of events until their remote genetics melt into a single format, the same gestures, the same voice, the same stories. Just as husbands and wives can become each other's offspring, each other's siblings, so basalt can come to look like granite, and quartz like flint if enough waves pass over them. A Jewish Hungarian Catholic from Westchester like me can begin to look and sound like an upstate New York Protestant like my husband, Bill—and vice versa.

Sometimes when my mother told a family story, I could hear my father's voice. Their voices were nothing alike—his Hungarian accent, low voltage, ironic, slightly gravelly; her Austrian accent, always intense, pausing for dramatic effect, seeking your assent, your response, pressing forward with the facts, with her own conclusions. But she would quote him sometimes, and then I heard him too. "Here on this hill, your father kissed me for the first time," she said after we'd climbed the ridge above her family's hometown in the Czech Republic. "Later on, when we became engaged, it was here that he said: 'You know, you are not marrying a smokestack.'"

I could hear my father's voice saying it, pithy, clever, knowing, seductive, mystifying. This was my father's kind of wit—so Hungarian in its juxtaposition of the concrete and the absurd, in its ironic tone, in its sophisticated way of sounding like an ancient peasant proverb. The smokestack he referred to was just below them, the central architectural feature of her family's match factories. My grandfather was a prominent, wealthy industrialist; my father a partner in a small commercial bank. Daddy was crafting this little proverb for her by way of predicting the life they would be living together in Budapest, a comfortable, elegant life, similar in some ways to that of her parents, yet different too.

My father's confident predictions did not come true, at least not in the long run. It all turned out differently. Their lives, our lives, were overturned, violently redirected by war and immigration, but saved too by my father's stubbornness, his knowingness, his ability to predict—or at least to guess right—just when it counted most. Solid as a rock: My mother often used the metaphor when looking back on their passage from one culture to another. "He was," she said, "my Rock of Gibraltar."

When you look at stones from a beach, it is probably good to find a geologist who can tell you what you are looking at—granite or basalt, quartz or flint. Otherwise you will see the rocks merely as curiosities, a comfortable weight in your hand. With family stories, there are no experts—or perhaps, you could say, anyone can pose as one. But there are some facts, hard, smooth, rocklike: In October of 1942 my maternal grandfather was imprisoned at Drancy, a Nazi concentration camp in France. His first wife, my grandmother, killed herself in July 1931. My parents, with my sister, Doris, and me, immigrated to the United States in April 1939.

What do these facts do to each other? How do they fit together? Which ones are most important? Which ones made me who I am or define what we call a family? How does the water of time and retelling flowing over and around them change their shape, remove their sharp edges, domesticate them, make them fit together in the palm of my hand, in a sunny corner of my side porch? There are real stones in my family stories—grave markers, the facades of buildings, precious gems. And there are missing stones—the grave of my grandfather in France, for one. Not all stones or stories are comforting. Some seem like prehistoric tools, made only for scraping, digging or cutting, still others for tearing from the pavement and hurling through windows. Some stories inhabit the shady, cobwebbed corners of memory; others, like huge ancient menhirs or dolmens, dominate the landscape with a capacity to measure time and space, to offer a reference point for where we are or have been. I offer these family stories in hopes of locating myself and others in the tides of time. Perhaps these stones will speak.

There are people who are, from an early age, by nature and inclination, attached to the past—anthropologists, historians, archivists, novelists and poets of their own lives, keeping meticulous or quirky records, looking back methodically or nostalgically or satirically. They go back to their hometowns, sniff the air for change or continuity. They keep in touch with their earlier selves. My husband and youngest son are among this tribe. I never was until I was well into middle age. I was simply too busy, too engaged, too willfully intent on the here and now to do much meditating on where I had been. I must have had a sense, too, absorbed from my father's spoken and unspoken injunctions, that the past might be a painful place, better avoided than confronted. It was better to keep looking forward for fear of seeing something terrible—what was it? something dangerous, forbidden. If I looked back, I or someone else might be destroyed. Remember the fate of Lot's wife, of Eurydice.

Still, after 50, it seems, almost everyone becomes a memoirist. Is the impulse simply hormonal, physiological, the flagging of desire, a weariness of the flesh that makes what has happened seem more exciting than what is to come? Or is it the acknowledgment, finally, of one's own inevitable death that brings the wish to set the record straight?

I had been interested enough in my family's past to encourage my father to write a memoir in his later years. But it was not until after his death in 1988 that I felt that interest turn to a mandate. I traveled a number of times to family homes and workplaces in Central Europe. I started learning Hungarian. I read and reread letters and other family documents. I bothered people, especially my mother, with questions. I took notes and photographs, kept journals and wrote essays. I haunted certain sections of the library. I was, it is true, a little obsessed. I needed to know more about my family's lives in a world that had been destroyed by war.

It was relatively easy to ask questions and guess and speculate about my parents,

My grandmother's ring, given to me by my mother.

whom I thought I already knew pretty well. But my grandparents' generation was truly a lost continent to me, a place that I had never seen and would never reach. The lives of those people, their voices, their rages, their charms, their joys, their habits, their gestures — these are as remote to me as the time in which they lived. Yet, mysteriously, as surely as if they had instructed me, I have learned from them.

"You act as though you grew up with a lot of servants," a neighbor with a wicked tongue once said to me many years ago. I was probably out in the yard in my jeans and workshirt, raking leaves or replacing a bicycle chain, trying to keep track of three small boys, trying to keep my sanity. But she had picked up something in my tone, in my bearing, an attitude of entitlement — not evident to me — that gave her an inkling of a life I had not even lived. It's true that my parents had been comfortable in their suburban New York existence, that we had a solid middle-class life, even some hired help. That was between 1941 and 1954, when a not-so-wealthy, one-paycheck family could easily afford a maid. But by the time of my neighbor's comment, my husband and I were living on his assistant professor's salary, plus what I could earn as a part-time schoolteacher. Still there was, evidently, something osmotically remembered, something in my manner that rubbed this woman the wrong way, and that something had been transmitted—as I now guess—from my magnificent grandmother through my mother to me. Call it a form of inheritance. But since my grandmother's virtues are not admired in a democracy, except in celebrities or movie stars, my neighbor's assessment confirmed the earlier opinion of my schoolyard days, where the consensus had often been, to my sorrow, that I was conceited, stuck-up. It was this grandmother, Elza Roheim Fürth, who became the subject of one of my first efforts to write about my family. Elza's suicide was in 1931, when she was 54, five years before I was born. Because there are so few stories about her, I cherish the ones I have.

Sometimes, when I wear her big ring, I try to imagine Elza Fürth, even though my mother's hand was the one I saw wearing it nearly every day during my child-hood. My mother, Eva Fürth Perl, had a hand a lot like mine, square and functional with roundish fingernails. I can see the ring on her neatly manicured hand or on the kitchen windowsill where she used to put it when she was scrubbing potatoes or mixing up a meatloaf, or on the glass-topped, chintz-skirted dressing table where she left it at night.

The story of the ring goes like this: Grandmother bought it—an index-finger-nail-sized sapphire encircled by diamonds—after winning at baccarat in the casino at Monte Carlo. She was there with her husband on holiday and had already spotted the big blue chunk in a jeweler's window. She went straight from the gaming tables to make her purchase. That was like her, the family commentators say, perfectly in character—impulsive, vain, beautiful, showy, extravagant.

She was also famously, embarrassingly, inefficient—my mother's word—not a good housekeeper, unable to plan ahead, careless of details. She would neglect to count up how many were coming for large dinner parties and so there would be confusion and quarrels with the servants, too few places set for the guests, not enough chairs to go around. And every July when she left for her four-week stay in one of Europe's grand spas—Marienbad or Carlsbad or Bad Kissingen—she could be counted on to forget some essential piece of clothing. Grandmother would leave from the railroad station of Sušice, site of the Fürth family homestead in Bohemia, with steamer trunks and hatboxes full of belongings, wearing a traveling suit that had an identical second skirt into which she could change en route, so as to arrive unwrinkled. And every year, at the first railway stop, she would remember that she had forgotten some crucial item. The next day a postcard would arrive for Madame Schmidt, the Belgian housekeeper: "Chère madame, envoyez moi …"

When I married, in 1957, my mother gave me the big sapphire ring. I rarely wore it until I was past my mid-50s, older than my grandmother was when she died. It seemed inappropriate for the wife of an English graduate student, inappropriate later for a teacher in the public schools, and later still for an editor at a small daily newspaper. And in any case, not really my style. Although I like large rings, I prefer the colorful opacity or low-intensity glow of semiprecious stones — amber and onyx, dark coral and lapis. Gemstones with their cold flash have no special appeal for me. But I wear this one because it is part of my history, and because I like the way it sits on my hand, and because I think it should not spend its life in a safe deposit box.

Perhaps where suicide has been ritualized and given a meaning, it is less troubling. Think of the proud Roman choosing death over slavery, Socrates drinking his cup of hemlock, Japanese kamikaze pilots going down in flames for their emperor. Even now, the families of Islamist suicide bombers seem persuaded that their children have died in a worthy cause. But in our Western, Judeo-Christian culture, suicide invariably brings with it a load of confusion — shame and anger and remorse and blame. How could she do this to herself? How could she do this to us? How could we have let this happen?

Still, there is surely also a measure of relief. Finally, she solved her problem, our problem. She was too unhappy to live, too sick. No one could have helped her. Now at last we can go on with our lives. But can we? Or does this impulse, this sickness, run in the veins, corrupt the very air? Are we, too, infected with the disease of despair? What will happen to us, to our children, our grandchildren? Is the ring that I wear poisoned, as in some dreadful fairy tale? Can I break the spell by saying the magic words? And what are those magic words?

The most vivid connection I have with my grandmother is a large pastel portrait that greets me from the bottom of our staircase. Made by Clemens von Pausinger, a fashionable portraitist, in 1917, the year she turned 40, it depicts a woman of the world, high-spirited and flirtatious, wearing a brown velvet suit that shows off her small waist and generous bosom. A dyed-to-match fur collar and dark brown

One of the only photos we have of my grandmother.

wide-brimmed hat with a large white bow at the back complete the outfit. A lorgnette in her hand is tilted teasingly outside the compass of the picture.

My grandmother is largely missing from the family photo albums—strange for a family that enthusiastically embraced the camera. There are both snapshots and formal photos of my mother, of her sister, Gretl, of my grandfather Ernst Fürth, and other friends and relations, but only a couple that I have seen of Elza. It seems she avoided the camera, perhaps preferring a medium over which she could exercise greater control.

Grandmother was Hungarian, from the city of Mohács, a place with an unhappy history, site of the decisive 1526 defeat of the Hungarians by the Turks. After Elza married, her family, the Roheims, descended upon the Fürth household in Sušice every summer, with "their Magyarian appetites and loud manners," as my aunt Gretl described them. Elza's mother, my great-grandmother Roheim, had, like her daughter, a fine mezzo-soprano voice. This accomplishment was taken seriously, and the summer entourage always included their singing teacher from Dresden. Great-grandmother Roheim was undisciplined and often alarmingly uncorseted. She was also greedy, famous for complaining loudly at meals about missing items. The story goes that no matter how much food was already heaped on her plate, she would exclaim: "I didn't get any mushroom sauce yet," or "What? No red beets today?" The Roheims were not only numerous and disruptive, but also in a perpetual state of financial collapse. Great-grandfather Roheim was a "loser and a hapless speculator," writes my aunt. The family required continuous support from their son-in-law, my grandfather, an heir to his family's thriving match industry.

Despite her disheveled family, Elza must have seemed a fine bride for Ernst Fürth. She was vivacious, charming, fashionable, the product of a finishing school education that included French and English. Heads turned when she entered the room. Although she didn't play games herself, she followed the new British fashion by having a tennis court built for family and guests on the grounds of the match factory. And she knew how to get her way: Summer squashes were planted over the factory's steam lines so that she could eat like a Hungarian despite the chilly Bohemian climate. She could also be the philanthropical society lady—especially later, when the family moved to Vienna—working during World War I to raise funds for the Red Cross and the Vienna Choir Boys.

She was a woman with many admirers but no friends, and clearly too self-centered to be much of a mother. She consigned the care of her daughters to nursemaids and governesses, as was customary for women of her position. But she seems to have gone well beyond conventional detachment. She was not attentive, not loving, not even particularly companionable to her children. By contrast, my grandfather provided daily company. My mother remembered walks in the park and trips to museums and sitting after dinner at the dining room table while he read his newspaper and she did her schoolwork. There were few such memories of her mother. Still, both my mother and aunt recalled the pleasures of trying on elegant shoes and gowns in their mother's dressing room, one of the few places where Elza felt truly at home. It was here that she previewed outfits before a trip; here that the hairdresser came every morning. In the closets, writes my aunt Gretl, "there were colored silk stockings, and always a box of Gerbeaud chocolates behind the stacks of lingerie. I sometimes got a piece to eat; they smelled more of perfume than of chocolate and were a little stale, but that's just the way I liked them." And eight decades afterwards, my mother could still express a small child's delight at lying on the lush white bear rug in her mother's bedroom.

Both daughters disapproved of their mother's carelessness and excesses, and modelled their own lives in conscious opposition to these qualities. My grandmother's worst, unhappiest self seems to have been self-pitying, vain, dissatisfied, "hysterical"—a wild woman to be feared and avoided. Her own inner turmoil brought her to the final, despairing, defining act of her life.

The physicians did not have a name for it, the illness that caused my grandmother to lose drastic amounts of weight, that brought on a plague of disfiguring liver-colored blotches all over her body. My mother believed that, among other things, her mother's troubles were related to menopause, and that Elza could not bear the idea of getting old, of losing her beauty. She had always been "nervous," probably always prone to manic depression. Did she know that her husband was most likely involved with another woman? Or was the marriage of her younger daughter the final blow, the unmistakable end of her youth? On my parents' wedding day, always described like something from a dark gothic tale, Elza tried to talk my mother out of marrying, insisting that the bridegroom still had a mistress. She tried to keep Mother from putting on her wedding gown. Elza was accompanied to the wedding by a physician who was prepared to give her injections if necessary.

Perhaps my grandmother could also be seen as one in a long parade of talented, energetic bourgeois women who never found work equal to their capacities. Extravagant purchases, the manipulative exercise of charm, and explosions of rage seemed to be her only outlets. And perhaps spiritual fulfillment, even sanity, were all the more difficult for a beautiful woman in a society that valued beauty so highly. It was too easy for her to be purely ornamental. She may have been a jewel in her husband's crown, but she was ultimately a hungry soul. When I read of the treatment given to "nervous" women of her class in that era—treatment consisting largely of inactivity and isolation—I feel a great sadness for her.

On July 16, 1931, Elza Fürth jumped to her death from a window of Vienna's Cottage Sanatorium, a glorified spa where people went for rest cures, to recover from unhappy love affairs or too much good food and drink. She had been sent there with a private nurse who was supposed to administer medication and keep an eye on her. The nurse had gone to breakfast when Elza ended her life.

The suicide occurred only two and a half months after my mother's marriage to George Perl. The young couple had set up housekeeping in Budapest, my father's home city, and my mother, 24, was just pregnant with my sister. When my father got the news in his office, he phoned the dentist where my mother had gone for an appointment, telling him to keep her there until he could arrive to deliver the news in person. He and my mother traveled quickly by train to Vienna, then took a cab to the morgue of the cemetery, where the body had been laid out.

Surely my grandmother's suicide came as a shock, like any suicide, but it was also, like some suicides, no great surprise. Elza had threatened it for years, although the doctors—those great Viennese experts—had said it was just talk, not a real danger. In fact Vienna was suicide capital of the world at the time. It was a kind of grisly fad. Almost every family my parents knew included someone who died this way.

My mother believed that before her mother's suicide, my grandfather was already involved with Ella Siebert, the woman who became his second wife, and who was deeply resented—*despised* was Mother's word—by both of her future stepdaughters. Unlike my grandmother, she was unafraid of the camera, and appears in a number of photos as a strong, rather horsefaced, elegant woman. She was eminently sane, a fine bridge player (my grandfather loved bridge), and extremely—once again my mother's term, this time pronounced with considerable venom—*efficient*. The family saw her as opportunistic, gold-digging, and perhaps, worst of all, utterly unrefined. She was—and this became important only later—a Gentile. She remained loyal to my grandfather to the end, traveling with him from Vienna to France after the Nazis took over Austria, helping to keep his life bearable in exile, probably engineering his release from the Nazi camp at Drancy in December 1942, and finally, burying him just three weeks later on French soil. But it was because of Ella, my mother believed, that her father could not be persuaded to come to the United States before the war when the rest of the family did, not wishing to endure his daughters' animosity toward his second wife. After the war, it was Ella who inherited most of the remains of Grandfather's fortune—his real estate in Vienna and his valuable Austrian pension.

But my mother and her sister had their mother's jewels. After Elza's death, their father called his two daughters into his office, where the jewelry lay in a pile on his desk. With a single swift gesture, and without a word of explanation or discussion, he divided the pile in two, one for each daughter. And so, in what has always seemed to my mother an irony of fate, it was the much-maligned extravagance of my grandmother that survived the war and the loss of the family fortune. It was Elza's expensive, showy jewelry—my big ring among others—that, for all they knew in their early immigrant years, comprised almost all the material benefits my mother and her sister were able to salvage from the wreckage of that past.

Not all family pasts result in so much wreckage. Not all families leave behind such eloquent and painful remains. As a writer and amateur historian, I sometimes feel like the grubbiest of treasure hunters, picking through the rubble of terrible disasters for human remains—wedding rings, old coins, bent silver spoons, bits of torn clothing and crumpled photographs.

Fortunately for me, ours is a family of many writers—correspondents, diarists, memoirists. This has been a comforting habit for immigrants, people who have lost their homelands, friends, relations, wealth, standing and material possessions. My mother kept every word my father ever wrote to her from their first flirtation until his final illness. My aunt Gretl recorded memories of her early life. I have my father's memoir and my mother's recollections written during their later years. I have many of the letters my parents wrote to me and those I wrote to them. And here I sit at a keyboard. All this ink on paper or in the electronic ether gives detail and dimension to a past that cannot otherwise be revisited.

Both of my maternal grandparents' lives ended in dramatic and terribly sad ways. Elza Fürth's drama was largely internal, a theater of her own making, yet probably also beyond her control. The short account of her life given here is as close as I can come to a full portrait. My grandfather's last years, by contrast, were part of huge public events—World War II and that cataclysm of evil we call the Holocaust. My grandmother died because she could not bear to live any more; my grandfather perished a victim of history, a Jewish refugee trapped in Nazi-occupied France.

The disastrous endings of both lives tend to blot out their individuality—all their nobility and frailties, all their strange quirkiness, all the odd or conventional elements of their distinctive personalities. In writing about these forebears I have hoped to rescue the complexity of who they were from the dreadful oversimplification of their deaths—to find the wedding rings and spoons, and, yes, flesh and bones, buried in the rubble. For my grandmother's story, I have used the small shreds of information available to me. Because there has been no way to let her speak for herself, she remains a static if vivid figure in the background. Telling my grandfather's story—the catalyst for this book—has involved the opposite process: trying to compress, narrate and make sense of an immense volume of written material along with my mother's amazingly detailed recollections. Because so much is known, written and remembered about him, because he exercised such a strong, conscious influence on both of my parents, and because his last years were played out during some of the most important moments of the past century's history, Ernst Fürth has come to take center stage in my family story.

Like so many assimilated, middle-class European Jews of the time, my grandfather saw himself as more Austrian than Jewish. His education was classical, his inclinations highly ethical but thoroughly secular. For several generations in his family, there had been no formal religious observance, except for marriage and burial. And although Austria-Hungary was rife with anti-Semitism, Ernst Fürth had moved easily in an elite, integrated social world. He avoided the tribal, the parochial, the narrowly provincial. He was an agent of change, an actor on the great stage of industrial progress. His life had seemingly described a steady march forward. A successful man of the world, he had been able to control what happened to himself, to others, to large quantities of essential goods. He had led an active, socially useful daily existence, enjoying the comforts of life and the company of lively, intelligent and (preferably) attractive people. The first 70 years of his life gave no outward clue to its end. But the triumph of fascism altered everything. The protections afforded by all that the Fürth family had built up and valued most highly over the generations—wealth, status, education, culture, taste, manners, progressive attitudes, community service, decency—these were as nothing in the face of Hitler's insane campaign to destroy those he had designated as his mortal foes: the Jews. My grandfather saw himself as an individual, as did millions of others. Yet they all became part of a huge, sometimes undifferentiated flood of suffering.

As conditions deteriorated and it looked more and more as though Ernst and Ella Fürth were not going to get out of Occupied France, my grandfather predicted sadly in one of his letters to my parents in the U.S. that for me, his youngest grandchild, "the memory of me will soon vanish, unless it is possible to renew it in this life." Part of my effort here is to revoke that prediction, to enlist the transformative power of words to resurrect memories that I never acquired in the ordinary flow of events. My hope is that by redefining "this life," I can expand it to mean not just my grandfather's life, nor even just my own life or the lives of my children, my sister's children and grandchildren—but the longer and endlessly renewable life of a book.

The story told in these pages is one of war and exile, of identities lost and found, of uprooting and assimilation, of family ties and family alienation, of losses and gains, of growing up and growing old, of permanence and change, war and peace. Common themes, yet like all individual stories, their mingled strands are as distinctive as any fingerprint. My family were not typical immigrants; their histories were odd and special. My sister and I did not simply become "perfect American girls," in my grandfather's touchingly hopeful words. And my grandfather was not just one of the people destroyed by the Nazis. Like stones in a stream, a family's stories need to be turned over and looked at in different lights to bring out their flaws and strengths, their striations and shimmer—their particulars.

Eva and George Perl were married for 57 years. George died in 1988, Eva in 2003.

2

Inheritance

HERE ARE SOME OF THE PARTICULARS. It is the summer of 2001. I am having dinner, which I have prepared and am eating with Mother. We sit at the counter of her kitchen pass-through. She faces the living room and I look into the tiny, somewhat gloomy kitchen of her condo, where at 94, she still lives alone. I have made one of the meals she can still eat—sauteed scallops with plenty of lemon on the side, boiled rice, and steamed, chopped spinach. She has a full set of dentures, which can no longer be made to fit well, the dentist says, because of bone loss and weight loss. She now has trouble chewing, and lately has begun to have trouble swallowing as well. There have been a number of choking incidents, some, to her particular dismay, in restaurants, where she now goes only infrequently. She still cooks for herself and continues to do it inventively and well, but I have arranged to come several times a week and join her to make and share an evening meal.

Mother has lived in this condo in Amherst, Massachusetts, since 1984. She has been alone in it since 1988, when my father died of congestive heart failure at 92. His was a mostly gradual but sometimes dramatic decline, with trips to the emergency room, a heart attack and several cardiac "versions," those procedures so popular on TV where the patient's heart is jolted back to life by electric shocks from paddles to the chest. Considering how little time she spent on her own before her husband's death, Mother has managed her widowhood with relative contentment. That is not to say she has become less demanding of perfection or attention from the people around her, but she has shown no signs of the depression and lethargy that sucks the life from many people's final years. A while back she had a highly successful hip replacement, but now, following a period of restored mobility, she suffers terribly from arthritis in her spine, and more recently in her knees. For a time she used a cane, and now needs a walker. Surgery has been suggested both for her knees and back, but she has refused. Although the doctor praises the strength of her heart and lungs, she is too old, she thinks, for another major operation. After an active and vigorous earlier life that included many years as an excellent tennis player, she has followed a routine that has involved regular physical therapy and daily swimming at a local health club, which has kept the worst at bay until recently. She now takes heavy-duty painkillers, narcotics such as OxyContin that she balances carefully to provide relief without too much dulling of her extremely sharp wits. It is a fine line that sometimes gets crossed in either direction.

After some consideration of the alternatives—we had looked at assisted living arrangements, which she rejected—she has had stairlifts installed on both of the staircases in her three-level condo. This was a considerable expense, $18,000, but still cheaper than moving and paying rent for a tiny room, especially, she decided, when you consider the enforced sociability and substandard meals. She makes her own

Eva and George shown pursuing different sports before their marriage in 1931.

decisions, although she discusses these matters with my sister and me. It is understood that I will help her stay in her home as long as possible—until the end.

Mother has lived carefully within her means for many years. When my father's finances collapsed in the '70s, he never fully discussed it with Mother. That would not have conformed to the rules under which he operated: It was a husband's job to make the money, a wife's to make the life. Instead he turned to my sister and me for help. My mother knew approximately what was happening, but not why or to what extent. She became skillful at living frugally, even within their expensive milieu of Scarsdale, New York. When my parents arrived in Amherst in 1984, they were still driving the Plymouth Valiant that they'd had for 18 years, but because they had sold their small house in the suburbs, they could easily afford this condo in Amherst. In any case, they found that life here in a college town was culturally rich and, of course, much less materially expensive than in their home of over 40 years.

The trajectory of their economic lives had described great peaks and valleys. Mother was the daughter of a wealthy industrialist. Ernst Fürth had been the director of all match manufacturing in the Austro-Hungarian Empire, and Mother grew up during the First World War in Vienna in an atmosphere of restrained luxury. There were servants and a grand apartment where balls were held. My grandmother was able to indulge her taste for fabulous jewelry, and there was regular travel. Nevertheless, both daughters attended state schools and despite their mother's extravagances, were warned against conspicuous consumption. Though he himself had been an officer in the Austrian cavalry, Ernst did not let his daughters ride horseback, because he felt it was too showy during World War I, a time of terrible want. Still, Mother knew where she came from, and had expectations that her life would be made easy by the family's wealth and position.

My father's pedigree was less impressive than Mother's, though his resume was distinguished. He was Hungarian from a solidly bourgeois background, and had attended Budapest's best secondary school, the Evangelikus Gimnazium. (Other graduates included famous and infamous scientists and mathematicians, Leo Szilard, John von Neumann, Edward Teller.) As a young man, he had managed his grandfather's agricultural properties in eastern Hungary, then made his way on his own into the world of finance. He held a law degree, and with his two half brothers had founded a successful merchant bank in Budapest that specialized in agricultural loans. He was an official with the newly founded Hungarian stock exchange, while

A parlor in the Fürth house in Sušice, now in the Czech Republic.

also keeping up his interests as a literary intellectual. When he married my mother in 1931 — she was 24, he 36 — he was a person of substance, already on his way up.

When they left Europe in 1939 to come to America, my father was able to bring with him enough money, about $20,000, to support his family of four for three years without working. I remember his description of a conversation with an unfriendly cab driver who took a classic anti-immigrant stance. "You immigrants are going to take jobs away from us," the cabbie said. And my father replied: "No, on the contrary, I hope to hire you." He had looked into the world of agriculture, mainly because he and my mother and sister and I had been admitted to this country on the strength of his "agricultural specialist's" visa. But he soon gave up that idea and moved back into finance, finding a desk in the old New York brokerage firm of Haydn, Stone, where he worked as an independent investment counselor. For a long time he prospered

The corner of the room with Grandmother's desk.

there, making it possible for him and Mother to travel in Europe every summer, stay in good hotels and live comfortably at home. In London, they often stayed at the Dorchester, Elizabeth Taylor's favorite hotel. My sister and I did all the things middle-class suburban girls did—took piano and riding lessons, were sent to good summer camps and to college at Wellesley and Radcliffe.

As I said, the topic of money was not discussed in our house. That would have

Ernst Fürth with his daughters, Eva, left, and Gretl.

been considered crass or bad manners. Instead the conversation was supposed to operate on a more elevated plane, and we participated in a very European atmosphere of high expectations and high culture. The house was full of books, and we made regular trips to Manhattan for museums, concerts and operas. During the years we were growing up, there always seemed to be enough money to do what we wanted. We knew that the world was full of people with more money than taste, and that taste was by far the more valuable commodity. I can hear my mother declaring that someone's clothes or house were "tasteless," like an evangelical Christian pronouncing damnation. So although we knew not to be flashy or extravagant, I can't ever remember being told, "We can't afford that." Then at some point, Daddy guessed wrong about the timing of one of the economic downturns and sold too soon. By the time our parents arrived in Amherst, they were living on greatly reduced means, although my father managed to rebuild his stock portfolio enough that Mother could have a more secure old age. And she, as it turned out, became quite adept at managing that portfolio after he was gone.

After my father's death, I found that I wanted to know more about his family.

That realization was sparked by a trip to Hungary in 1989 with my mother and sister. After that I took several more trips to Hungary and decided that I'd try to learn Hungarian, which my sister Doris—always known as Dodo—and I had not learned as children. This involved weekly sessions with my mother and my good friend Cathy Portuges, a film historian with her own Hungarian roots. I soon began writing about my experiences in Hungary, and before long my interest branched out into my mother's Austrian family. In 1996, I published an essay about Mother's mother, trying, among other things, to make some sense of her suicide in 1931. Shortly thereafter, for my birthday, Mother presented me with two of her father's letters from Occupied France. She had a cache of these letters, but had not looked at them in some 50 years. Thus began a major project for the two of us. Together we worked our way through the letters, more than 200 of them, she translating in her slanted hard-to-read cursive on yellow lined pads, I transcribing them to my computer. In between we discussed and tried to unravel the details of my grandfather's sad existence from the time of his departure from Vienna in the spring of 1938 until the time of his imprisonment in the French/Nazi concentration camp of Drancy and his death in 1943. By the time of her death in 2003, I had written several hundred pages, incorporating selections of the letters into the makings of a family memoir.

While Mother and I are finishing our dinner, deep in conversation—she is a great talker—the phone rings. I answer, and a voice identifies itself as a representative of Blake & Blake, a Massachusetts firm of genealogists. This outfit had been sending me what looked like generic glossy brochures, as they had my mother, sister, and cousin Fredi Strasser. What is a genealogist? Someone who offers to take you to Ireland to show you your great-grandfather's grave? Who wants to send you the family coat of arms? We had all been throwing their materials out. After I hear who it is, I say we aren't interested and hang up the phone. About ten minutes later, the phone rings again. "Please don't hang up," the woman's voice says. "Is this the home of Eva Perl, and is she the daughter of Ernst Fürth who died in France in 1943?" Now she has my attention. All of these communications, she says, have to do with a property in Vienna that my mother may be heir to. She says the address, and my mother immediately knows what this is about.

The five-story building at Schmidgasse 14 is substantial and impressive, a broad-shouldered neo-Renaissance stone palazzo; but because it stands in a narrow street, it's hard to get far enough away from it to take in its scale. From the back you can get a better sense of it, with its open courtyard and large garden where staff and patients of the Sanatorium Fürth, a private clinic built in 1887, might have taken the air or gone for a short stroll. Mother was born in this building, had her appendix removed here, and recuperated here after an automobile accident. The building was bought in 1895 by her father's brother, Julius, a physician who had attended medical school in Vienna. Sigmund Freud, a classmate, spoke at Julius' funeral. Julius Fürth ran the clinic, now known as the Sanatorium Fürth, and his family lived in an apartment attached to the building. Mother often came to play with her cousin Lothar in the garden. Lothar was the eldest of her many cousins, and he, too, became a physician and succeeded his father as director of the sanatorium. Mother remembers that later, when she was studying for a social work degree, Lothar helped her study for her anatomy exam. The Sanatorium Fürth was known as a lying-in hospital, but also as an international center for medical education. Doctors from all over the world came to learn modern techniques there.

On March 12 of 1938, the Nazis arrived in Vienna, bringing with them a well-documented reign of terror against Jews. Jewish physicians like Lothar Fürth were no longer allowed to practice. The building was "Aryanized," seized from its rightful owners. A few weeks later, in one of the Nazis' favorite forms of humiliation, Lothar and his wife were made to scrub the sidewalks outside the clinic while a jeering crowd watched. The following day, Lothar entered the clinic with his wife, and injected them both with fatal doses of morphine. They died there on April 3. An article in the April 4 *New York Times* mentions their death.

The building was held by the Nazis during the war, and afterwards their successors, the Austrian government, leased it out. In a turn that still strikes me as ironic, it became an annex to the American embassy, housing the Fulbright Commission and U.S. Information Agency, among other offices. My mother, sister and I visited there in 1989, when we spent a few days in Vienna en route to a longer stay in Hungary. Mother had written ahead to the embassy to ask if we might visit the building, telling them something about its—and her—history. The stiff, formal reply was that we were welcome to visit, but, because of security concerns, could only come into the public parts of the building. So we walked around in the elegant entrance rotunda, but were not permitted to set foot in the garden or any other part of the building.

Following the phone call from Blake & Blake, mother is excited by the unexpected news that she might at this late date be named an heir to the sanatorium. But her response is wary as well. Since the end of the war, she has lived through many ups and downs of this sort, many raisings of hopes and expectations only to have them dashed. My father had spent decades filing claims against various governments and entities to reclaim property and wealth that had been lost during the war. He did his research carefully. I remember, for instance, his going to the library to learn the details of a tank battle between the Russians and Germans that had taken place on or near one of his grandfather's agricultural properties in Hungary. He and his brother had a claim for the restitution of that property. Eventually, when he was 90, the Hungarians released $20,000 of the $100,000 that he had claimed. It was to be parcelled out to him in annual payments of $1,000! He died two years later. None of the rest was ever paid.

There had been other, more successful claims, but on the whole my mother had come to think that her husband's time could have been better spent than endlessly working on what she saw as hopeless projects. He had a tiny Dickensian room at the back of the house behind their bedroom, where he kept the files of these cases—"the messy room," Mother called it—and neither she nor any housecleaner was allowed to touch his papers.

In a small but rich collection of items I have from my mother's house, I find several folders labelled in my father's late shaky hand. One says "Hungary," and is the record of the exchanges about his last claims for properties there, another says "Czech," and is about the claims Mother and her sister, Gretl, had for stock in their family's match manufacturing business. The money retrieved from the Czech claims helped my parents move to Amherst. There is another folder, too, labeled "Immigration 1938–40," and it contains not only the documents submitted for our citizenship, but many others as well. Especially poignant to me are my father's applications for sea transport from Europe, which begin in March 1937. There seemed to have been at least two different sets of reservations, the second of which, in April 1939, we used to make our departure from Le Havre for the United States on the S.S. *Manhattan*. There is a lading list, with all the baggage that the family carried, which was to be collected from Pall Mall Deposit at 10 St. Alban's Street, London. Some of this must have been sent directly from Budapest after we left, because I remember being told that when the family left for Switzerland, shortly after New Year's, my parents carried only suitcases, as if for a winter vacation, so as not to attract unwanted attention. The lading list, by contrast, includes eight trunks: One is described as black brass-bound, another green canvas brass-bound, and among others, there is a wardrobe trunk. I remember that trunk well, which sat in the basement of the house in Scarsdale in which my sister and I grew up. It was one of those early-20th-century marvels, black with prominent wooden ribs. It stood up on its end and had many drawers and even places to hang clothes on special small hangers. Also listed is a black typewriter case, which no doubt held the small machine with Hungarian accent marks that I knew in later years. There is a large wicker hamper in a crate, and a pram. That last would have been for me; I was only two and a half at the time.

Just naming these objects is affecting. These were the things they brought with them to start a new life. Even more affecting are the things they left behind, the life they could never retrieve or revisit, but most heartbreaking of all are the people that were lost.

In the summer of 2001, as we are learning about the Schmidgasse legacy, Mother is living on her Social Security check, plus a modest amount of income from her stock portfolio, a total of about $36,000 a year. She is proud of being able to manage in the condo, which is fully paid for, although there are property taxes and a monthly maintenance fee. She no longer travels, but there have begun to be major expenses connected with her failing health, and she worries about being able to keep up with them. She has hired someone to help her get bathed and dressed in the morning. Soon she will need help cooking her meals, and not long after the news about the building in Vienna, she will begin to have serious falls. She cracks a rib in her bathroom one Christmas Eve Day and spends Christmas the next year in rehab after injuring a knee. Now she will need round-the-clock care. Not long ago, at her request, I had sold two big pieces of her mother's jewelry to cover some of these

We sold the emerald turtle.

growing expenses. This selling of jewelry — most of it from their life in Europe — was something my parents did from time to time during various downturns in their fortunes. It was never a happy experience. My father always felt it went badly, that they had been cheated, that they sold at the wrong time or to the wrong buyer.

For me, the project was an anxious affair. I asked a friend with a great deal of experience in buying antiques what he recommended. He said there were highly respected dealers worldwide that I could contact and then send the pieces to. I'd have to put them in the mail? I asked, stunned. Oh, yes, people do that every day, he said. You just insure it at the post office for whatever you think it's worth. For a few dollars you can get thousands of dollars' worth of coverage.

I had no idea what they were worth, these two big emeralds. One was in a ring, dime sized, a round, faceted stone surrounded by a circle of diamonds. The other was a carved stone, much bigger, the size of one of those dime-store turtles they used to sell in my childhood. In fact, it was the figure of a turtle, a Fabergé-style piece, made to be worn as a pin. The turtle's back was grooved to show the pattern of its shell; its legs and head were hinged to move back and forth, and it had tiny ruby eyes. There was a gold grillwork on the underside holding the pin and clasp. For a time in the '20s, while she was studying in Paris, Mother lived as a paid guest in the house of an elegant French lady, Mme. Hirsch, a friend of her parents. She once appeared at a formal dinner wearing the turtle. The lady of the house took one look and sniffed: "My dear, if you are going to wear fakes, do not wear such big ones!"

I finally decided to take the two pieces to Boston to get an estimate from Shreve, Crump & Low's estate jewelry department. This slightly stodgy Boston firm has been doing business since the 18th century. Bill and I had bought our plain gold wedding bands there in 1957. I invited a friend to join me on this venture, but I still felt very vulnerable carrying these two valuable pieces in my purse, a hiker's black nylon fanny pack with lots of convenient compartments. I zipped the two pieces into one of these interior niches, then carried the pack more tightly and self-consciously than usual, feeling rather like an international spy with bits of radioactive materials on my person. A pleasant, businesslike gentleman took a careful look at the two objects with his loupe, and matter-of-factly made me an offer of $15,000 for the two. I could contact him any time, and bring—or mail—the pieces to him if my mother decided to sell them. I thanked him, took the jewelry back to Amherst, and asked Mother what she thought. These were parts of the family's history, but $15,000 would buy a lot of hours of personal care in these declining years. Mother was not sentimental about them. Sell, she said. So I took some pictures of the jewelry so that I would at least have those, and went back to Boston.

Hearing about the potential inheritance of Schmidgasse 14 opens the floodgates to all sorts of feelings. Mother remembers details of the building and the prestige of the institution, how Arabian sultans used to bring their children there to be treated for congenital hip problems, how she had met and gone to parties with young physicians from all around the world who were studying and observing at the sanatorium. It opened the gates to other kinds of feelings as well—expectations of unanticipated inherited wealth. These were feelings I had never harbored, since I had long known of my parents' straitened finances. They were feelings that Mother had surely suppressed after all these years of losses and disappointments, dangerous feelings, as anyone knows who has ever waited with bated breath and mouth watering for an inheritance. I found myself calculating, pricing, adding, subtracting, multiplying and dividing. What would a large building in central Vienna be worth? How many heirs would there be? We knew that my sister and I would inherit equally from our mother, and there was our cousin Fredi, the only survivor of Mother's sister, Gretl. But how many others? Our grandfather was one of eight siblings, and most of these people had offspring, though Mother knew of only a few of them. The diaspora of war and succeeding generations had spread them around the globe. Still, when we were growing up we had a running joke that we could not go anywhere with Mother without encountering one of her cousins. I myself had once found myself on a ski lift in Vermont with a previously unknown relative.

We filled out the forms Blake & Blake had sent us and set the ball rolling. But what kind of a ball was it? Perhaps, like Sisyphus, who was punished for being avaricious and deceitful, we had been assigned to a stone that we could push partway up the hill, only to have it roll back on us. Would this inheritance be nothing but a burden, bringing out only the worst in us? Sisyphus was not the only archetypal account of the wages of greed. There were all those fairy tales, the one about the fisherman's wife with a magical fish that fulfilled all her wishes until she went too far and found herself back in the hovel where she'd started. We know that the expectation of inheritance can have a corrosive effect on family relationships, sometimes even destroying the character and lives of prospective heirs. Dickens made this condition legendary in the endless case of Jarndyce v Jarndyce in *Bleak House*, which he introduces thus:

> This scarecrow of a suit has, in the course of time, become so complicated, that no man alive knows what it means. The parties to it understand it least; but it has been observed that no two Chancery lawyers can talk about it for five minutes, without coming to a total disagreement as to all the premises. Innumerable children have been born into the cause; innumerable young people have married into it; innumerable old people have died out of it. Scores of persons have deliriously found themselves made parties in Jarndyce and Jarndyce, without knowing how or why; whole families have inherited legendary hatreds with the suit. The little plaintiff or defendant, who was promised a new rocking-horse when Jarndyce and Jarndyce should be settled, has grown up, possessed himself of a real horse, and trotted away into the other world. Fair wards of court have faded into mothers and grandmothers; a long procession of Chancellors has come in and gone out; the legion of bills in the suit have been transformed into mere bills of mortality; there are not three Jarndyces left upon the earth perhaps, since old Tom Jarndyce in despair blew his brains out at a coffee-house in Chancery Lane; but Jarndyce and Jarndyce still drags its dreary length before the Court, perennially hopeless.

> Jarndyce and Jarndyce has passed into a joke. That is the only good that has ever come of it. It has been death to many, but it is a joke in the profession.

For several years, Mother and I worked through family documents.

Unlike the characters in *Bleak House*, we are managing, for the most part, to keep family relations in good order — no legendary hatreds brewing. So far, so good. One important preventive against getting into trouble is to be sure everyone is kept equally well informed. Quite quickly a lot of information begins flying around. We are soon in touch with a variety of enterprises and people: the legal genealogist in Vienna who uncovered the legacy; a legal practice that will handle the case; the government agency in charge of restitution. My sister, our cousin Fredi and I agree that we will keep each other posted about any news. E-mail is a great help here, since we can simply copy and forward to each other any communications we receive or send. Fredi is crucial to our enterprise since not only has he had wide experience in the business world, but even more important, he speaks and reads excellent German, and is willing to summarize documents for Dodo and me. In the meantime, it is hard to keep from imagining what we might do with a large sum of money that could drop into our laps. Mother, quite sensibly, is hoping to have extra money to pay her growing medical expenses. And like the little boy who was promised a rocking horse, I am already imagining spending my inheritance on a pied-à-terre in Portland, Oregon, where our youngest son and his family live.

A few months later, we receive some news from an unexpected quarter. Harry Moses, a producer from the CBS show *60 Minutes* wants to talk with us about a possible feature on this inheritance. Harry visits Fredi to discuss his ideas, then gets in touch with me as well, since I have become the informal family historian and know a great deal of Fürth family lore. Harry thinks the story of Schmidgasse 14 is pretty interesting. He has been there and seen the outsized photos of George Bush and Dick Cheney's faces hanging in the entrance rotunda. Like us, he finds it ironic that American government officials are working in a building that had been "Aryanized," and never returned to its rightful owners. But information keeps unrolling. He has a special interest in this story that is new to us. There are two brothers living in California, Chris and Rich Andrews, ages 47 and 51, who have learned that they, too, are heirs to this building. Did we know them? No, but we learn that they are the grandchildren of one of our mother's many first cousins, a woman who lived in New Jersey and whom we had met a few times during our childhood. She was Marie Redlich (née Fürth), known in the family as Mädi, a stylish woman who had been a wonderful tennis player in her youth.

The Andrews brothers had a terrible early life. They had lived with their divorced mother, a woman who suffered from schizophrenia, and at times the three had lived in extreme poverty, surviving on welfare and food stamps. During their mother's frequent hospitalizations, they had been farmed out to various other families. Eventually, when the boys were young teenagers, their mother committed suicide. Yet they had managed to thrive and make their way as adults, Chris as a technological entrepreneur and Rich as a tennis coach. (This seemed an interesting sidelight. They hadn't known their grandmother, the fine tennis player, but could it be that there was a tennis gene in the family? Mother had been a good player, too, and Dodo and I were still playing in late middle age.) They had received a similar letter to the one we'd had about the building in Vienna and were simply bowled over by it. They had known nothing of their prosperous forebears, nor had they known—equally astounding to them—that their mother had Jewish roots. As they put it, "We never knew we were Jewish."

Moses wants to interview the brothers and us, especially Mother. She is frail, but fully lucid. He plans to tell the story of the building and of Lothar Fürth's sad fate. Then he wants to stage a "reunion" between us and the Andrews brothers here in Amherst. My sister is at first highly resistant to the idea, but is eventually won over by my cousin and me. What do we have to lose? we argue. Perhaps the publicity will embarrass our government into putting pressure on the Austrians.

The *60 Minutes* troops come on fast and furious with an enormous show of power, technicians, equipment, schedules that swallow up any lives we might have thought were our own. We are not to communicate with the Andrews brothers, something Harry feels would spoil the "spontaneity" of the moment of meeting. So we bow to his request. We learn that Scott Pelley, a *60 Minutes* mainstay, will be conducting the interviews, one of them with my mother at her condo. The production people take one look at her carefully appointed living room and decide that it needs a few changes. We send Mother upstairs for a nap while they do this, since it seems best to avoid upsetting her. This is a woman who does not want even the position of a vase of flowers changed on her dining room table without her permission. In fact, the crew rearranges just about everything in the room so there will be space for the lights and camera people. They close the curtains to her beloved deck to keep the sunlight out. We now have a TV stage set.

The producers have done their homework, have been to Vienna, studied the archives, interviewed people connected with the building and its current fluid status. I have given Harry my writing about the family to read by way of background, and in the completed script, he will quote from it—unattributed, to my annoyance. Scott Pelley shows up. Mother by now is downstairs, quite at her ease, seemingly not bothered by the total transformation of her home. "I don't know what everyone is so nervous about," she observes calmly. "And you must be the interviewer." "How do you know?" asks Pelley, in his oleaginous, slightly pompous manner, his chin elevated a little more than necessary. "The double-breasted blazer," she says. I can hear her slight mockery, though he seems only to detect charming flattery.

Pelley interviews Mother for almost an hour. She is alert, composed, articulate, though slower than in the past. He asks at one point what she thinks should be done with the building, since up to this time, the Austrians have refused to hand it over. I can tell that he wants her to make a self-interested, acquisitive response. He wants her to insist that the Austrians return the building to the family so that she can profit from it. But she surprises him, reflecting on the family's commitment to social service, sidestepping the hoped-for personal gain. "I think," she says, "it should become a school or a library." This response does not make the final cut. What does make it, and this, it turns out, is the heart of the film, is the story of the Andrews brothers. They have been interviewed at length at home in California, telling the sad story of their childhood, and then in a cemetery, weeping over their mother's grave.

That evening we meet at Amherst's Lord Jeffery Inn for our much-hyped reunion. I have arranged for Mother to have a special menu, some kind of cream soup, so that she will not have to be embarrassed by her inability to chew an ordinary meal. She finally arrives and the cameras roll as Chris and Rich Andrews introduce themselves to us and vice versa. "Hi, I'm Chris," he says to Mother, bending over her in her wheelchair. "Hmmph," she says, nodding just barely graciously, but clearly unimpressed. At a certain point, Pelley raises his glass and intones, "To the Fürths!" and we all follow suit. It is a good meal, with plenty of filet mignon and nice wine, and we joke that even if the inheritance never comes through, at least we will have had a free dinner.

Naturally we were disappointed with the outcome. To tell a complicated story in

My cousin Fredi Strasser is interviewed by Scott Pelley of 60 Minutes.

12 minutes of TV time is simply impossible. Although the video contained many evocative images and some well-documented background history, what the producer mostly did was tell a simple story about the Andrews brothers and the discovery of their heritage. All subtleties were rubbed out, any smaller gems ground down to dusty clichés under the wheels of the great simplifying medium. Mother's hour-long interview was reduced to a 15-second sound bite. The segment was filmed in August of 2003 and aired in November as part of a program that included a piece in which Dan Rather interviewed a black family that had had to give up its children after nearly starving them to death. A friend who does not watch much television afterwards observed to me: "Marietta, everyone cries on that show." We did not cry. Those tears had long ago been shed, and they were for people, not for buildings. Mother, who was by then bedridden, saw the show, but I'm not sure how much she took in, since she had slipped badly both physically and mentally by then. She died a few weeks later, on December 9, 2003.

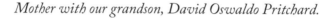

Mother with our grandson, David Oswaldo Pritchard.

When I visited there in October of 2007, the building at Schmidgasse 14 was empty.

3

A Building, Entanglements

A LOT OF WATER HAS FLOWED OVER THE DAM in the years since our TV appearance in 2003. When Chris and Rich Andrews came to Amherst under CBS' auspices, they spoke warmly and enthusiastically about the fact that they were now being reunited with their family and that this was after all the only important fact about the discovery of this inheritance. But differences soon began to emerge. For a time, we made jokes about settling into condos in "our" building, but Fredi, who had been a young teenager when his family left Europe, made it clear that he did not want to own any property in Vienna. His parents had never returned there as a matter of principle, and he had no special affection for the city. Quite the contrary, he believed—correctly—that the Austrians had been willing participants in the Nazi disaster. He thought the building should be sold, as did my sister and I. Chris disagreed, arguing that it should be kept in the family and turned into some sort of museum commemorating the accomplishments of the Fürths. He was himself prepared to raise the money, to buy the rest of us out, he said. This seemed an unlikely prospect, but at the time, all proposals were equal, since in any case we did not own the building yet.

Chris was an enthusiastic e-mailer, to put it mildly, often sending us three or four missives a day. He and his brother had visited Vienna as soon as they learned about the potential inheritance and had done a great deal of research on their own, making contact with government officials, giving their own regular interviews with the press. The Andrewses would not join us in making use of the Viennese representatives, despite initially agreeing to do so, but would work on their own, thereby avoiding the substantial one-third contingency fee. We had signed on for this representation and

Herbert Gruber, a legal genealogist, located and verified the heirs.

decided — despite some irritation with our lawyers at times — that it was worth it to have someone else on the scene doing the work for us. Chris was determined to do things his own way, and we struggled to come to some sort of cooperative equilibrium with him. But things spiralled into more serious kinds of misunderstandings, with accusations and even threats. Eventually my sister, Fredi and I decided that we could not usefully make common cause with the Andrews brothers. After several years of exchanges, we wrote Chris to say that from now on he should communicate only with our representatives.

Meanwhile, the battle to retrieve the building from the grip of the Austrian government continued. Our lawyers and legal genealogist had mounted a well-researched response to the government's claim that the building had been willingly sold to the Nazis and so was legally the property of the Austrian government. Lothar Fürth had been in bankruptcy, the Austrian officials countered, and needed to sell the building, so the government was entitled, as successor to the wartime regime, to keep possession of it. Our representatives quite properly replied that because of the anti-Semitic edicts that forbade people from frequenting Jewish doctors, Lothar was unable to conduct his business, and so had been made to give up the building. His financial distress had been forced upon him by cruel and illegal laws. The Austrians had been slow in facing up to restoring the wartime losses of Jews and others. It was only under pressure from the Clinton administration that they finally—almost 50 years after the end of the war—agreed to acknowledge the country's culpability and set up agencies to make good at least a fraction of those losses. One of these agencies, the In Rem Commission, was in charge of dealing with both real property and artworks stolen during the war. The commission eventually agreed with our claim, and the building was officially returned to the family in November of 2005, four years after we first heard about it.

After such a long wait, we were delighted by the decision. Once the Austrians had relinquished the building, the general view among the heirs was that it should be sold. Potential buyers were on the horizon, but it was clear that none of them would agree to take over the massive structure as long as it had a tenant. Finally, after a number of delays, the American government employees vacated the building in the spring of 2007.

But not so fast. The ownership was still only on paper and there was a long road yet to travel. The commission needed to be certain that all living heirs had been found. This was an enormous project, taken on by Herbert Gruber, the legal genealogist, who would study records of births, marriages, deaths and wills all over the globe. On our side of the family, our grandfather was one of eight siblings. All of Lothar Fürth's cousins and their descendants needed to be found and certified. Then there was the less numerous side of the family, Lothar's mother's descendants, the Rosenbergs. Each side was eligible for half of the legacy, according to the standard legal formula known as *per stirpes*. In February of 2003, I'd had an e-mail from Mr. Gruber listing nine heirs. By the time he finished his work at the end of 2006, the list numbered 38 heirs, some with shares as large as one-fourth, some, out at the ends of the family

The former sanatorium's courtyard had a garden where patients could sit or stroll.
On my visit in 2007 it had already begun to go to seed.

tree's branches, with shares of $^1/_{368}$. My own fraction was $^1/_{48}$.

Within our smaller group of heirs—my sister and I, our cousin Fredi, the two Andrews brothers and Marc Richter, a young Swiss lawyer—we eventually agreed that the building should be sold. So, despite the uncertainty about the final roster of heirs, we asked our representatives to look into selling the building so that we could get an idea of what the market might bring. They collected a number of bids, the best of which was 10 million euros (around $12 million at the time) from Alpha, a Ukrainian real estate developer. Even with the substantial contingency fee to be paid to the law-

The neo-Renaissance building is an imposing presence.

yers and genealogist, it was a lot of money, enough for a great many rocking horses.

Gradually the list of heirs expanded, and in general it seemed that all were in agreement about what should be done with the building. A sales agreement was drawn up with Alpha, who seemed likely to convert the former clinic to deluxe condos or a boutique hotel. All seemed to be moving along smoothly. Even the Andrews brothers had stopped complaining.

Then things took another turn. In December 2005, Mr. Gruber informed us that there was a newly identified heir, one Helene Templ, living in Vienna, who was

A skylight provides daytime illumination for the central atrium.

represented by her son, Stephan, a journalist. This new addition began to make waves. We had seen plenty of waves before. But this was something entirely new. Stephan Templ seemed determined to have our enterprise fail, but not before tying it in knots. Ironically, he is a writer about architectural history who has co-authored a book called *Unser Wien* (Our Vienna), a catalog of the Viennese buildings "Aryanized" by the Nazis. Schmidgasse 14 is one of the buildings listed in that book.

Templ refused to agree to sell, then refused to give his reasons, refused to communicate in any way with us or our lawyers, referring us to his lawyer, to whom he gave no authority. Of course, we all understood that no one would want to buy a building if one of the heirs was a holdout. Various meetings were set up, but Templ would either not show up or would appear and refuse to agree to anything. At one point he claimed to have another buyer, whom he would not name. This buyer would allegedly

Wrought iron scrollwork lines the main staircase.

pay considerably more for the building than Alpha, and Templ would agree to the sale, but only on condition that he would get much more than his legal portion. We were asked to put up nearly 2 million euros (about $3.3 million) toward his inflated share. After much consternation and discussion over this astonishing and outrageous demand, we and our representatives agreed that spreading out the cost among nearly 40 heirs was still worth it, if it meant the building could be sold quickly. Templ at this point withdrew his demand, but still refused to sell, still refused to give reasons. Marc Richter, who had been acquainted with him earlier, tried to reason with him, making, among others, the strong humanitarian argument that there were a number of financially needy, ill and elderly heirs whose situations could immediately be alleviated if this sale went through. Both Fredi and Marc tried phoning Helene Templ, and Marc even showed up at her apartment in Vienna in an attempt to persuade her to deter her son from his stalling tactics. Mrs. Templ seemed sympathetic at the time, but soon afterwards cut off all contact with any of the other heirs.

From time to time the media took an interest in the story of Schmidgasse 14 and our tangled claim. Austrian journalist Bernhard Odehnal wrote a long, well-researched article in *Die Presse* in March 2007 summarizing the history of the building and its current status, along with some background material about the Fürth family. Most recently, an article appeared in *Profil*, a Viennese publication, clearly based on interviews with Templ. The article described the "vultures" who make money from Holocaust victims. These vultures included genealogist Herbert Gruber, who was subjected to an interview that I can only describe as an ambush. At one point the article refers to "the only heiress living in Vienna," who is described as having suffered at the hands of the Nazis and still not recovered. What a collection of ironies! First of all to speak as if Helene Templ were the only heir to have suffered at the hands of the Nazis; but more to the point, to ignore the fact that it was Templ himself, with his mother's collusion, who was now causing suffering, victimizing the victims, their children and grandchildren.

October 2007. I have come to Vienna to see for myself some of the assorted characters in this ongoing—endless?—drama, as well as to see again "our" building, which I had briefly entered with Mother and Dodo in 1989, a time when we could not have imagined this rollout of events. So many dark clouds are hanging over our enterprise. So much business is unfinished and looks now as though it may stay that way for a good long time. Will we ever see the fruits of this inheritance? Will our children? Our grandchildren? The weather is appropriately grim, as my computerized weather forecast has promised—cold, windy, rain verging on snow and the general darkness of short autumn days. Vienna's latitude is somewhat north of Montreal's. But I am ready for it.

Using the Internet, I have found what looks like a nice apartment for the week in walking distance from Schmidgasse 14. I am nothing if not nervous. I have often traveled on my own, but usually meet up with someone at my destination. I've only rarely stayed alone, and never for this long. So this is a test of a variety of sorts. The large, comfortable apartment gets good grades and I manage to pass the test pretty well, too. Sleeping is not great—I hear the apartment's and the street's every sound—but it's evidently adequate since I don't feel tired during the day when I am out and about, interviewing Herbert Gruber; our lawyer, Julia Andras; our potential buyer, the Alpha representative, Maxim Slutski; Hannah Lessing, the head of the Nationalfonds, the agency responsible for restitution, and a group of her staff. In addition, I have a tour of the building with Fulbright director Lonnie Johnson; and I spend part of another day with Bernhard Odehnal, the journalist who has written about our case. Bernhard has prepared a little tour of places in Vienna that he thinks will interest me as a Fürth family historian. I cover a lot of ground, even have a half day left over to visit museums.

During my week, I tramp about for many miles, and soon learn to use Vienna's dependable subway system. I make use of the tiny but efficient kitchen in my apartment for breakfast and supper, and I eat my lunches out in the city. I try eating dinner out alone, but find myself too self-conscious, not enjoying the food, so return to my solo practice. Food in restaurants is on the whole a disappointment. I have tried to order several of my favorite nursery-type foods that Mother used to make— *kaiserschmarrn, eiernockerln, palatschinken*—at solitary noonday meals in small, simple eateries, hoping for comfort in culinary recollection. None has filled the bill. All are too tough, too floury, overcooked. So much for recovering childhood pleasures. Mother was not an ambitious, but a delicate cook. Getting it just right, consistency, timing. That made meals a little fraught—you had to be there at just the proper moment. There was no extra sitting around having a drink at her dinner parties. But there would be no tough *kaiserschmarrn* either.

My best food experiences in Vienna come under several categories. There are the simple cold cuts and raw veggies I buy at the local Billa market and assemble for supper in my own apartment kitchen—excellent liverwurst or salami or prosciutto on sturdy, fine-textured dark bread with superb European butter, a red pepper on the side, followed by a pear and a couple of cookies and a cup of green tea with honey. Then there are the two fabulous meals—sophisticated international cuisine—that I have with my daughter-in-law, Mo, who is here for a conference. And I eat one perfect plate of *dobos torte*—my favorite Central European dessert—at the Kunsthistorisches Museum on my last day there.

Naturally I think often about Mother, about her life in this city, about why she didn't yearn to return. It seems obvious to resent the place that treated you and your family so cruelly. Yet there was also what seems to have been a happy childhood and young girlhood. Still, she never made much of a fuss about the loss of her home city. I remember her saying only that Vienna after the war was like a Tyrolean town — provincial, without Jews. It was this lack of mourning, of going back over the troubles of the past, that our father insisted on. It was like the way he didn't hang around saying good-bye when leaving someone's house. No vestibuling. Make a clean break. I had a sense of his sorrow only once, when he was an old man, talking with friends of ours about their visit to Hungary, his native land. "It was a beautiful country," he said, his voice breaking.

As I make my way around the city, I remember how close Mother had been to her father, a relationship of mutual admiration. They hiked and traveled together, went to the theater, to concerts and museums. Ernst and his brother Bernard used to meet young Evi when they left the office and after her school day to walk on Vienna's Ringstrasse together, then go for a late afternoon *jause* of hot chocolate or coffee and pastries in their favorite cafe. Ernst encouraged his younger daughter to capitalize on her skill in languages and study in France so that she could get a certificate to teach French. Then, after a further year studying in London, where she was strongly influenced by issues raised by Britain's General Strike of 1926, Eva asked if she could help set up a social services center at the factory in Sušice. Ernst said she could do it, but only if she became properly credentialled in social work. She took a two-year social work course in Vienna, then returned to the family's hometown, where she helped design, plan for and put into existence a center for the match factory's workers, which included day care for nursing mothers, a cafeteria, a medical clinic, and dormitories for single workers. She was still finishing up her work to open the new center days before her marriage in May 1931. This center was greeted with considerable fanfare as a model of progressive social service. Its opening was attended by Alice Masaryk, daughter of the republic's president, as well as by Edvard Beneš, who would succeed Masaryk.

Of course, Grandfather was proud, too, of his daughter's beauty and verve. She loved being in company, loved also the outdoors, hiked, swam in the freezing waters of Sušice's Otawa River, and played tournament-level tennis. She was bright, popular, sought-after. There was never any question, evidently, that once an eligible husband appeared, she would give up her social work to become the lady of someone's elegant house, a charming and vivacious hostess, a wife and, of course, a mother. In Budapest, it was unlikely that she would ever have a profession of her own. Hungary was much more conservative than socialist Austria when it came to women working outside the home. Besides, even after seven years there, she was still trying to master that intractible language.

Then came the abrupt change, one I believe she never could fully accept. From being the privileged daughter of a well-known industrialist married to a promising young businessman living in high style in Budapest, she had gone directly to being the chief cook and bottle-washer in an American wartime household. Her new role as suburban housewife was one she eventually came to take seriously, but never enjoyed. She performed her tasks with a high degree of perfectionism, just as she did anything she undertook, but as long as my sister and I lived at home, there was always an air of martyrdom about her domestic persona. There was, it seemed, no sorrow like unto her sorrow, no insult like the ones she endured. To a small child, she seemed at times as dangerous as a caged lioness. Sometimes her rage was aimed at my father, whose standards of household orderliness were at least as high as her own. Sometimes they were aimed at my sister and me, childish begetters of work, confusion and disorder. We were made to understand that she was made for better things than cleaning up after us, taking care of us when we were sick. Her social work training was not supposed to have prepared her for *this*. It was supposed to have resulted — as indeed it did for a brief shining moment — in public, institutional success, with prestigious backing, with protection from disrespect, uncertainty and grubby daily struggles. Our mother wasn't afraid of a certain kind of hard work, mental and physical exertion, but this business of becoming a servant, a slave to unending menial tasks, this seemed beyond endurance.

A fearsome kind of psychological blackmail enforced our childish obedience: What might her anger produce? I can remember her screaming and weeping and striking out at us, and asking "Do you want me to go away?" What did that mean? Was it a suicide threat? What was my mother afraid of? Being dragged down by disorder and unpredictability in the form of unmade beds, stains on carpets and late arrivals? Perhaps. It may be that the image of her own mother's dissolution lay behind her need to have absolute control over every detail of daily life. Routines were crucial, along with high levels of success, beauty and good health. Mother's response to illness, especially my father's, always seemed excessive, frightening. No illness could be as serious as any of his. I can still hear the sound of her voice over the phone when

I was a young wife and mother, with three small runny-nosed boys under the age of six, announcing to me — tragically — that my father had a *bad cold*.

This time in Vienna, unlike on previous visits, I don't visit the family's apartment in the Alserstrasse, nor do I go to the Gregor Mendelstrasse, where Ernst and his second wife, Ella, lived, nor to the former Cottage Sanatorium, the site of Grandmother's suicide. I don't visit any cemeteries. This time I call up the family ghosts without visiting their former places of habitation. Except for Schmidgasse 14. There I think of Mother, playing in the garden with her cousin Lothar and his sister Hertha. Mother said that when she was in the hospital after a car accident with a fractured vertebra, lying on ice, she could feel the vibrations from her mother's step in the room, but not her father's light tread. The floors of the rooms are all still parquet, as they surely were in her day. Imagine, a hospital with parquet floors. Floors of the hallways are checkerboarded stone, red and tan, all as it likewise must have been from the beginning. Outside, above a window, on a frieze of harpies, acanthus scrolls and urns, it says 1887. There is elegant wrought iron on the staircases, above the entrance rotunda and in the back on the terrace, all very restrained, keeping the function of the building foremost. White tile is still in place on the walls of the former operating room of this building that was so familiar to Mother, but that she had never expected to inherit.

I am accompanied on my visit there by Lonnie Johnson, who has moved out of the building a few months earlier after directing the Fulbright office for 10 of its 57 years there. He has now moved to a more central location in the Museumsplatz. Lonnie has arranged for me to join him and a gentleman from BIG (Bundesimmobiliengesellschaft), the government office that now has charge of the building. I have a new digital camera, bought for this trip, and I take lots of pictures and then we take pictures of each other. I am the sturdy gray-haired person in a black raincoat standing at the top of the stairs to the garden that is already overgrown and untended. A pile of neatly stacked firewood stands near the stairs. It is a melancholy scene. Unhappy ghosts inhabit it.

How many degrees of separation do I have from this building? In what sense is it mine to inherit, to own? We laughed at Chris and Rich Andrews' naive assertion when they visited it first, saying to the guards at the door: "We own this building." Well, sort of, and along with more than 30 others. It was never a sure thing. Even now, it remains a troubled enterprise, with the incomprehensible actions of a single heir seemingly preventing a peaceful and worthwhile resolution.

The story of the building in Vienna and its tangled history represents one kind of inheritance, the legal transference of tangible things — buildings, money, objects — from one generation to another. Who gets what? But what does it ultimately mean to own family property, riches, objects that other people have lived with? How do questions of property and inheritance affect people's characters and lives? These can be fascinating, often troubling matters. In the case of Nazi Austria, the troubling aspect runs even deeper than usual. Historian Lisa Silverman writes: "[T]he elimination of Jews from society was integrally linked with the confiscation of their property." ["Repossessing the Past? Property, Memory and Austrian Jewish Narrative Histories," *Austrian Studies* 11 (2003): 138–53.] Indeed property ownership itself was only made available to Jews in Austria in 1859–60, as they moved toward full citizenship. So-called Aryanization, Silverman writes, was a first step in "isolating and separating Jews from the community in order to facilitate their eventual elimination from society." The story of the inheritance of this Austrian building carries heavy and tragic freight.

Yet, there is also another kind of inheritance, the abstract, intangible kind. What the CBS filmmakers were celebrating, in part, was a newly acknowledged family connection, a sort of instant legacy. Here are your cousins, your relatives, your family, they were saying. You are about to become a single indissoluble unit. But in our case, these simple formulations quickly proved to be unsound, the expected union largely unachievable. Joining a family is not just a matter of genealogy, of acknowledging a family tree. It is also about recognizing attitudes and relationships acquired over generations. Make an assumption about family dynamics and you are likely to get it wrong. This is a strange life form, with its own traditions, habits, affections, prejudices, resentments, enthusiasms — histories, in a word. Like any other ancient organism, family trees tend to be full of knots, scars and treacherous roots that are easy for the unwary to trip over. It takes time, attention and patience to get to know them, to make peace with them.

In the way of all offspring, I have surely inherited many intangible things from my parents. From my mother, a belief in high culture, a facility with languages and a love of physical activity, most specifically, tennis, swimming and walking. From her also, some skill at making one's surroundings attractive, and a strong inclination toward including oneself in that effort. No doubt there are other qualities that I can't see myself, or perhaps would prefer not to. In the early days of our marriage, when Bill used to say, "You sound just like your mother," it was not a compliment.

What, then, if anything, have I inherited from my father? Harder to say. Perhaps I can see in myself his ironic, skeptical eye, his unwillingness to join any crowd, his resistance to creeds or closed systems of belief. I did not get his mathematical or analytical skills. No chess or bridge player I, and not a good reader of history or philosophical essays. I did not pick up his resistance to green vegetables, nor can I remember a joke, of which he had a great store. But his voice and attitudes are in my head forever.

When I read and reread my grandfather's letters, I feel I have inherited, too, a great weight of sadness. Never to have known this intelligent, elegant, accomplished, humorous man is a tremendous loss. And yet I have the letters and have been able to come to know him through them.

But there are, too, smaller-scale inherited objects. What about them? There are only a few of my parents' things that I wanted to make room for in my house: books, artworks, a chest of drawers, a small American antique table that my father used as a desk, a square flowered china serving bowl, some jewelry from my parents' and grandparents' generation, only a few pieces of which have meaning for me. They no longer hold the weight of class and status that meant so much to earlier generations, although some have monetary value. For me they are mostly curiosities or, much more important, bearers of stories.

There is the story of the single diamond earring, one of a pair my sister and I divided at Mother's death. The large diamonds, almost four carats each, were replacements for ones my father had sold early in his life. It was 1916 and he was 21 and suffering from a "shadow on the lung," a euphemism for tuberculosis. It wasn't that he was avoiding military service, although his father had already used his influence to keep him out of the army. Before he left Budapest, his grandmother, who had raised him and his sister after their parents' divorce, gave him her diamond earrings to sell to cover his expenses when he went to a Swiss sanatorium. He sold the diamonds in Zurich, and the proceeds paid for his medical care, room and board, yet he always felt cheated by the man who bought them. He vowed then, he said, that he would do everything he could to become both healthy and prosperous. Later in his life, when he had recovered fully and had become a successful young banker, he took the empty earring settings and had them refilled with diamonds of the same size to give to his new wife. The stones my sister and I own are attached to a romantic tale and gesture, the kind of thing my father especially enjoyed.

The story of my grandmother's sapphire ring, mentioned earlier, has recently taken a slightly different turn. Concerned about my own children's inheritance and curious about the value of the various ancestral ornaments, I had them appraised. The appraiser expressed interest in the items. Several of them show very fine work and are unusual because of their history and provenance. It would take her a little longer than usual to produce a report, she said, because there were no hallmarks or indications of metal content. But she called me the next day to say she had found something interesting about my grandmother's ring. The workmanship was very fine and the small diamonds were real, though not particularly good, but the blue stone is a fake, a synthetic sapphire—a very good fake, but synthetic all the same. I gasped a little, then laughed. First I thought, what a letdown. And then, what a story. But what did it mean? Did my grandmother know it was fake? Did my mother? I had heard of rich women having their jewels exactly copied so that they could wear them without fear. Was this a copy of a real sapphire, a twin that my grandmother had had made, the original of which still existed somewhere else in the world—a safe deposit box in Budapest or Vienna? On someone else's hand? Did it change the story of how she had bought it after winning at the casino in Monte Carlo? Had she been cheated? Had she kept it as one of the family secrets that she took with her to her unhappy death? I wondered how my mother would have reacted. I think she would have been surprised, then appalled, then she would have laughed. The ring, if its stone had been a real sapphire, could have paid for a year of someone's college education. It is just as beautiful as it ever was, but now it is a handsome piece of costume jewelry with a great story attached. Perhaps the story is worth more than the imagined stone.

And what about the building in Vienna? The building carries a different weight, not just because of its size and potential value. Unlike the other items handed down from my family, it has a public as well as a private history. The early public history is proud—the success of a well-respected medical enterprise that provided a useful service—and then tragic—the seizure of family property by a ruthless and brutal regime. The private, family aspect of its history is no less full of contrasts, beginning with a belief in professionalism and progress, then, in these last years, descending into disrespect and even betrayal. Perhaps here, too, the story is worth more than the building.

Ernst Fürth

4

Homesickness;
Meeting a Grandfather

YOU NEVER KNOW when revelation is going to sneak up on you. A few years ago, I was dutifully going through the motions at a reunion at my husband's college. A man I'd never met and haven't seen since was telling me about his plans to move back to this New England valley. He felt "at home in the landscape," he said, then described what seemed welcoming to him, geological and human features I know well, since I've lived here myself for over 50 years. I listened with some interest, the polite, low-level listening one perfects over decades of attending such occasions. Then, to my surprise, there in the noisy hallway of a former fraternity, with both of us holding paper cups of something, he aimed an authentic question at me: "Have you ever felt really at home somewhere?"

"Yes," I said, "on the plains of Hungary." And as I said it, it felt right, even though I'd never put it just that way before. Later, in a more reflective moment, I decided that feeling at home may be a little like falling in love, both of them connected to precipitous and distinct sensations, both dangerously tinged with myth, cliché and longing.

The Great Hungarian Plain, the *Alföld* or *puszta*, begins in Budapest, just east of the Danube, as soon as you cross one of the many bridges connecting the green hills of Buda with the flat bustling center of Pest. Keep heading east and the land stays flat, the sky huge. Go east another 100 kilometers and you will reach Hungary's other major river, the Tisza, an often muddy, sluggish stream that runs roughly parallel to the Danube before joining it in the former Yugoslavia. You will have passed through some of the richest land on our planet, flat and fertile, a dark, alluvial soil capable of growing almost anything.

In 1991, my mother, my sister, Doris, and I visited the match factory in Sušice.

Although I was born in Budapest, I had not been back to Hungary until 1989, the year after my father died. And although I had lived most of my childhood in the same suburban house, there always remained that residual sense of being a bit of a foreigner. I could not say that I ever felt fully at home in Scarsdale, New York.

But my first trip to Hungary had hooked me; I kept being drawn back. I loved Budapest—still war scarred and a little shabby in 1989, but dressed, like Scarlett, in a ball gown made of the old parlor curtains. Budapest was a vibrant stage set, hospitable, stylish, the place my father had grown up, the place my parents had launched their marriage, and where my sister and I had been born. I also felt a kind of elemental attraction to the Great Plain. The attraction surely was, in part, the romantic lure of tracking ancestral footprints in *the land*, where there were fewer signposts.

In 1991, I had headed out this way with my husband. As I exclaimed over the beauties of the landscape, Bill hunched further down behind the steering wheel, resisting my efforts to include him in my quest for family footprints. He was not moved by the red-tile-roofed villages or the acres of vineyards, nor the rows of poplars lining the small country roads. He was not enjoying the hot sun and the flatness. He was not amused when we had to wait most of an hour on a dusty riverbank to put our rented car on a rickety raftlike ferry to take us across the Tisza River.

Unlike me, Bill has had all the roots he has ever needed or wanted. When I first visited his family in a small city in upstate New York, I was amazed to discover in what proximity they lived to each other. Amazed and, I'll have to admit, appalled. From the backyard of his parents' house, you could yell down two houses to where his three aunts and grandmother lived. "I see you're hanging out your sheets today," his Aunt Romayne would call from her back porch. "Yes," Bill's mother would shout back. "I thought the wind would dry them nice and fast."

"What are you fixing for supper?" Aunt Romayne would call out next.

"I'm planning to bake a ham. Then we can have it cold and for sandwiches for the rest of the week. I got some apples and corn on the cob over at Portz's farm stand, and I'm fixing an apple crisp."

The concept of privacy, the none-of-your-business attitude that so pervaded my continental/suburban upbringing, seemed utterly foreign here in Johnson City, N.Y. But it also meant a kind of clarity about who you were and where you took your place in the world. The people in this family had continued to live within a 20-mile radius for several generations. In a half-hour's drive, you could visit the graves of all of my husband's known ancestors. He had no need to go looking for his past. It was right there in plain sight. And although from time to time he liked to revisit it nostalgically, he had always intended to move beyond its provincial flatness. He couldn't fathom why I had suddenly become mesmerized by my past.

What I was suffering from, it seems to me now, is a long-term case of homesickness, that dangerously weighted longing for unattainable completion. All immigrants suffer from homesickness as they look back to the familiar world they've left behind. And although the sense of loss in a child raised by immigrant parents is less immediately apparent, yet it is no less compelling. For me, there were no coherent memories of the old world, no deep roots in the new one. Like a climber queasily suspended over a ravine, I found, past the middle of my life's journey, that I needed to struggle to find my footing.

Nineteen ninety-one was also the year of my first trip to Czechoslovakia, as it

A 19th-century engraving shows the factory complex. Schüttenhofen was the German name for Sušice.

was still called then. Before the visit to Hungary described above, I went to Prague and then to Sušice in the company of my sister, Doris Ablard, my mother, and my sister's daughter, Katie. We made a lively quartet. Mother, at 82, was physically slowed up by a hip that would soon be replaced. Her vision was reduced by one blind eye and one that would soon need cataract surgery. But she was psychologically and mentally indefatigable. Her grasp of events, names, and locations, both past and present, was absolutely secure. She was always fluent in German, English, French, and Hungarian. And during this trip, even after a 50-year interval, she discovered that she could

In 1991, the smokestacks were still there.

still make her way in Czech, a language she had not needed since early childhood.

My sister, Dodo, was 59 that year, athletic, slim and youthful looking, despite the family trait of early white hair. A specialist in early childhood education, she is the mother of three grown children, of whom Katie is the youngest. Dodo is a fearless traveler, whose determination overcomes all linguistic barriers. In Czechoslovakia, where her knowledge of the language was limited to "hello" and "thank you," she was able to arrange for a private toilet for our mother in our small hotel, where such luxuries were generally reserved for visiting royalty. I also watched her persuade a

Matchboxes came with colorful labels.

Czech ticket-seller to accept the wrong passport for travel out of the country. This was all done using her patented combination of basic German, sign language, and refusal to take no for an answer.

Katie, who was 23, had graduated in anthropology from Bates College, and was teaching English to Hungarians in Budapest while learning Hungarian and traveling all around, often on her own. She joined us in Prague, arriving there from a quick trip to Cracow with a knapsack full of excellent Polish fruit juices.

I was 54 that summer, and had recently left my job as an editor at a daily newspaper where I had worked for 13 years. As a freelance writer/editor, I was hoping to find time to do more of "my own" writing, even, in Proust's words, "mere family history." Sušice was one of the places where I needed to spend time. There I began to understand more about my mother's early life, and about where the Fürths stood in the scheme of things. When we visited the match factory in the early morning, the three managers who took us around first toasted us with *becherovka*, a sweet, tonsil-clearing Czech schnapps. They all knew the Fürth name. Even after the German occupation, the war, and 40 years of Communism, everyone in town knew the name. The Fürths were a postindustrial version of lords of the manor—first citizens, factory owners, the people who had brought prosperity to a sleepy country town.

A book published by the Diamond Match Company in 1926, titled *The Romance of the Match*, begins with pictures of noble heathens, the kind that embellished my early education—elegant Egyptians, high-domed Mayans, athletic Greeks. All are engaged in the effort to produce fire, the mythic goal, the stolen secret for which Prometheus suffered on the rock.

Now take a look at the portrait of my great-great-grandfather Bernard Fürth that hangs in Sušice's museum. Not an ounce of romance there, a face that gives nothing away. The eyes look straight at you, the slightly crooked mouth lends a determined set to the jaw. A gold watch chain crosses his vest under the dark frock coat. He wears two rings on his right hand. This is a man, orphaned early in life, who founded a thriving enterprise. And, although it is hard to imagine in this day and age, matches truly were a necessity. For three-quarters of a century, until the invention of the butane lighter, central heating, and the electrification of the countryside, no household could survive without a reliable source of fire. Everyone needed, by one estimate, five matches a day.

At the Great Exhibition of 1851 in London's Crystal Palace, "lights" from all over the world were on display: "Fürth of Schüttenhofen [the German name for Sušice], in Bohemia, seems ... to have been the principal exhibitor with his dozen

Fürth matches were sold all over the world.

Bernard Fürth founded the industry in the 1850s.

boxes with 80 lucifers, or 'Congreves' in each, for one penny, also 'ladies' lucifers' at about double that price." These matches in their wooden boxes with colorful labels were sent all over the world. My mother as a child collected the different labels.

Sušice is a pretty town folded into the valley of the Otava River in the shadow of the Sumava Mountains, a countryside loved by hikers and cross-country skiers. From the hilltop pilgrimage chapel of Angela Strazte (guardian angel), you can look down at the panorama of the town—red-tile-roofed houses, the river snaking through, the hills rolling away in all directions. The town center is a charming cobblestoned square with a church, a town hall, a hotel, the museum (the former pharmacy), and my grandparents' house, divided up at the time of our visit into offices. But what you see most strikingly from the top of the hill, rising up from the middle of town, are the tall, tapered factory smokestacks, a few in an ornamental 19th-century red and black brick, the rest in drab gray modern concrete, both still emitting a heavy, palpable smoke from their coal furnaces. The enterprise was manufacturing other wood products besides matches, but it still went by the name of Solo, just as it did in our grandfather's day.

Other things remained the same too. The top of this hill, it seemed, was still a favorite spot for trysts. As my mother, my sister, my niece Katie and I reached the summit, a young couple in mid-embrace, startled by our arrival, disappeared into the woods. It was here, my mother says, that my father first kissed her. And it was here, after their engagement, looking down at the factories below, that he issued his warning about "not marrying a smokestack."

My mother was indeed the daughter of a smokestack, of three generations of smokestacks, people who took trees, stripped, peeled and sliced them into tiny sticks, combined them with quick flaming chemicals, put them into pretty wooden boxes, and sold them to the rest of the world. Over several generations of hard work, the Fürths had grown to be aristocrats of merit, vigorous and assured, the equals in most ways of the hereditary, inbred, exhausted Austrian aristocracy. They were at ease with diplomats, with professors of philosophy, with great physicians and artists. And, like all aristocrats, they were snobbish.

When my mother brought home her first serious love, a man whose family owned an elegant store in Vienna—a cross between Tiffany's and Gump's—her father said: absolutely not. This man, Paul Förster, might well be an intelligent, attractive person, amusing and good company, part of Ernst Fürth's bridge-playing group, even. He might well be a person of good character. But he would not do as a serious suitor, because, as part of his family business, Förster dealt directly with customers: He sold things. He was, as the British say, "in trade." He would not do for the daughter of the Fürths, who were connected to the great international industrial world, far above the mere selling of pretty knickknacks. Although for a time my mother continued to see Förster in secret, he was never welcomed back to her parents' house, and she eventually bowed to her father's wishes.

Ernst Fürth, right, at ease with my parents, George and Eva Perl.

My father, on the other hand, was a thoroughly acceptable prospect. It was from the top of this hill overlooking the Fürth family's match factories that he had warned my mother that finance was not the same as manufacturing, that bankers and investors didn't see a physical product, that the risks and rewards were different. He was a young man with a thriving career, but he wanted her to understand that when she married him it would be a different sort of life from the one she had grown up with. He was imagining a comfortable, high bourgeois existence in Budapest with perhaps the addition of a small working farm in the country where the children (he was already planning a life for his unborn children) could enjoy the fresh air, learn about animals and crops, and escape the bustle of the city. He did not imagine the uprooted life of immigrants as he courted my mother in 1930. And my mother surely never imagined that she would end up living where nobody knew who she was—among strangers.

In 1941 my aunt Gretl Strasser, my mother's sister, wrote a series of recollections of her childhood in Sušice, an account with the flavor of a cheerful folk tale. All the characters are fully formed, defined by just a few anecdotes, a few quick strokes. If there is sorrow, it doesn't last long. The benevolent order of things is well established, and a child's mischief only reinforces the knowledge that all is under control.

Gretl writes at some length about her grandfather Daniel Fürth, Bernard's son and heir to the match factory. When her parents, Elza Roheim and Ernst Fürth, married in 1898, Daniel gave the newlyweds the family house on the town square as a wedding present, keeping an apartment in it for himself. Daniel had already turned over the running of the factory to two of his sons, Ernst and Bernard, but he still enjoyed his life. He especially liked playing cards with his cronies. So when the young bride complained about the old man's noisy card games and the accompanying cigar smoke, Daniel moved into the building next door.

Here is my aunt Gretl on the subject of her grandfather Daniel:

> Grandfather was the center not only of Sušice but of my own life. Why people thought him an angry, stubborn old man will always be a mystery to me. He was the epitome of kindness to me, as old as the world and just as eternal. His life was so orderly you could have set a clock to it. When my memories begin of him, he was already in his 70's and he had long since given the factory to his sons. Nevertheless he had a desk opposite my father's where he sat every day.
>
> He had lunch at noon sharp, then took a nap for an hour. Then the *tarok* [a card game] party arrived. Sometimes I was allowed to sit as a silent spectator, and I always shuddered a little when Grandfather started to yell so loudly about his partner's mistake that I thought the game wouldn't end without murder this time. At four o'clock the three had survived the game and Grandfather returned to the factory to read his afternoon mail. At six, he left the factory along with the workers. On the way home he stopped at the druggist and bought two pieces of candy for me. "Well, my little golden cap," he said, and sat down at the big table in the children's room. Then Mama and Father came in, and at seven o'clock sharp Grandfather left the house.

The world described here by my aunt Gretl, this beautifully ordered existence with people knowing and, for the most part, keeping their places, formed the backdrop of my mother's childhood. In 1913 when she was seven, the family moved to Vienna. They kept the house in Sušice and the daughters returned there every summer for country vacations with their children, even during the summer of 1938, after the Nazi takeover of Austria and just before the outbreak of war. That summer, in the midst of rumbling on every front, my father—who generally stayed in Budapest to work during the summer—sent my mother two sets of tickets: train tickets back to Budapest; or, if that proved impossible, plane tickets to Zurich, from where we would all leave either for England or America.

No wonder my mother both resented and revered my father. He had snatched her from the world that her family had been building for generations. He had dragged her away from the places that had defined her existence. And yet he had saved all our lives, seeing clearly what most of his friends and relations had been unable to see—that their comfortable existence in those countries was over, that the beautifully ordered surface was about to be rent by unimaginable events, and that the only way to escape these irrational forces was to leave for a new world, never to return.

The death of my father in 1988, in his 93rd year, opened up many unasked and unanswered questions for me. The anchoring rock was no longer there. My father's firm, sometimes forbidding presence was gone. Surely this is, in part, why I was drawn back to Central Europe, to Hungary, to the Czech Republic, to wander around the places in which my past had been made. The itch was grounded in simple curiosity. But it contained also an effort to locate myself better—to acknowledge and eventually dampen the fires of homesickness.

In 1996, Mother and I began our work on her father's letters. Not only could she read the Gothic script in which my grandfather wrote—it is as unreadable as Cyrillic or Greek to me—but even more important, she could fill in details about people, events and the implications of things said and unsaid. Not only was I able to depend upon her erudition and vast linguistic skills, her astounding memory and tenacious energy, but also upon her unqualified trust as I set out to tell these stories.

In addition to my grandfather's letters from France, Mother and I worked our way through the sequence of letters that went the other way, the ones my parents wrote to France during the summer of 1940, and which were returned to them when the mail was blocked after the German occupation. There are also the letters of Frederic Reyfer, a decent and tireless Frenchman, who we now believe was a member

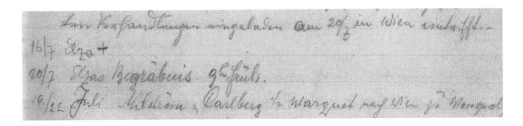

Grandfather's diary entry notes the date of my grandmother's death.

of the Resistance. Reyfer set up a system for putting my parents back in touch with Ernst and Ella Fürth after 1941, and tried to shield these elderly exiles from disaster.

We also looked into a diary that Ernst Fürth kept from 1916 to 1938, which is mainly concerned with business, with his travels to match factories in Austria, Hungary, Yugoslavia and Slovakia, with shipments of wood and chemicals. The diary is impersonal, external, although occasionally you get a glimpse of the man, when he writes, for example, about intervening with the government to allot larger food rations to the factory workers during World War I. You can also see his restraint—or perhaps just the limits of human expression—when he marks his wife's suicide with the following cryptic entry: "Elza +." The diary gives a sense of the busy life of a vibrant man of business, an industrialist, who worked hard, yet left plenty of time for enjoyment, vacations, travel, relaxation. But it is a terse record of events only, unadorned by opinion, humor or emotional color. Although he would never have seen himself as a particularly literary man nor as a self-conscious "witness" to terrible events, the letters from France offer a nuanced picture of a complex person, determined to articulate his experiences, thoughts and feelings in a coherent way to his beloved daughters. Stripped of virtually all that he once took for granted, my grandfather nevertheless made a life where he could. Deprived of his children and grandchildren, moved from place to place, lacking the company of his peers, lacking, eventually, the most basic human freedoms, he rejoiced in the latter days of his exile when he and his wife were able to put together a foursome for bridge.

It is no exaggeration to say that my mother idolized her father. I cannot remember her ever addressing a serious criticism toward any aspect of his character. He was, from all she has told me, kind, generous, cultivated, elegant, modest, humorous and good company. Trained as a chemist and by temperament a practical man, he was a vigorous natural athlete, who loved to hike and was self-taught at tennis. He kept up with politics and literature, and took an observer's pleasure in Vienna's thriving cultural life—music, art, opera, theater. When he came out of a musical event, says my mother, he could whistle the new tunes he had heard.

Ernst Fürth was handsome and intelligent, an international figure in the world of match manufacturing. He was a man of his time, his place and class, a man who held firm views about how the world should be arranged, a patriarch in an era when "paternalistic" was still a term of praise. As long as there was access to large supplies of timber and a reliable workforce—both of which were plentiful in 19th- and early-20th-century Bohemia—match-making was an industry to depend upon, offering an ever-expanding market and a reliable route to prosperity in a wider world.

Emblematic of that sense of wider belonging is the inscription on the grave of Ernst's father, Daniel Fürth, who died in 1911, and whom we meet in my aunt Gretl's affectionate recollections. Below his name and dates on the simple polished gray stone oblong is the German word *Fabrikant*, industrialist; and below that, in Latin, *Non omnis moriar*, I shall not wholly die. The German designation looks back proudly and forward optimistically to a world of material progress. The Latin, taken from one of the odes of Horace, is part of the richly secular, European, humanistic tradition with which the Fürths identified themselves. Emblematic too, of the catastrophe to come, is the fact that the stone stands in Sušice's New Jewish Cemetery.

Born April 8, 1865, the youngest of eight children, Ernst Fürth was sent to board with a family in Vienna at the age of 11 after his mother's death. His education included eight years of Latin and four of Greek at Vienna's Akademische Gymnasium (Mother called it "the best school in town"). He took his degree in chemistry at the University of Vienna, spent a year serving in an elite Austro-Hungarian cavalry regiment, then went on to further study in Berlin at the Kaiser Wilhelm Institut. He returned to Sušice to work with and eventually succeed his father as director of the Bernard Fürth match works. The factory's old-timers scoffed a little at the young, overeducated boss with his newfangled innovations. But he overcame their resistance, modernized the production system, and earned their respect with his humane practices. Benefits to workers included family medical care, accident insurance, residences for employees, and after 1931, as a result of my mother's work, a social service center with a clinic, cafeteria and day care for nursing infants. In 1913, when Ernst Fürth became director of a newly formed corporation called Solo A.G., linking all the major match factories in the Austro-Hungarian Empire, the family moved to Vienna, although they kept the house in Sušice. From then until 1938, Ernst Fürth traveled all over Central Europe, visiting factories under his aegis. Earlier, he had been to England to see the great Bryant & May match company, to the United States to learn about assembly lines at Diamond Match. In the '30s he went many times to Sweden, where "match king" Ivar Krueger had devised what turned out to be an ill-fated scheme to bail out countries damaged by Europe's Great Depression. A few years after the suicide of my grandmother, Elza Roheim Fürth, and over the objections of his family, Ernst married Ella Siebert.

For me, it has surely been true that working my way through these facts, studying these letters, photos and diaries, getting to know my forebears' voices through their own words and the accounts of others has formed an irreplaceable piece of my inheritance. It is a precious legacy that, unlike buildings, works of art or jewelry, cannot be stolen, undervalued or contested in a court of law. Meeting my grandfather in this way has, in some measure, helped to assuage my homesickness.

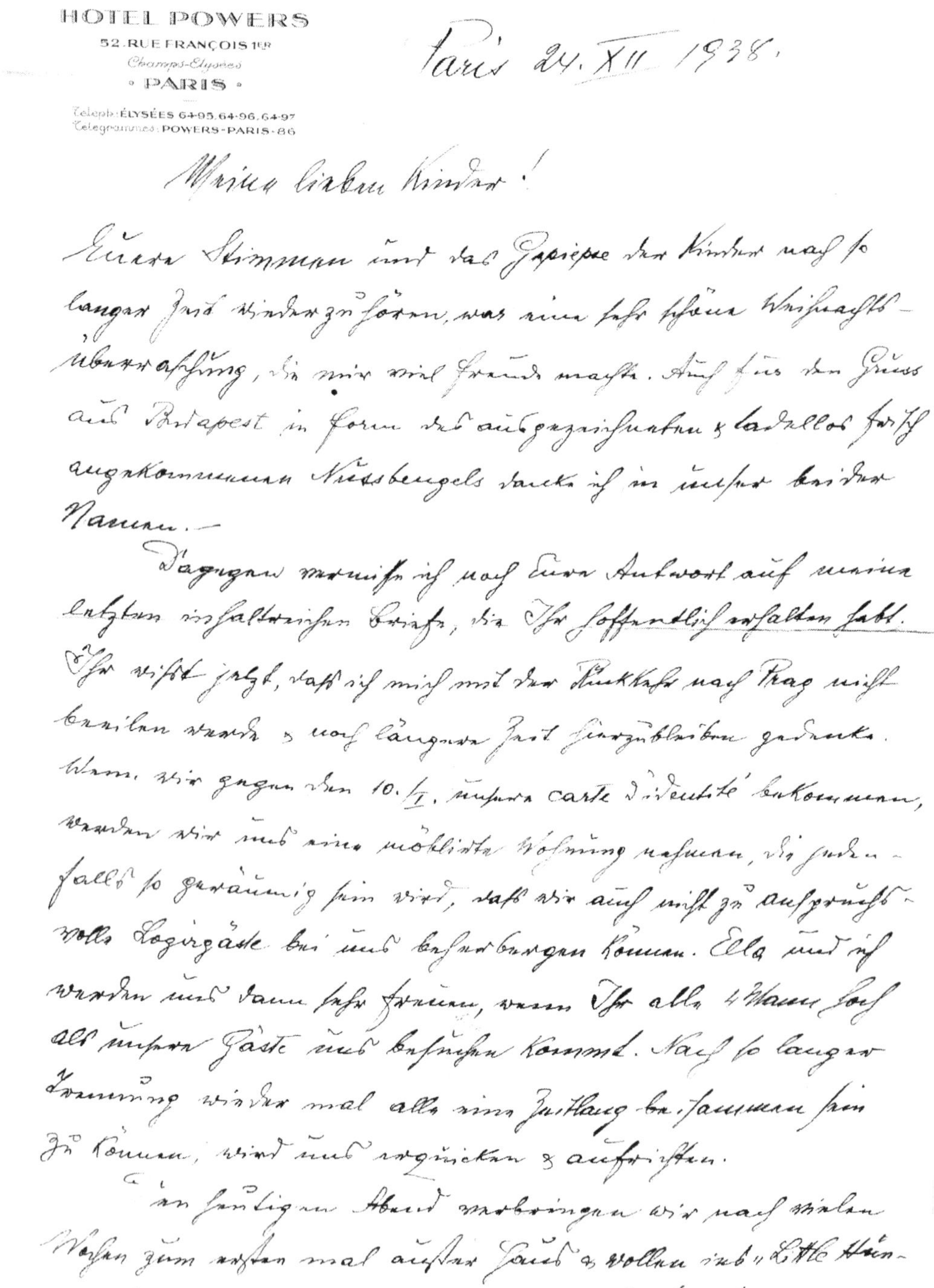

HOTEL POWERS
52, RUE FRANÇOIS 1er
Champs-Élysées
• PARIS •
Téléph. ÉLYSÉES 64-95, 64-96, 64-97
Télégrammes: POWERS-PARIS-86

Paris 24. XII 1938.

Meine lieben Kinder!

[handwritten letter in old German cursive script]

Grandfather writes from Paris, Christmas Eve, 1938.

5

Catching Up with the Past

ON CHRISTMAS EVE OF 1938, Grandfather wrote from a hotel in Paris to my parents, who were still in Budapest. After Ernst and his second wife, Ella, left Vienna in the spring, they had gone first to the family homestead in Sušice, and from there to Switzerland, a place that might have provided sanctuary during the war. But it wounded my grandfather's dignity to have to report to the Swiss police every week, and so he left for Paris, where, he was convinced, foreigners were treated better. His Christmas letter from there shows that he has every intention of staying. That letter, the earliest in our collection, is an energetic introduction to a man determined to continue enjoying a life—albeit a diminished one—over which he expects to retain a considerable degree of control.

Dec. 24, 1938

My dear children!
Hearing your voices [they must have phoned] and the chirping of the children again after such a long time was a very nice Christmas surprise and gave me great pleasure. Also I thank you in both our names for the greeting from Budapest in the form of an excellent and perfectly fresh *nussbeugel* [a nut-filled pastry].

On the other hand I miss your answer to my last very extensive letter, which I hope you received. You now know that I intend to stay here for some time. When we get our *cartes d'identité* about January 10th, we plan to rent a furnished apartment, spacious enough for not-too-demanding houseguests.

Ella and I would be delighted if all four of you would be our guests. After such a long separation, it would be refreshing and raise our spirits to be together again.

Tonight, after many weeks at home, we will have dinner at Little Hungary, perhaps we can get a *halászlé* [a Hungarian fish soup]. Thanks for the subscription to the *Neue Züricher Zeitung*, but please inform the newspaper office of our correct address, which they botched up.

A thousand hugs for big and small
from your faithful
Father

My parents were only three weeks away from leaving their own apartment in Budapest forever. On January 13, 1939, they packed their suitcases and left for Switzerland with my sister, me, and our nursemaid, Nene. Mother—who impulsively packed the Christmas tree ornaments in the suitcases, the only household objects she carried—remembers that the mistletoe was still hanging over the doorway of the apartment.

Before they left, Grandfather wrote again from Paris, outlining what he knew about one of the very good reasons for our departure: Hungary's new Jewish Laws. My parents, though thoroughly assimilated and secularized through several generations (note the Christmas ornaments), and more recently converts to Catholicism, might nevertheless be powerfully affected by these laws. Of course my father, who had already made up his mind to leave, was all too well aware of the gathering clouds. Indeed it was he who had urged my grandfather to leave Europe. Here is my grandfather from Paris:

Dec. 30, 1938

My dear children!
Today I read a very thorough report about the new Jewish laws in Hungary and I have come to the conclusion that from now on for Jews, not only will social and political life be restricted, but also economic progress—the aim of honorable work—will be made impossible. But why should I make your hearts heavier than they already are by lamenting and complaining? Rather, I am all for your making the energetic decision to emigrate as soon as possible and to start a new existence

over there. In the provisional bill I read a passage that intends to facilitate emigration for Jews. That, hopefully, means that they will be permitted to take with them a certain percentage of their property in one form or another. As clearly as the rest of the bill is written, this portion is left unclear, and I put little hope in the law's mercy.

But even in the most unfavorable case, you should stick to your decision. You know that when I left Vienna I could only rescue a small, modest fraction of my possessions. Still you can count on me over there. Even if I have to reduce my own needs, I'll help you out until you manage to earn your own living.

Find out whether Gretl has a small wish and put it on her birthday table in my name.

By spring of 1939, Ernst and Ella had moved from Paris to Nice, seeking a better climate and better company for their bridge game. By now they had been joined by Ernst's widowed sister-in-law, Cecile Fürth. Ernst was no doubt also looking for a place where they could live more economically than in Paris. As he says, he had been able to rescue only a small fraction of his wealth. Despite his initial confidence, these funds eventually ran out. As long as he could, my father saw to it—until it became illegal—that my grandfather was supplied with money.

While my sister and I stayed with our nursemaid in Switzerland, our parents went to England for three months to consider whether they should immigrate there. My father, given his experience managing family farms in Hungary, was looking into the possibility of growing sugar beets in the northwest of England. Plans were afoot to renew farming in these "distressed areas," former mining territories. And although he established an important business connection, he was not able to get a work permit. Even more importantly, he was uneasy about British laws that put immigrants "at the pleasure of the Home Office." Still, Mother had spent a happy year studying in London in 1926, and so she lobbied strongly in favor of settling in England. But, as my father wrote in 1971 in his memoir—his written English, like his spoken, strongly accented with Hungarian: "If I go with my three girls, they should be safe to remain. The only country, the only one on the globe is the United States of America. If you enter with an immigration visa, you are a permanent resident. You can be interned, you can be jailed, but you cannot be thrown out." And so my father decided,

My mother in what my father later described as their
"somewhat palatial apartment" on Budapest's Andrássy út.

over my mother's opposition, to bring his young family to America. After the German invasion of Czechoslovakia on March 15, 1939, my grandfather cabled my parents in London strongly backing my father's decision: "Take the next boat."

Leaving Hungary for America must have been a terribly lonely decision for my father. My parents had been married for seven years, and had made a place for

My father with his beloved books.

themselves in Budapest society. My mother, who spoke several other languages, was working hard to master Hungarian. My father's career, as my mother put it, was "at its peak." The charming young couple had a seven-year-old daughter, Doris, a two-year-old (me), and had recently redecorated what my father described as a "somewhat palatial apartment," on Budapest's Andrássy út, the city's grandest boulevard.

Budapest, 1938, my mother with my sister and me.

In spite of what was happening elsewhere in Europe, none of their friends saw any reason to leave Hungary. But my father had gone to Vienna to confer with my grandfather a few days after Hitler took over Austria in March 1938. "What I saw," he wrote decades later in his memoir, "is difficult to describe. Soldiers with steel helmets were standing guard before most public buildings, machine guns on the corners, the swastika all over the place, people in black uniforms (S.A.) in open trucks carrying people. Singing, chanting: *Ein Führer, ein Reich.*" On his return from Vienna, my father went straight to the American consulate in Budapest to apply for an immigration visa for the U.S. Nine months later, we were on our way.

A letter from my grandfather, dated April 17, 1939, reached my parents on board the U.S.S. *Manhattan*, sailing from Calais the next day. He refers to my father, Gyuri (the nickname for György, George in Hungarian), commending his intention to study agriculture at an American university. My father was being admitted to the United States through a special immigration quota for agricultural experts. This was a piece of phenomenal luck for us because it permitted us to enter the country even

*When my father returned from visiting Vienna in 1938 after the Nazi takeover, he went
directly to the American consulate to apply for immigration status.*

though the Hungarian national quota of 473 people had already been filled for that
year. (My mother, my sister and I were admitted on a German quota, since Austria,
my mother's home country, was now in German hands.) But my father took the
agricultural classification seriously, believing that he would be required to follow this
line of work. In fact, it turned out that although U.S. officialdom was concerned that
we should not become public charges, it did not care how my father earned a living.

Here is my grandfather's letter to my parents as we were about to sail to the New
World:

> My dear children!
> Your intention, Gyuri, to reeducate yourself before starting out in a foreign land,
> whose climate and soil are so totally different from Hungary's, and to have some
> practical experience, is certainly wise. With your previous knowledge, you certainly

Nizza 17. April 1939.

Grandfather says farewell to his children.

will be able to shorten the schooling and acquire the necessary knowledge in a few months. Of course you will want to leave New York soon. What can the turbulent city offer, when from morning to night you are occupied with small children and are unable to undertake much? In a small, quiet town you will be able to find a less stormy life than you have had during the last months. Especially I would like to ask you not to overburden Evi, whose physique is not strong enough to keep pace with her ambition. Care of the children, secretarial services, household duties, and service for her husband in the long run are more than she can carry out, even if she does it all gladly.

Your report about England was of great interest to me and I assume that what you started there will continue to fruition even during your absence. I followed your advice and converted my Swiss francs into dollars and gold. In any case it is a comfort to know that the Glarona interests [his bank account in Zug, Switzerland] can be transferred to America, if Switzerland no longer functions.

Ella thanks you for taking her jewelry and asks to have it handed to Erich [her son], who most likely will meet you at the pier.

Still one request: please write frequently and about everything. I would not want to lose the close attachment we have had until now. I want to be informed about every detail of your future life.

And now I say goodbye fondly to big and small, happy sailing and future; perhaps we will see each other again happily; but if not, keep in good memory your faithful
Father

In his formal, dignified farewell, Ernst expresses—not for the last time—his confidence in my father's judgment and ability to make his way in the world. His protective solicitousness about Mother suggests a perceived fragility that may reflect more about *her* mother than about her own staying power, which, in the long run, turned out to be considerable. On the other hand, my grandfather had a point. Though energetic, vivacious and intellectually ambitious, Mother had led a protected and privileged life. There had been serious education, but with it regular travel and an easy access to high culture and the people who exemplified it—writers, artists, musicians, not to mention the upper echelons of business, government and the

Last visit in Sušice. Left photo, grandfather and his wife Ella Siebert with my sister, Doris, and our older cousins Erna and Fredi Strasser; right photo, Ella with Erna and Fredi and their mother, Gretl Strasser.

professions. Mention important figures from that era—Thomas Masaryk, Richard Strauss—and my mother had some kind of contact with them. And although my grandfather disapproved of ostentatious displays, the wealth was certainly there: Comfortable vacations in attractive locations, good clothes, good food, well-made and beautiful possessions and the society of one's social peers was taken for granted. In addition, the family always had a solid buffer of servants to perform the kinds of tasks my mother was now being called upon to handle. Before she came to the United States, she had never, for example, cooked a meal nor made a bed. In addition, and perhaps most importantly, there was the matter of status. It went without saying that in Europe, the Fürths were *somebody*. A humorous skit performed at my aunt Gretl's wedding cast her as "The Solo Princess." Here in this country, my mother—like all immigrants before or since — had to struggle to redefine herself, to free herself from the oversimplifications of "refugee" and "enemy alien." She even had to free herself from the category of "Austrian." As in: "Oh, you're Austrian. Then you'll want to meet Frau X. She's Austrian too." Well, maybe, maybe not.

This letter from my grandfather also brings up the perennial business of the jewelry. The last time my mother saw her father was May of 1938 in Paris. She had gone there after traveling to London with her sister Gretl, where the two had taken their jewels for safekeeping. As it had been for my grandmother and other well-to-do women in many eras, substantial jewelry was the outward and visible sign of their place in the world, as well as a conveniently compact form of durable wealth. For refugees of any social or economic standing, no valuables were easier to transport than a small packet of gems. And of course, nothing was more eagerly searched for. In January 1939, as they left Hungary forever, my mother was asked to remove her shoes at Hegyeshalom, on the Hungarian-Austrian border, in case she had valuables hidden in hollowed-out heels. She remembers the experience as frightening, but surely it was a modest form of harassment compared to the full body searches conducted later on. That jewelry must also have been part of the reason our parents went to England after depositing my sister and me in Switzerland. Evidently they were able to take it from there without any questions asked.

Another letter, mailed at about the same time, introduces us to Ella, whose two sons were already in America.

> Dearest Evi,
> As you see we are always with you, and you mustn't take the farewells so tragically; perhaps it is only for a few weeks and you will see father again! Perhaps it is better, Evi, that you did not come here, since it would have been very upsetting for father! I have already been through all that and know how it hurts!
>
> The politics and uncertainties take a toll on one's nerves, even if one believes one can handle it. For that reason one should steer clear of sentimentality! You will be fully occupied with the children, and we hope that the boat offered peace and recreation. Dorli and the little one, were, I hope, not seasick. I wish for you, my child, that as soon as you set foot in the New World, you will spend happy times with your loved ones. One can be content any place, and you have much time ahead of you.

Grandfather with our nurse, Helene Nedela, known as Nene, who holds me.

Although we did not always understand each other, Evi, it was mostly the mistrust that you bore me. But I hope that you people have begun to see and know that I mean well toward you and am fond of you!

Now my dear, go happily toward your goal, my warmest wishes accompany you all!
Cordially your
Ella

I send hugs to my boys and wait till they make me a gift of the villa! I'm afraid that will be a long wait.

Ella's rare pieces of correspondence are especially fascinating to me, since I never heard about her from my parents in any but derogatory terms. The name itself was always pronounced with a harsh propulsive sound, a kind of snarl. So it is illuminating to see her slightly untidy handwriting, hear her epistolary voice. In this letter, she takes up some of the same themes that appear in my grandfather's farewell letter, but without his elegance, his verbal finesse—without his deeply felt love. This is a big, unpolished voice, speaking in clichés and slogans, full of her own experience and self-professed wisdom. It is interesting to hear her acknowledge the rift between her and her stepdaughters—and to blame it on their misjudgment of her. Notable too is the reference in the postscript to a piece of real estate, which she had received as a gift from my grandfather, and which she evidently made over to her sons for safe-keeping, now that they were in America. She is already—a bit blatantly, I'd say—looking forward to repossessing her possessions. This made additional trouble between her and my family. After the war she came to the United States to visit her son Erich. (Her other son, Herbert, had joined the U.S. Army and died in the Battle of the Bulge.) She came also to demand from my parents the contents of Ernst's Swiss bank account, threatening legal action against them. That account had, in fact, been depleted during the war. But the whole performance left a permanent bad taste in everyone's mouth, since Ella had inherited several valuable pieces of real estate in Vienna—the aforementioned villa, among others—along with Ernst's substantial

Grandfather's last passport.

Austrian pension. The Czech properties, which had been left to Mother and Gretl, had already been expropriated and collectivized by the Communists.

But there is no denying the energy in Ella's voice as it rings out from her infrequent letters. No denying either that this is a woman who would have liked in April 1939 to find a way to be on better terms with Ernst Fürth's children—for whatever reasons. But her priorities now and until the end of Ernst's life were simple: her husband's comfort and their joint survival. It was in this role that she functioned so admirably, a role for which my mother eventually accorded her a grudging respect.

The Perl family arrived in New York harbor on April 24, and stayed for 10 weeks in a dreary hotel called the Franconia on the West Side, where, for the first time, my mother had to contend with being a full-time parent without a nursemaid. (They had said good-bye to Nene in Switzerland, and she returned to Budapest.) My grandfather writes from Nice a couple of weeks later, responding to my mother's description of their crossing and arrival. He worries, among other things, about how soon Gretl's Hungarian husband, Paul Strasser, will be able to follow her. Paul had been unable to get a visa because the Hungarian national quota was filled, and, unlike my father, he could not claim any of the "specialist" categories. Paul eventually reached the U.S. in January 1941, traveling east from Budapest via the Trans-Siberian Railroad, through Yokohama, then across to San Francisco. Gretl and her two children, like my mother, had been admitted to the United States under a German quota.

May 7, 1939

My dear Evi,
To my great pleasure I received your letter written on board the "Manhattan" with your traveling impressions yesterday evening. I can well imagine how cumbersome and tiring it was to transport the children and all the luggage. You probably will have trouble finding enough space in the cramped apartment at the Franconia Hotel.

I would never have imagined that, along with the weather, the general atmosphere on shipboard would be so cold, and that people of your caliber with two such charming children would be treated like second-class citizens. In similar situations the French have more charm, and even at the Prefecture [police headquarters], where the employees have to deal with rather repugnant refugees, the tone is pleasant and obliging. Hopefully you will soon get into surroundings where you will be considered as *pares inter pares*. Because otherwise *warum hätte man die Krot gefressen?* [Why did we eat the toad? (Why go through the whole ordeal)]

How is Gretl going to fare, who will be without male protection and support? She and the children are due here on the 16th and I'll have the pleasure of their company for five days. At the moment, we seem to have been given a small breathing-time. The speech of Beck [probably General Ludwig Beck, former German chief of staff, who opposed Nazis, then headed the plot to kill Hitler in 1944] was not published in the German press. Who can imagine what Hitler is plotting in Berchtesgaden? What is America's opinion? I'm of the impression that the people are not completely behind Roosevelt and that the majority would prefer not to be involved in Europe's troubles.

Write frequently, even short cards.

Reading this letter with full knowledge of what the French were capable of after the German occupation, I have to shake my head as I hear him compare American rudeness with official French "charm." *Vive la différence,* I say.

The next letter to Mother in New York is dated May 24, 1939, and describes the visit of Gretl and her two children.

Yesterday evening we took Gretl and the children to the railroad station and bravely took leave of each other. We had five *gemütlich* days to discuss the present and plans for the future. All along I had to admire Gretl's equilibrium, confidence and courage; it was almost contagious and made the parting easier. Her determination to forge ahead, although there is no guarantee of success, should help her overcome many difficulties. May the Lord help her!

Erna and Fredi [Alfred] are nice children, but for their age [15 and 12] rather immature and childish. It is the result of [their governess] Anny's years of guardianship that left its mark. Let's hope they won't take too much time to get up to the American speed.

Your children, by contrast, seem to have an innate urge for independence and won't take long to become perfect American girls.

After many dreary, rainy days, today we have the first warm, sunny one. Tomorrow I will acquire a bathing suit and then we can go into the water daily. There are no large bathing establishments, but quite a few small, nice spots, with sandy beaches that are inviting.

In a letter brought over the frontier Mrs. Cižek [wife of the director of the two Sušice factories] describes life in Sušice in gloomy colors. Shortages of food, high prices, hermetic sealing of the border of the "Protektorat" on the German side. In front of Jewish stores there are the usual posters, but that doesn't stop people from shopping there. From other sources I hear of the Czech population's great dissatisfaction, especially with the enforced Germanization.

This last letter seems particularly rich. I am especially touched by my grandfather's wish that my sister and I should become "perfect American girls." It certainly was a goal that my sister and I both eventually struggled to reach in our own ways, and one for which, it now seems to me, our parents sacrificed a great deal. All parents, to some extent, lose their children to the next generation's prevailing culture, and all children, to some extent, inhabit a different country from their parents. But for children of immigrants, that contrast is even more striking. My parents, for instance, took the advice of their first good American friend, a teacher in Cornell's laboratory school, in which my sister and I spent the summer of 1939 while my father studied agricultural methods there. This woman strongly advised my multilingual parents to speak only English to my sister and me, so that we would not be ostracized for speaking with a foreign accent. This seemed especially convincing to my parents, who, because of first Austria's and later Hungary's alliances with Germany, eventually bore the classification of "enemy aliens." And so, to ensure our assimilation, our parents never spoke to us in either German or Hungarian, their own mother tongues. It is hard to imagine what this must have felt like—perhaps somewhat akin to a pair of robins who find themselves hatching cuckoo's eggs.

For most of my life, it was just fine by me to be a cuckoo in a robin's nest— the perfect imitation of an American girl, maintaining a steady contrast, a steady pressure against my parents' elaborate European social expectations and high standards of achievement. Paradoxically, as I succeeded at becoming captain of the cheer-leaders, strove to be fluent in teen talk, popular with everyone, easygoing and casual, I also worked to keep up accomplishments my parents could approve of—learning to perform Schubert lieder, to read Shaw and Molière, to speak and write in French. It was easy enough when I was a little girl to fulfill everyone's expectations, to gain approval from adults and children alike. But it grew harder when I became an adolescent.

I look at a picture of myself in a strapless evening gown toward the back of a dance floor at a formal dance. I am about 15, a part of the picture, yet not a part. Everyone else there seems to be blond and energetically engaged in conversation—about country clubs? We didn't belong to one. About their debutante parties? I wasn't going to be one. About their summer places? We didn't have one. I look distracted, disengaged. I am there only in body, and trying to make that body look as Anglo-Saxon as possible. A glint of shine from my dark head reminds me that I used to wrap a scarf tightly around my wet hair to flatten out my strong natural curl, thereby imitating the look of straight hair—at least for a few hours. Meanwhile, my biggest and least attainable romantic interest around that time was a broad-shouldered, slightly dishevelled young man who attended the High School of Music and Art in New York City. I'd only encountered him a couple of times—he was a friend of a friend—and he had never phoned me, but I had a terrible crush on him, wrote his initials all over my notebook. (Like many American teenage girls of the period, I spent a lot of time next to the phone, waiting.) He was serious, talented, a musician, bohemian, Jewish. Perhaps I was not serious enough for him, not perhaps sexy enough, probably not Jewish enough. I was passing in all sorts of ways, ways that I didn't even recognize at the time, and was not to come to terms with until many years later. Was I a robin or a cuckoo? I was a pretty good mimic, but I had no idea what kind of a bird I was.

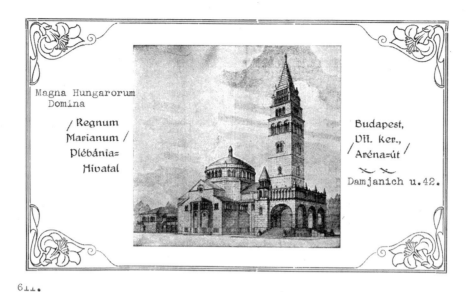

Magna Hungarorum
Domina

/ Regnum
Marianum /
Plébánia=
Hivatal

Budapest,
VII. ker.,
/ Aréna=út /
Damjanich u. 42.

611.
.... sz.

ÁTTÉRÉSI BIZONYITVÁNY.

Alulirott hivatalosan bizonyitom,hogy a mai napon Dr.PERL GYÖRGYNÉ,született

Furth Éva Gizella urnőt,aki mint Dr. Furth Ernő és Roheim Elza szülöknek tör-

vényes leánya Wien-ben /Oesterreich/ 1907.március 27.-én született és Budapes-

ten,VI. Benczur u. 45. sz. alatt lakik,-miután az 1868.évi LIII.tcikk 5.§.-á-

nak a levéltárunkban levő két jegyzőkönyv tanusága szerint eleget tett,-a ró-

mai katholikus egynáz kebelébe felvettem.

Budapest,1936. november 26.

Dr. Némethy Ernő
plébános

In November of 1936, my family converted to Catholicism. My mother's conversion
document refers to her as Perl Györgyné, the Hungarian form of address for married women.

6

Mixed Messages

IT WAS NOT UNTIL MY SECOND YEAR IN COLLEGE that I learned about my Jewishness, a "fact" about me that many others apparently recognized right away. From the moment I arrived in Cambridge, well-meaning acquaintances had been fixing me up for dates with nice Jewish boys, for the most part boring young preprofessionals, earnest overachievers from the Harvard Law School. My family name was Perl; without knowing it, I'd simply been taken in by the Jewish social underground. One of these dates expressed dismay at the sight of a tiny cross I was wearing on a gold chain around my neck. This pretty tourmaline ornament was something my father had bought for all three of his "girls" as a baptismal gift. The family had converted to Catholicism several years before my father decided to leave Hungary, and my sister and I had been raised in the Church. The young man insisted that my family name was not only German, as my parents had always told me, but indisputably Jewish. He definitely got my attention. I began to ask my Jewish friends how you defined being Jewish. What was a Jew? Who was a Jew? I was trying to get a simple answer to that most complex of questions—fascinating to rabbis as well as to anti-Semites—a conundrum that even the state of Israel has trouble solving. Finally I approached my parents with questions I should have known to ask—that they should have filled me in on—much earlier. My mother's father was Jewish. I had known that since I learned of his imprisonment in a Nazi camp; but how many other grandparents? I'd never asked that particular question. The answer: all of them. Yes, my parents agreed, in a certain way, in the eyes of certain people, that made me

My sister, my mother and me dressed for church in the U.S.

Jewish too. But they had never seen themselves as Jewish in any important way, never wanted to agree to a racial definition, to a definition that took away their choice in matters of religion or in any other aspect of their lives. Of course this illusion of choice was just that—an illusion. The larger, pre-existing choices in my family's life had already been taken away by the war, by Hitler, by the destruction of their way of life. Meanwhile, they had allowed me to take part in the family high-wire act, a risky game in which we made up the moves as we went along. Suddenly I saw I was working without a net.

For me, the news of our Jewishness came first like a kick in the teeth; then it became more like a decades-long underground fire, flaming up always in a new place, causing the ground to cave in under me where the smoldering had passed unseen. Only much later—only after digging deeply into the family's history— did I begin to understand the cultural and historical reasons that led my parents to what seemed to me then such a wounding decision. And finally, now that I am in my eighth decade, it has become a source of a muted, bittersweet pride, the pleasure of taking part—however peripherally—in yet another rich tradition.

But how could I be Jewish and not know it? Until that moment in college, my naive understanding of Jewishness was that it was a religion, freely entered into, that one could become a Jew the way one might become a Presbyterian or a Catholic. Wrong, wrong, wrong. Jewishness, I was finally learning—painfully, angrily—may have nothing to do with religion. It surely never did for my parents, nor for the generations of secularized, assimilated Jews who were my grandparents and great-grandparents in Central Europe. Instead, my family's Jewishness was a cultural, some would say a racial, fact, determined by parentage, acknowledged, even reinforced, insisted upon by society, by governments, by institutions, by lovers of tribalism, by racist bigots, religious zealots and ethnic watchdogs on the one hand, and by reverencers of tradition and community, historically attuned believers on the other. The war had been over for 10 years before I understood that my mother's beloved father had not been persecuted by the Nazis for his religion, but for his ancestry. I was a good student at an elite college, yet this basic concept had somehow eluded me. It was the family secret, kept even from me, kept, perhaps, from me by myself.

Jewishness, I was to learn, is an unshakable historic burden. You could be a pious Catholic—as I had been—but you remained a Jew. As a lapsed Catholic you remained a Jew. The fact was, you *could* be a lapsed Catholic. You could never be a lapsed Jew. It was a permanent number tattooed on your wrist.

On a shelf in my study, between *Roget's Thesaurus* and *Gray's Anatomy*, stands my Douay Bible, the one that Catholics are supposed to read. Its dimpled white leatherette cover is cracking, the spine yellowed from the light. Somewhere else, in a box with my childhood memorabilia, are two first communion gifts, a rosary and a prayer book covered in a nacreous swirl of imitation mother-of-pearl. These things remain a part of my life, despite the fact that I am no longer a believer and that a loosely linked structure of my own convictions now stands on the site where the great baroque pillars of the Church once held sway.

Downstairs with the rest of the reference books, dressed in sober black cloth, sits my Protestant King James Bible. As pencilled marginalia in a round girlish hand witnesses, this is the one I once read as part of a freshman college course called "Ideas of Good and Evil in Western Literature." The Douay Bible had been given to me six years earlier when I was confirmed, but it never seemed to have a real function, except for private study—something Catholics were not, in any case, encouraged to do.

Now, decades later, I learn from its introduction that the difference between it and the King James is one of scholarly traditions. The Catholic Bible includes more—the books of Tobias, Judith, Wisdom, Ecclesiasticus, Machabees I-II, Baruch and sections of Daniel and Esther. The paradox of the book, like the paradox of Catholicism, is its claim to inclusiveness, to a universality that embraces all human possibilities, all races, all nations.

Not in my youthful experience of it. My sense of Catholicism was of exclusion, of keeping people out, of paring things down so fine, making the rules so hard to follow, that no one could win—as Robert Frost says, "so the wrong ones can't find it / So can't get saved as St. Mark says they mustn't." The Irish priests in our suburban New York parish expressed three main interests: denouncing Protestants, denouncing Communists and raising money. Raising money, though boring, now seems to me comparatively harmless, the only one of the priestly concerns with a positive trajectory, the only one that didn't encourage us to hate somebody. We were issued little cardboard boxes with a year's worth of envelopes, into which we put our weekly "offering." The envelopes protected you from the embarrassment of letting everyone see that you were dropping a mere quarter into the long-handled basket passed down your row, but more importantly, they were a way of keeping people serious about giving to the church. I know that the envelopes were dated; what I can't remember is whether they were numbered, coded, identifiable. Had we made a pledge of a certain amount each year? Catholics were always making these pledges and promises. It was never enough merely to confess, to look back and take stock of your shortcomings, to make an act of contrition. You had also to do penance and then look ahead to the life you could be leading, promise to be better, make a vow, renounce your old ways, give things up. It was a strenuous spiritual life.

As new immigrants, my cultivated European parents were appalled by the vulgarity of our priests. Father Madden, pastor of Our Lady of Fatima Church, was a fleshy lout, a football player gone to seed, a coarser version of Karl Malden or Joe McCarthy. European Catholicism, my parents explained to my sister and me, represented a much more spiritual, more aesthetic and intellectual tradition. Still, they made no move to protect us from these weekly insults to our intelligence and sensibilities. The alternative seemed to them unacceptable, an American Protestantism that they saw as almost entirely social—all church suppers and basketball teams. At least Catholicism reminded them of something familiar. The unmagical Protestants

First communion, 1943; high school cheerleader, 1953.

were just too foreign. My family continued to go to the Catholic church every Sunday. My mother wore elegant clothes, including wonderfully becoming hats with small veils and those fur scarves made of little foxes with fake glass eyes that ate each other's tails. She often cried during the service, which I took to have something to do with the war and the fact that her father was suffering in Europe and that she might never see him again. But then she cried a lot when I was growing up, usually about her children's impossible behavior or when she was fighting with my father. I never thought to ask why she was crying in church, for fear it might somehow turn out to be my fault.

As the other formal part of our religious life, every Friday afternoon until I was in junior high school, a group of us were carpooled to religious instruction. The local church, though good enough for Sundays, for delivering the sacraments, was evidently not deemed high toned enough for our spiritual education. For that, we were taken to two very serious Catholic places. The first was the Cenacle of St. Regis, on Riverside Drive and 140th Street. That building, seen in the 1990s from the West Side

Highway, was a burnt-out shell, bare ruined choirs that you could look all the way through. But back in the late '40s, in this severe, slightly damp, dark gray and brown stone building, we were taught the distinctions between venial, mortal and original sin by aging, sorrowful nuns and the occasional unthreatening priest. Here we learned of the only truly powerful act that a lay Catholic could perform, that of baptism, but only in cases of the greatest emergency, in extremis. For instance, if we happened upon an unbaptized child who had been hit by a car, and there were no priest around, then we could legitimately baptize. We could administer the sacrament just by saying *Ego te baptizo in nomine Patris, et Filii et Spiritus Sancti.* When it was a case of saving a soul from eternal damnation, any Catholic—even a woman—could perform this priestly act. These bits of arcane knowledge with their attendant unlikely case histories were fascinating, but what I remember most about religious instruction were the drives back and forth, with my mother being not at all amused by the shenanigans of the rowdy McCaffrey and McCall boys in the back seat. I was always embarrassed by Mother's lack of cool. She was too easily bothered by rowdiness. Her emotional temperature rose too quickly and by too many degrees, it seemed to me. Other mothers in the carpool—real Americans—seemed to take all this wrestling and punching in stride.

Later there was a longer trip to Greenwich, where we paid weekly visits to the Convent of the Sacred Heart, a posh girl's boarding school that we were delighted not to have to attend. The nuns here were much more worldly and stylish in their starched, pleated coifs. They treated us kindly, but with a touch of condescension, as though they were dealing with little heathens, charity cases from a distant benighted continent. After all, our parents had already failed in their Catholic duty by not sending us to parochial school. Yet despite the chaotic car trips and the hauteur of the nuns, I took all this instruction seriously. I wanted to get it right so I could excel, get straight A's and blue ribbons the way I did in everything else. Religion, like other areas of my life, involved finding out what the rules were, arguing strenuously about their lack of reasonableness, then assiduously following them.

When it came to religion, it turned out, it was not so simple to follow the rules, even when you thought you knew what they were. Take confession, for instance, an experience I grew to detest and avoid. In many ways this is the cornerstone of the Catholic experience, a uniquely Catholic drama, reenacting the glorious promise that Jesus made to wash away the sins of the world. Other Christian churches celebrate the sacraments of communion, baptism and marriage. Only Catholics confess. Confession is supposed to be anonymous, optimistic, spirit-lifting, a chance to wipe the slate clean and start afresh, the Church at its most generous and humane. To me it never felt like that. There in that stuffy little box, through a screen that was meant to conceal our identities, I was bound by my faith to enumerate my transgressions to a priest whose voice I knew all too well, and who probably also recognized me. The confessional, built like a vertical coffin, always reminded me of death. It was supposed to: What would happen if you were struck by lightning or in a plane crash and you were unconfessed, with your soul in a state of mortal sin, like Hamlet's murdered father, "unhouseled, disappointed, unannealed"? Answer: You went directly to hell. With the help of confession, you had a chance at least of purgatory—just as unpleasant as hell, we were told, but with the consolatory knowledge that eventually it would end, and your soul would rise to heaven.

You could not take communion without having first confessed, and you were expected to take communion regularly, perhaps once a month, although the absolute minimum was once a year—your Easter Duty. It was hard to know what to confess, if you hadn't done some obvious thing like tell lies or take money from your mother's pocketbook. Neither of these sins were my style. I can remember confessing fighting with my sister, talking back to my mother and thinking bad thoughts about people. I never would have mentioned the word masturbation or necking, although I knew that almost any form of sexual pleasure outside of marriage was considered a sin. And I didn't even recognize subtle transgressions like coveting my neighbor's bicycle, cashmere sweater or boyfriend. It got so that I simply avoided confession, letting huge stretches of time elapse between visits, meaning that when I said: "Bless me, father, for I have sinned. It has been a year and a half since my last confession," I was in for a scolding for the length of time I'd stayed away. Meaning that next time I'd stay away even longer. I remember one particularly brutal haranguing I got when I was a young teenager. It was not our regular priest, but the older, more distinguished pastor of a parish across town that we were attending while our church was being renovated. The priest made it clear that he knew who I was, and that the only unforgivable sin I'd confessed was the length of time I'd stayed away. That was my last confession.

I left the Church in an extended fit of adolescent despair over its inability to deliver what I thought it had promised—believers who acted on their beliefs.

In high school I began noticing that not everyone took the rules as seriously as I did, that the fast, sexy Catholic girls in my class were the ones who were also the most sanctimoniously observant, who took communion every week, who fasted for days at a time during Lent, who went on retreats. I began to see that for them, confession before communion on Sunday was primarily a matter of clearing the decks of whatever it was they'd done during the week before. Going all the way was rumored to be part of what they did. I was genuinely shocked. These girls were saying one thing and doing another. Naive and unprotected from such doubleness, I had come smack up against hypocrisy and was prepared to blame the Church for it.

My last official participation in a church event took place the spring of my freshman year at Radcliffe, an Ash Wednesday mass somewhere in the vicinity of Mount Auburn Street. I emerged from the brief morning service into the damp cold of a Cambridge February with the mark of penitential ash burning on my forehead. It might as well have been the scarlet letter. I wore it with the gloomy knowledge that I was lying about my relationship to the Church, that I was faking it, that I was no longer a believer.

Faking it was not then and never has been a happy mode for me. I am not a good liar. Deception, though not without its potent thrills, exacts too heavy a toll. Even at the level of small-scale politeness, I lack the impulse to be tactful, have no easy grace with compliments I don't feel. When someone asks me: "How do you like my new dress?" I find it hard not to be frank. Yet, as I soon learned, the deception was even more complicated than I thought. I was not merely *no longer* a Catholic, but in the deepest sense, I never had been one. The whole thing was a lie, a pretense, a performance, a cover-up.

Maybe there was a level at which I didn't want to know about our Jewishness. It would have made playing by the rules all the more difficult. Could I still have been a cheerleader? Still have been popular? My sister claims to have known all along. Why didn't we ever talk about this? Was she burdened with the family secret in ways I wasn't?

I learned that my parents had converted in 1936, baptizing my sister and then me, when I was born a month later. The rabbi who they needed to sign their conversion documents was someone they didn't know, since they practiced no form of religion. When they went to see him about the necessary formalities, he spat in their faces.

The conversion was clearly an act of expediency, although my father would never admit it in so many words. If they were going to live in Hungary, it was becoming increasingly uncomfortable to do so as a Jew. Anti-Jewish laws had been in existence since after Hungary's one-year Communist "revolution" of 1919. More serious restrictions would be imposed in 1938 and 1939, making it harder for Jews to be professionals or to hold and sell property. Indeed the growing official anti-Semitism, along with the rise of fascism, had pushed my father not only to Catholicism, but more importantly toward the decision to leave Europe. Unlike many of their acquaintances, he became increasingly convinced that war was going to overtake Hungary. Did he foresee, too, the horrors, the systematic destruction of the Jews? A visit to Berlin in 1934 had alerted him to the power of Hitler's brown-shirted thugs marching in the streets. And harassing visits from the Hungarian secret police looking for evidence of illegal business dealings had clearly strengthened his resolve.

As the facts piled up for me about my parents' decision to leave Europe, about the subtle and not-so-subtle growth of anti-Semitism, I began to understand their decision to put behind them a life in which all their important documents were marked "Israelite." Yet at the same time, I still had my own questions. Where did I fit into all of this? What did it mean for me? Was I a lapsed Catholic or a Holocaust survivor? At first I was simply furious for the confusion my parents had thrown me into, for what I saw as a deliberate lie. In their effort to protect my sister and me, they had obscured, tried to blot out an identity that had, they argued, never identified anything they cared about. But what does it mean to "pass," to blot out an identity, to invent a new one?

Since then I have read many wartime accounts of "hidden Jews," mainly children, whose parents turned them over to Catholic families or convent schools to raise in safety, protected from Nazi horrors. Usually these children knew of the lie they were living. They had to know so they could keep the secret and survive. But there were and are other sorts of hidden Jews, families who have sidestepped or denied their historic links to Jewishness. Former Secretary of State Madeleine Albright is perhaps the best known in recent years. One friend of mine, born in this country to Austro-Hungarian parents and raised in a noisily fundamentalist Christian church in California, learned about her family's Jewish connection only when she was in her 40s. A cousin in Budapest took her to see the grave of their mutual grandmother, who was buried—to my friend's astonishment—in a Jewish cemetery. Even then, her family denied it all, continued to try to disavow the past, even as she unearthed and confronted them with school certificates and passports marked "Israelite." For them—as for my parents—the great Jewish motto "Only remember" had become "Better to forget."

Secrecy is not a function only of wartime, nor is it a specialty of Jewish or crypto-Jewish families. It is embedded in the human condition, and families are among its most fertile breeding grounds. Children may have their secrets, but most of all it is the adults who get to control and conceal powerful information. The young child gets fleeting glimpses of adult life, voices raised or hushed behind closed doors, shadows on lowered blinds, one half of puzzling phone conversations. There is the great secret of sex between one's parents, the secret of their fights, the secrets of family feuds, of why one relative is preferred over another, the secret of one's own standing in the household: Is one loved? admired? accepted? favored? In a bourgeois household, there are all the secrets related to money: How much is there? Where does it come from? Is there enough? How much is enough?

In my family the mysteries were compounded by the fact that my parents spoke to each other in languages—Hungarian and German—that my sister and I could not understand. The degree of confusion was compounded, too, by my father's love of speaking in parables, his love of complexity, his love, in short, of secrets. At some level I must have known that there was something hidden about who we were, but until I was an adult, I didn't know what it was.

Jewishness, for my father, had been drained of positive value, had never been more than a largely meaningless affiliation. He saw it almost entirely as an obstacle, a handicap. It had encumbered his life and he didn't want it to encumber ours. It was better to bypass it, to leave it out of the equation as long as possible. Perhaps, eventually, it would go away. My father saw himself as a Hungarian, but his strong skepticism made him wary of all forms of tribal or nationalistic zealotry. Though he had a deeply spiritual side, he was not religious, preferring his own rituals and rules to those of any external institution. He would not have denied the existence of a higher power, but would have put it in philosophical, intellectual, even mystical clothing, choosing always the ambiguous, civilized utterances of Rilke and Emerson over the dogmatic pronouncements of Moses or Pius XI. (In one of the last years of his life, he reread the Old Testament and pronounced it brutal and boring.)

As for me, although I was a lively, outspoken, tomboyish girl, I was also a profoundly dutiful daughter. And I was a sucker for Catholicism, easily hypnotized

Trauungs-Zeugnis.

Von dem Unterzeichneten wird bezeugt, daß laut hieramtlichen Trauungsbuches *Pro.*

Reihezahl 109/31 am *fünften Mai* Eintausend

neun hundert *ein u dreissig* 5 V 1931 das nachbenannte

Brautpaar nach den Gesetzen des Staates und der Religion getraut worden ist.

Bräutigam:

Dr Georg Perl, ledig

geboren *in Budapest am 18 November 1895*

zuständig nach *Budapest*

wohnhaft in *Budapest*

Sohn des *Dr Sama Perl*

und der *Lenke geb. Jakabfy*

Braut:

Eva Fürth, ledig

geboren *in Wien am 29 März 1907*

wohnhaft in *VIII Alserstrasse 45*

Tochter des *Dr Ernö Jakab Fürth*

und der *Eliz geb. Roheim*

Die Trauung wurde in Gegenwart der Zeugen *Edmond Fürth*

und Dr Anton Lukacs

von *Herrn Rabb Dr J M Bach*

in Wien I *Seitenstettengasse 4* vorgenommen.

Matrikelamt der israelitischen Kultusgemeinde in Wien.

am 6. *März* 1931

beeideter Matrikelführer.

My parents were married by a rabbi, and their marriage license was registered by Vienna's official Jewish authority.

*"Non omnis moriar," a quotation from Horace, is inscribed
on my great-grandfather Daniel Fürth's gravestone in Sušice.*

by incantation, by repetition, by music, by the light through stained-glass windows.
I pledged my faith early and with the greatest seriousness. Meditation and detachment
seemed to come naturally. Sitting through mass as the priest droned on in Latin was
not so unlike thinking my own thoughts at a dinner party where all the grown-ups
spoke Hungarian. Later I learned to understand much of the Latin of the mass, and
in my postpious years have sung many choral settings of it. No question, it is powerful theater, but for me that's also part of the problem. One reason that I avoid church
services even now is that I am too quickly moved when I hear a psalm read, when
I hear, or especially sing, a stirring hymn. The music and the words still connect me
with irresistible early longings. What happens is a kind of aesthetic and emotional
melting that has nothing to do with belief or conviction, nor with the willingness to
join a group seeking systematic guidance from a higher authority. No other religion
could ever earn my allegiance. *Once a Catholic, always a Catholic* takes on a nice double-
edged irony in my case.

When looked at from a safe distance, my anguished departure from the Church seems inevitable and predictable, simply a return to the skeptical, humanist culture I had belonged to all along. It was surely my fate. Remember that my great-grandfather Daniel Fürth's grave bears an inscription from Horace, not from the Bible or Torah. Still, at age 19, I felt myself in the middle of an emotional and meta-physical whirlpool. It was a little like trying to work your way through those circular arguments Catholics used to have about the relation between free will and predestination: How can man (yes, then it was always man) be said to have free will if an omniscient God knows how it will all turn out? Where, in any case, did I belong? And did I have a choice, free will, anything to say about it?

A letter of my father's to my mother in 1935 gives a sense of the studiedly detached tone he took toward the act of conversion. My sister, Doris ("Dorli"), would have been three years old at the time, and had been attending occasional church services with Nene, the nursemaid. Evidently my father was prepared to use my sister's interest in church as a way of justifying the conversion. In his letter my father avoids any mention of Hungary's anti-Semitic atmosphere and the excellent practical reasons for converting to the country's official religion. Or perhaps he simply preferred not to commit these reasons to ink and paper. There is no question that the detachment is studied: My father had already begun looking at non-Hungarian options, putting money into a Swiss bank account, as had my grandfather and many others. It was this money that our family lived on for the first few years in the U.S.

The letter reached Mother in Sušice. Daddy had been attending to the harvest on a farm he managed in Hungary. He writes in some detail about his trip from Budapest into the country and of the medical attention being given to his brother for a case of swollen glands. Then, quite offhandedly, he brings up "our christening."

> Concerning our christening, indeed we did not discuss it, since we had only half a day to ourselves. I will inform myself about the procedure, and as godmother I would suggest Mrs. de Hazay, who is a Catholic. In case a man is needed it could be Petényi. Do you agree?

> The amazing urge of Dorli for church perhaps makes our decision easy. On the other hand for us it is perhaps more an administrative act than an emotional one. I do not know what my mother would have thought about it. My father would have basically not been opposed. The same is true in your case. It is not cynicism,

but it belongs to the matters about which I have no opinion. The push has to come from outside, perhaps from Dorli.

I hear Berti's carriage arriving and interrupt this letter.

My father has set the terms for how this change is to be seen: no big deal, just an administrative matter; we'll let the child's impulse guide us. Please don't think I'm being cynical, he says; it's just that this is not a terribly important inner event for me. Still, he brings in some heavy guns from the realm of family mythology to back him up: his parents (both dead), Mrs. de Hazay, the mother of his late great mentor. His didactic tone is not peculiar to this occasion, since even in his most casual letters to my mother, while he continues to court and woo her, he continues, above all, to teach, counsel, correct and advise her.

Fifty-three years later, in one of our last conversations, when he was 92 and near death, he expressed his annoyance to me. My nephew Jonathan, my sister's son, had been asking him lots of penetrating questions about the family's Jewishness. I can imagine my father's reply, describing the good life he wanted to create for his family, his efforts to avoid the pain of exclusion involved in acknowledging our Jewishness. My guess is that he never mentioned his and my mother's own brand of anti-Semitism, a finely honed scorn for the vulgar Eastern European shtetl Jews, "not our sort." Yes, he was a snob, had never wanted to belong to the club that would have him as a member, especially if that club admitted other Jews. He did not, early in his career on Wall Street, accept an invitation to join the prestigious firm of Kuhn, Loeb. It was simply too Jewish.

Nor was this wish to stay separate from the Jewish crowd new to life in the United States. In an early letter to my mother, some time before their marriage, my father describes his return from a summer visit to her family in their Czech country homestead. After a happy time there in that pastoral paradise, he speaks of finding himself back, as he puts it—shockingly to me, though surely intended with ironic black humor—in "Judapest."

Whatever he said to my nephew Jonathan, it was supposed to be the last word on the subject. It was not; Jonathan persisted, spoke with my aunt Clary, my father's sister, who had survived the war in a safe house in Budapest, thanks to Raoul Wallenberg. My father was irritated, told Jonathan to leave Clary alone, to put this subject to rest. Why was this young man bothering everybody with these old questions? Wasn't it right, my father asked me angrily, to have wanted a better life, to have wanted to be able to stay at a good hotel, to associate with the people you liked rather than having them chosen for you by some meaningless connection? He did not—he never did—mention the Holocaust, matters of life and death. Avoiding death, it went without saying, was the reason above all reasons to escape from their old life. But once safe on the other side, it was books, travel, domestic ease and a modest level of social acceptance that made my father's life worth living. Surely Jonathan could see that; surely I could.

When my parents came to this country, they were surprised to find that upper-crust American Jews were "much more Jewish," as my mother put it, than the assimilated Jews, the *haute juiverie* they had known in Hungary. The Warburgs and the Lewisohns, German-American Jews whom they occasionally encountered, were not only rich and cultivated, but also overtly religious. They advertised their pious Jewishness. In Hungary, by contrast, many Jews had taken Hungarian, Magyarized, names, and few educated Jews—certainly not the ones my parents associated with—were religious. When Hungary became an independent partner with Austria in the Dual Monarchy in 1867, the national-liberal aristocracy had made a deal with the Jews:

> The Jews would adapt their religious and communal life to modern society, under state supervision, and in return would be encouraged to participate in national development in practically all spheres, particularly economic and cultural. There being no native Hungarian commercial or industrial class, the Jews gladly welcomed the opportunity to fill the vacuum. Many Jews also enthusiastically accepted the offer to assimilate, which meant adopting the language and national identity of the majority.
>
> This compact was not as neat as it may sound. . . . legal emancipation did not guarantee social acceptance . . . nor did it eliminate anti-Semitism.[*]

No indeed, there were always those loose ends, always a little residual anti-Semitism, always, finally, the lack of social acceptance. Here, too, in the Land of the Free,

[*]Charles Hoffman, *Gray Dawn: The Jews of Eastern Europe in the Post-Communist Era* (New York: HarperCollins, 1992), p. 60.

my parents struggled with those same forces, often finding themselves on the fringes of something they wished they could belong to. Although they were rejected for membership in a shore club in Westchester (what were the reasons? was this xenophobia, anti-Semitism? did these people *know*?), my father kept up his dues in the Public School Club in London, long after it was clear that the infirmities of age would never allow him to return there. My mother continued to have the feeling that there was a really interesting party somewhere to which she was not being invited. For both of them it must have been a great relief when my sister and I married the most WASP-ish of men and settled into what looked to them like lives of easy acceptance, me in the ivy-clad precincts of academe, my sister inside the Washington Beltway in the company of ambassadors and Supreme Court justices.

In so many ways I have been lucky in the man I married. A person with a subtle, literary, unideological mind, Bill is at home—sometimes infuriatingly so—in ambiguity. He does not ask for resolution or simplification. In relation to the complications of my background, this has been reassuring, a comfort.

When we first met, I was 18, a Radcliffe sophomore; he was 22, an English graduate student at Harvard. We checked each other out in various ways, including religious ones. He had left the Episcopal church several years before, choosing for himself rather a philosopher's and humanist's unaffiliated set of beliefs. I explained my complex religio-racial fate as I had recently learned it. It was OK with him, seemed to pose no problem. Both of us were mainly relieved to learn that the other was not an observant believer of any variety, not a churchgoer.

When he went home at Christmas to visit his family in upstate New York, he mentioned to them that he was becoming quite serious about a girl he'd met in Cambridge. "Oh," said his mother. "And what *is* she?"—meaning, of course, what religion? "Well," said Bill, "she's sort of Catholic and she's sort of Jewish."

"Jesus Christ," said his father (never much of a churchgoer himself, nevertheless a man who took these categories seriously). "There are two kinds of people I'd hoped you wouldn't get involved with: one is Catholic and the other is Jewish. And now you've managed to get yourself involved with both."

Bill's father had a point. It *was* confusing, especially if you needed to stick to the

Bill Pritchard when I first knew him in 1956.

old rules, according to which you married your own kind. These rules had served the Pritchards well for many generations — as, indeed, they had served my family too, depending of course on what you meant by "your own kind." But Bill's father was a pussycat in comparison to the card-carrying bigots I encountered later as I began to make my way as an adult Jewish/Catholic. Several of these people were colleagues or graduate school acquaintances of my husband's, some were friends of mine. And all were ferociously, defensively Jewish themselves, despite the fact that most were deeply secular, having given up any but the most perfunctory displays of religious affiliation. What did I mean, I hadn't *known* I was Jewish? Surely this was some sort of a pose. And even if it wasn't a pose, what was I going to do about it now? Didn't I have an obligation to re-enlist, to begin celebrating seders, contribute to the State of Israel? How could my parents not have spoken Yiddish? Weren't all Jews in the U.S. Marxists, and didn't they all come from the shtetls of Poland

Four generations of Bill's family, 1933. Bill's great-grandfather
Moses LaGrange; his mother, Marion Pritchard; his grandfather
Delbert LaGrange; and young Bill himself.

and Russia to the sweatshops of the Lower East Side?

When the news about Madeleine Albright's hidden Jewishness emerged, I raised a small cheer. We were out of the closet together. Her Czech parents had done something much like what mine had done—converted to Catholicism by way of shielding their family from danger, then stayed that way as American immigrants, raising their children under the new dispensation. Although it is somewhat hard to

Four generations, 1960. Our son David; Bill's mother, Marion; Bill; his grandfather Delbert LaGrange.

credit that such a sophisticated person could have been kept in the dark until she was in her late 50s, I can easily imagine that as a child, she went along with her parents' explanations of who they were. Why should children question what their parents tell them? I kept a file of clippings of the responses to Albright's refusal to apologize for herself or her parents. Many of those responses reminded me all too sharply of the kinds of sanctimonious disapproval I had encountered almost four decades earlier, and have continued, occasionally, to run into.

Does anyone still remember the "Ballad for Americans"? This stirring piece of music, a multicultural polemic, a fight song for the melting pot, was part of my family's collection of sheet music from which I learned to accompany myself on the piano as I sang. Downstairs in the linoleum-floored "playroom" that held our grand piano, my father's library and the ping-pong table, I would sidestep the Bach inventions or Chopin waltzes that I was supposed to be practicing in favor of tunes I could sing. I was not an especially good sight-reader, but I learned to make my way through the piano accompaniments of current show tunes, songs from *Carousel* ("If I Loved You") or *Bloomer Girl* ("The Eagle and Me"), wartime standards like "White Cliffs of Dover," and anthologies of traditional American tunes like "When Johnnie Comes Marching Home" and "Poor Wayfaring Stranger."

The "Ballad for Americans" was in that pile of sheet music, and we must have had the record that we played on our old wind-up gramophone, because I can hear Paul Robeson's voice as clear as day. What a rousing piece of music that was for me, the great bass voice alternating with dramatic speech by a chorus and narrator, describing the birth of our country, his, mine and so many others': "Nobody who was anybody believed him. / Everybody who was anybody they doubted it. / Nobody had faith." Robeson sang out for freedom, the new faith as defined by "nobodies" such as Washington, Tom Paine, Crispus Attucks and Lafayette. And he sang out for the idea that an American was a mixed entity: "I'm just an Irish, Negro, Jewish, Italian, French and English, Chinese, Russian, Greek and Turk and Czech and double check—*American*." I believed every melodramatic, cornball word of it. You started out with all these designations, labels, national and racial connections, and you gave them all up to become this new thing, an American. It was a step beyond the Horatio Alger myth of being able to accomplish anything you wanted if you just had the gumption and stick-to-itiveness. It was a myth that said you could not merely *do* anything, but as an American, you could *be* anything, anyone.

Such an optimistic, energetic sense of possibilities suited one aspect of the wartime gung-ho, we're-all-in-this-together spirit of the times. But not everyone saw things this way. For some people, what you started out as was who you were. The labels people wore were not optional; no changing sides in the middle of the game, no making up the rules as you went along. Once a Hungarian Jew, always a Hungarian Jew. Never mind about conversion, about baptism, first communion and confirmation. Never mind about naturalization, new citizenship, new lives.

Ours was—and is—a mixed marriage, Bill's and mine. But I have come to believe that all marriages are mixed in the most important ways. And that beyond that marital mix, the complications increase and multiply. All families convey to their children a series of mixed messages—some more mixed than others. My parents had sent many of the usual contradictory signals, most of them in the form of mandates:

Be good but not priggish; be clever but not a showoff; be obedient but not servile; be successful but not pushy; be popular but be yourself. Be independent but loving; be dutiful, neat, clean, athletic. Read books, learn a lot; yet be sure to spend time outdoors in the fresh air, excelling at sports, if possible. Express your opinion but don't be so tactless. Speak up; don't be so talkative. Be beautiful; don't be vain. Care about your health; don't be a hypochondriac. Tell the truth; keep secrets. And add to that list: Be a Catholic; be a Jew.

A social worker friend who wanted to disparage my husband's style as a parent used that late '60s term, *mixed messages*, to describe what he was sending our children. It was a time when we were locked in a difficult struggle with our eldest son, then a young adolescent: Your husband Bill must send a lot of mixed messages, she said. He works so hard, yet he doesn't seem to; he's very serious about what he does, yet the surface is all irony and throwaway. Her remarks were a reproach, an explanation, a diagnosis of why we were having this trouble. *Mixed messages* was the fashionable buzzword for being a bad parent—saying one thing and doing another. Do what I say, not what I do; do what I do, not what I say—these contradictory modes were alleged to be bad for children and other growing things. You were supposed to be consistent. When they sliced you open, you were supposed to be made of the same stuff all the way through. A very American conceit—consistency, sincerity, unmixed messages. A puritanical, high-toned mandate.

My friend was well intentioned, but she would never be able to see virtue in anything but simplicity. Though my husband's heritage represents, in part, just this kind of singleness, he diverges from it notably. It's true, he has his steady beliefs, his even steadier habits. He has been a devoted and generous father, a faithful and generous husband, a loyal and dutiful son, a hardworking and dependable colleague. But as a social and intellectual being, he is in love with ambiguity, resists the unqualified answer, the simple solution, resists, always, the fashionable, the politically orderly. It makes him infuriating to live with, because he can rarely speak straight, take a stand. He likes to be outrageous, to shock, to be anticonventional, politically incorrect, to say the thing that no one is allowed to say. He has an ingrained grudge against anything trendy; he eats red meat, drinks martinis. He's been known to be belligerent and illiberal, bigoted, obnoxious. Along with the Romantics—Wordsworth, Tchaikovsky and Rachmaninoff—he loves the macho S.O.B.s—Kingsley Amis and Philip Roth.

Perhaps it is this doubleness that has put him in an easy relationship with difficult aspects of his own past. He does not hold grudges or assign blame. He seems to have walked through the slings and arrows of his own family's troubles with a magic shield around him, like the hero of a folk tale. It is the shield of humor, of music, of literature, the shield of ambiguity. "Do I contradict myself?" asks Whitman. "Very well, then, I contradict myself."

Such a faith in largeness seems just as American as the naive faith in simplicity. It is the pioneer, improvising, moving freely through open spaces. Although it's hard to think of Bill as a pioneer, he has, in an important way, the courage of his own wildness, his own willfulness and originality. Both of our upbringings suggest similarly well-kept, well-controlled spotless interiors, yet Bill managed to escape into the messy landscape of the intellect, where he gets to be his own person. For me, despite my superficially rebellious spirit, the powerful mandate to be a dutiful daughter has usually prevailed.

My upbringing embodied thoroughly European values of a particular haut bourgeois type. Small, tidy, neat, orderly, rational, elegant, punctual, those qualities were encouraged, insisted upon. But there were other layers too. Below the smoothly controlled surface ran an irrational undercurrent, a dangerous riptide: my grandmother's legendary extravagance, her breakdown and suicide, my mother's terrible unhappiness. Holding some of this irrationality at bay, a seawall against the flood of tears, was my father's solidity. Like Bill (and it helped that they were alike in this way), he could and often did see both sides of things at once. It's true that his view tended toward the dark, the melancholy, the pessimistic. He saw corruption as utterly inevitable, a kind of original sin. In his eyes, all elections, all sporting events, were fixed or at least fixable; silver linings were usually closely accompanied by clouds.

I have always had, by contrast, a great tendency toward the optimistic, the once-born—wishing for consistency, for simple, clear explanations, for unmixed messages. Good or bad? Yes or no? Up or down? I wanted the answers, wanted the story to come out even. When I was little, I remember my father trying to help me out— trying to confuse me?—with the idea of Santa Claus. When I started asking questions, Daddy replied, Well, you could think of Santa Claus as a spirit. But was he real? I wanted to know. How old was I? Five? Well, a spirit was real, my father said, the spirit of doing good for others, of giving, of generosity. Yes, I shouted, but was Santa Claus REAL? This was a story told years later about me, the charming, stubborn child, wanting nothing more than the simple truth, when, as we all know—as I came to know eventually—the truth is never simple, or, at the very least, that all messages of any value are bound to be mixed.

Realizing this has made it easier to come to terms with the anger I felt toward my parents after learning about my heritage, my ancestry, my ethnicity, my religious or racial background—whatever you want to call Jewishness. That anger was fast and hot and furious. How could they have done this to me? They had left me out of their calculations. They had conducted a social experiment in which I had been the guinea pig. No one had asked me, and worse than that, no one had told me. What else was buried behind the wall of elegant manners? What else had they decided to keep secret? Although they must have felt a combination of relief and embarrassment at my discovery, they did not go far in trying to explain. The conversion was the right thing to do at the time. Since then, however, the experience of reading my grandfather's letters, of learning so much more about the atmosphere of that period, has led me to a new understanding of what they thought they were doing.

Parents think they know what the outcome of their efforts will be. They think they know how to raise their children. They do things for their own good, no matter how painful for everyone. My parents joined the Catholic Church, and kept attending it. They—my father in particular—thought it would be a way of leaving the past behind, where it belonged. I believe that my father meant well, as he used to say of my mother when she raged at us. The times were hard, and there was a war on. Why not enlist us in the safest army, dress us in a uniform that would blend in easily with our new aspirations as free people?

My sister and me, summer 1945.

7

Knowing Perfectly Well

"**Y**ou know perfectly well what I mean," my father used to say. I was a lippy teenager, an opinionated young matron; he, an exasperated parent, a wise older man. I was standing up for whatever cause I happened to be espousing—being allowed to wear lipstick at 13 or defending women's liberation at 35; he was putting in for traditional—he would have said *rational*—views of how to behave, how to run one's life.

Of course I knew perfectly well what he meant. We had fought our battles too many times, knew each other's moves, counterpunching and feinting with the greatest of ease, coming in for the ad hominem (or feminam) knockdown. Yes, we knew perfectly well what the other meant. Yet surely, in the deepest ways, we did not know. There was the usual gap, parent to child, older to younger, man to girl. But there was also a cultural gap—not to mention an actual language gap. My older sister and I were technically immigrants, but because we were so young when our family left Hungary, it was only our elders who seriously counted as foreigners. Maybe all parents are foreigners to their children, puzzling as Martians, embarrassing as circus freaks. I have certainly observed this with my own children when they were teenagers. But when the two generations truly speak different languages, a different kind of strangeness opens up. My parents had opened this gap intentionally and for our own good. It was wartime, after all, and the pressures to assimilate were even stronger than usual. My sister and I spoke only English.

Still, in our battles of the wills, my father continued to insist that I knew perfectly well what he meant. Then, as if to let me off the hook a bit, at the end of some of our

Our family's house in Scarsdale, N.Y., from 1941 to 1984.

more predictable standoffs he would step back, make a gallant verbal bow, offer me a chance to behave in a civilized manner. "So," he would say with his short, charming laugh, "we disagree." That was not usually enough for me. I cared nothing for diplomacy, for grace—since they looked to me just like subtler forms of bullying. I was a sore loser; I wanted to score points, to win concessions—to win, period. As my sister used to put it with her own brand of exasperation, I always had to have the last word. My father, too—let there be no doubt about it—preferred having the last word; but beyond victory, he wanted peace, or at least the elimination of open conflict. I found a note from him on a Christmas card dated 1955. I would have been 19, just about the age when I learned about my Jewishness. The note reads:

> This thing Xmas, I think is really for peace and some humility.* Then you feel easier, you do not resent and are not offended, and move in the family as if they were friends (as should you).
> L. D.
> * And some presents.

My mother at the front door in the '50s.

That was my father—charming, didactic, his English thoroughly unidiomatic, standing up for what are now known as family values, meaning a suppression of children's quirks and desires in favor of the good of the whole group; meaning, I would surely have argued, in favor of the quirks and desires of the parents. His benign-sounding "peace and humility" simply signified to me another brand of coercion, and that he was, as always, backing my mother in her ongoing complaints against my adolescent willfulness. My father's corrective last words often happened on paper. When I returned home too late from a date in high school, I could expect to find a note waiting on the hall table setting out the standards of behavior I had transgressed, then offering reasonable but severe reconciliation. It was supposed to finish the discussion, bring light to darkness, effect a transformation, a conversion, cause me to change my behavior.

My father's habit of teaching—a less sympathetic observer might call it preaching—was deeply ingrained. He had taken on family responsibilities early in his life, a role thrust upon him because of his parents' divorce when he was four, closely followed by his mother's death when he was eight. He never had a dependable, settled family life. Perhaps that was why maintaining one, with all the conventional trappings, meant so much to him.

An early letter to my mother finds him instructing her about the proper attitude to take toward a gift he has sent her, a pair of opera glasses. It is September 1925. My father is not quite 30 and my mother is 18. He writes from Görbesziget, one of the family farms on Hungary's Great Plain whose affairs his grandfather had sent him to set in order. My father's uncle, who lived there, had been mismanaging the place, losing money on horses, squandering it on women. My parents had met a few years earlier at a party in the apartment of my mother's sister, Gretl, who was eight years older than my mother, married to Paul Strasser, and living in Budapest. My father was a sophisticated young man-about-town; my mother a pretty, lively, perhaps somewhat naive Viennese girl of 16. In 1925, after an evening at the opera where Paul's "stone-heavy field glasses" had been passed around, it seems that my father had sent my mother some smaller, more elegant opera glasses. My mother wrote thanking him, but expressing embarrassment at the evident expense. My father replied:

> The gift had no other aim than to give you some pleasure. I consider myself a friend of yours and this is enough for me. The purchase value is unimportant. You make me ashamed and misunderstand my intentions if you speak about an "expensive" gift, specially in connection with gratitude. I would never send a friend a gift out of gratitude, since friendship cannot be paid for. And since up to now you have not been too nice to me, I can hope that in the future this will change without or in spite of gifts.
>
> My entire thought was to cause some pleasure. The enjoyment of unpacking a box with unknown contents. Nothing more.

Nothing more, indeed. My father's response can be seen either as pompous — the designation would have made him wince — or more accurately as elaborately flirtatious. In any case, it laid down the rules of acceptable behavior, rather like his later messages on the hall table to me. There were plenty of gifts to follow, plenty of misunderstandings in the course of a 57-year marriage, but I'm sure my mother never again alluded to the cost of a gift. She was always a good pupil. In that respect, my parents were extremely well matched, my father with his teacherly mode and my mother with her prize-pupil one. Both privately and socially they operated at high wattage. Friends

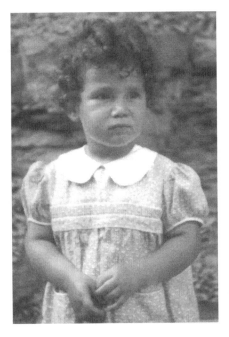

Two stages of my life: toddler and tomboy.

prized them for their wit, their intellectual energy, their charm, their elegance. They, in turn, expected an elevated standard of behavior, of conversation, of taste, of appearance from the people around them. They were not easy, relaxing people to be around. They worked hard at being entertaining, attractive, interesting, instructive. By the same token you could feel the gears of their judgment turning at every moment. I knew that they would invariably go back over any encounter with a friend or family member, rating it, grading the person for conversation, for appearance. "Isn't it impressive how well he knows his Dante," my mother would say. Or "Wouldn't you think they'd speak better French after spending a year there." "She's gotten very old," my father would say, as if a decline in physical beauty were an unforgivable gaffe, comparable to not making the proper response to a gift.

When Bill, my husband-to-be, first came to meet my family, he nearly lost the chance to win their favor because he failed to write them a thank-you note after his visit. These externals *were* important, my father would argue, when I stormed about, insisting the contrary. The outside, he would pronounce infuriatingly, is the outside

My sister, Doris, and me, "perfect American girls."

of the inside. If you have a choice, why not have friends who are smart, good looking *and* well mannered? Your friend Bill is very handsome, very intelligent, very musical. Maybe he can also learn how to behave properly.

If I have made my father sound like a stage Hungarian, all dark moustaches, hand-kissing and dogmatic pronouncements, then I have gone too far. These "outsides" do not give anything like a full picture of his "inside." He was also a witty, complex, sensitive man, who lived a rich intellectual life. During the years the young George Perl spent in alpine sanatoriums recuperating from tuberculosis, he had developed what every serious reader needs, the habit of sitting still. Later, during the time he was managing farms, there were six years with extended periods of solitude.

A bibliophile as well as a reader, he loved books, both as objects and as spiritual partners. He collected first editions of Virginia Woolf, George Bernard Shaw and Oscar Wilde. He loved his leather-bound sets of Racine and Dickens and the Hungarian poet Ady. He read constantly and widely—Nietzsche and Toynbee, Rilke and Tuchman, history and philosophy in several languages, as well as modern nonfiction, fiction and popular junk.

His personal standards were matters of the greatest seriousness. They included fidelity and a high level of responsibility toward others, first of all to those close to him. He was a person you could depend upon, and many people did. Leavening these substantial virtues, keeping him from seeming impossibly straitlaced, was a very Hungarian sense of irony that sounded to some like cynicism. It was, in fact, the farthest thing from it. He had few manual skills. He drove a car (awkwardly, I always thought), but could barely hammer a nail. He enjoyed swimming and walking and, for my mother's sake, played a quirky game of tennis, but although he believed in the value of sports, he was never anyone's idea of an athlete. Still, he was vain about what he could do, and was annoyed when, at age 80, the doctor told him, for the sake of his hearing, he had to stop diving into the pool where he swam.

He was, above all, a man of the mind. When I conjure up a picture of him, I see him, elegantly attired in the British country mode—corduroys, shetland sweater over a checked shirt, loafers. He is sitting in a chair, legs crossed, reading. During his working years, he read at least three newspapers a day: the morning *Times*, the *Wall Street Journal* on the train to New York, and the *New York Sun* on the way home. He did the chess and bridge puzzles and kept up on the fate of the Hungarian soccer teams. He read the modern fiction my husband gave him—Saul Bellow and John Updike and Anne Tyler—with varying degrees of pleasure, always responding in writing with his thoughts about any given or loaned book. In what now strikes me as a poignantly hopeful gesture, he once gave his copy of Mario Puzo's *Godfather* to our son David when he was a nonreading teenager. His curiosity about the world never flagged. He knew a great deal about agriculture and tried to keep up with science and technology. One of the last books he passed along to me was *Turing's Man*, an account of the development of the modern computer.

Part of him would have loved to make a living at writing and teaching, reading and thinking, the way my husband did. But history had not dealt him that card. In the turmoil of Hungary between the wars, his talent for business had brought him much greater security than he could have had at any university. Besides, there was already a quota—the *numerus clausus*—for Jews in Hungarian university professorships. Here in America, although he earned high praise in an economics graduate seminar in business cycles at Columbia, his lack of fluency in English would have made a professorial life an unacceptably long road. My mother remembered that when he gave a seminar paper, people laughed at his English. He was already 44 when he arrived here, and besides, he had a taste for luxury. Remember those small, elegant opera glasses.

In addition, he had a family to support in a scaled-down version of the style to which they had been accustomed in Hungary. He made the daily trip by commuter train and subway to the financial district, where he worked, self-employed, as an independent investment counselor. Being self-employed was crucial to him; he prided himself on never having had a boss, except for the few months that he worked in a library during Hungary's first brief encounter with Communism in 1919. When I was growing up, he made a good living handling investments for clients in different parts of the world.

In Scarsdale, the community they had chosen because of its excellent public schools, my parents lived comfortably. It's true that there was no chauffeured Mercedes as there had been in Budapest, no live-in servants to prepare sit-down dinner parties for 20. Still, my father earned enough so that he and my mother could buy the modest brick house they had been renting, send my sister and me to camp every summer, provide us with all the lessons required for suburban status—piano and riding and tennis and modern dance and ballroom dancing. They had household help—a black maid who came on the bus from White Plains several days a week, a laundress who came once a week, and an Italian gardener who did the heavy labor in the impeccable yard.

Since he could not have the life he started out with, this was the life my father agreed to want. He was able to live undisturbed in an attractive location that combined peaceful surroundings with what he referred to as "good air." He had a beautiful, well-dressed, vivacious wife, two healthy daughters who, for the most part, did what was expected of them. After the war, my parents were once again able to travel in Europe. They loved to go to the Engadin, a quiet high valley in Switzerland (a favorite spot of Nietzsche's), where they could hike and meet other Europeans in the slightly stuffy, well-appointed hotel. They went back to Italy and to Greece and

One of my favorite pictures of my father.

to London, and they visited Ernst Fürth's grave in France at a time when it could still be found. They went back only once to Communist-ruled Hungary in the 1960s, my father reluctantly and with predictably disappointing results. For me, it was a secure childhood, with a good measure of success in the things that matter to young people—friends, school, material comfort, the beginnings of sexual pairing-off.

Yet for my sister and me, there was an impossible conflict between being "perfect American girls" and living in a household with the highest continental standards. These conflicts sometimes grew explosive as we became teenagers. The place was filled with objects that could not tolerate a human fingerprint, much less a drop of water. Until I left for college, there was no television set, no feet up on the furniture, no helping yourself to food in the refrigerator, no food in the living room, no peanut butter or soft white bread to be found anywhere, rules about everything, absolute punctuality and mannerliness expected of all inhabitants and their visitors.

For many years, between late childhood and my early marriage, I struggled to escape from my parents, to get away from this overheated, overscrupulous, European atmosphere. From the fourth grade on, I spent as much time as possible in the house of my best friend, whose parents I secretly wished would adopt me. They were cut straight across the American grain, Henry Fonda and June Allyson—in my eyes the perfect sunny, humorous, unpretentious, understanding postwar pair. If something got spilled on the rug, never mind, it's just an old thing; we'll let the dog lick it up. If someone wanted to bring a couple of extra people home for supper, fine, we'll just make the hamburgers a little smaller. Easygoing, that's what they were, a description no one would have thought to apply to my parents. I longed to be like them, to live like them. My assimilation was nearly complete. By junior high school, I was spending most of my time and allegiance away from home—in school, at camp, at lessons, at other people's houses.

At 17 I was gone, off to college. And at 20, I married, finishing my last year of Radcliffe as the wife of a graduate student in a slightly seedy Cambridge apartment. For the next decade and a half, I worked hard to establish a life of my own amid the heavy demands of a prefeminist academic household, three sons in rapid succession and a series of part-time teaching positions. At 33, I found many of my assumptions about the world upended in a women's support group, part of the newly reborn women's movement. At 40, I found work that I truly loved on a daily newspaper, and moved into a different relationship with everyone in my life. Gradually I began to be curious about these difficult, complicated people who were my parents. When my father finally stopped going to work in the city at age 73, I encouraged him to write a memoir, a graceful set of installments that he completed over the next 10 years. And when he died at 92, I returned to Hungary—really you might say I went there for the first time. There I discovered that I wanted to know all I could about my father. Well into my 50s, I was becoming aware of just how imperfectly I had known what he meant. Why had I waited until he was no longer around? Something, perhaps, about doing this my own way, without his powerful laying down of the rules?

The first thing I did was to start to learn Hungarian. A language belonging to the Finno-Ugric family, it is more foreign than most. Because it has no Indo-European roots, anyone who doesn't already know Finnish or Estonian has to learn it virtually word by word. Its grammar is likewise unlike anything in English, Latin, French,

German, or Italian; its structure is described as "agglutinative," meaning that tiny, annoying elements pile up to form unique meanings. Learning Hungarian involves not only learning new words, but learning also a new way of thinking. Every once in a while, as I master a tiny corner of this language that no adult learner can know perfectly well, I sense a flicker of recognition. It is a small, happy "Aha!" from my father.

The dotted line shows where Grandfather spent his last years in France. Geneva and Annemasse were the places out of which Frederic Reyfer operated.

8

Assimilating

A FEW DAYS AFTER MY AUNT GRETL´S DEPARTURE for the other side of the world, Grandfather writes that he has bought himself a bathing suit and summer has arrived. His spirits seem high as he expresses his relief that at least his immediate family is well out of a Europe threatened by fascism, a place he seems to think — there on the Mediterranean — that he has left behind.

Reminding his daughter that our family has had better luck than many of his compatriots, he goes on to describe the troubles of friends and relatives in Czechoslovakia whose properties have been "requisitioned." A couple of months later, on July 26, 1939, he reinforces this theme:

> I was very pleased to see that your mood improves from day to day, and when Imre [Guttmann, my father's half-brother, recently arrived in the U.S.] starts to inform you about Hungary, you will realize that in spite of the fact that you abandoned much, you also won a great deal — your freedom and equality before the law. That is also our goal. For the time being we are not thinking about leaving Nice. We hear from all sides that the mountainous frontiers toward Italy are so fortified and garrisoned that the Italians do not have the least chance of getting through, and nowhere in the entire country is one safer from air attacks than here.
>
> And so we say *kismet* and endure our fate, together with millions of Europeans who cannot run away.

I could get an American visitor's visa within three days. I would only have to show them a round-trip ship ticket. Still, compared to an existence over there on a minimum of $200 a month, I prefer the life of a "middle" bourgeois citizen here in France—in spite of the menacing dangers of war. I have also convinced Ella of this view, although for months she has been flirting with the idea of leaving for America.

As I read Ernst's letter, with its confident explanation of why he is not coming to America, I am like a child at a melodrama who sees the train rushing toward the man on the railroad tracks. I want to shout, "Get out of the way! Run for your life!" But, in what feels more like a terrible nightmare, I am reduced to slow swimming motions. I can hardly move. My lips will not form the syllables. I cannot make a sound.

The summer wears on in the south of France, and Ernst and Ella are visited by Ella's Austrian niece, Andrea Roth, one of the people in Ella's opportunistic entourage of whom my mother and her sister so strongly disapproved. Ernst writes about Andrea: "Under pressure, she has become a German citizen and changed her social circle to 'Aryan.'" Grandfather's tone is neutral, not shocked, not reproving: People were doing what they felt they had to do. Not all of it was noble.

Changing the subject entirely, he describes his and Ella's still greater amusement at hearing that my father has bathed me and put me to bed, something he would never have been asked or offered to do in our genteel Budapest existence. "Poor Father," he says, quoting from a cabaret song, "how you have changed" [*Armer vater, wie hast du dich verändert*]. But the news from home continues to be dark: "From Sušice I hear that the son of the Solo employee Langhammer, Fredi's stamp-collecting friend, is sitting at the S.S. in Klattau, because he opened his mouth too much."

Our family is spending its first American summer in Ithaca, N.Y., getting introduced to the Northeast's extremes of heat and humidity. On the French Riviera, the climate, at least, is agreeable, with bearable heat, always a cool breeze from the sea. Still, he asks uneasily:

> But what is it all for, when the risk of war comes closer from day to day? The French do not believe in war. Yesterday at Lanquetins I played bridge with a general, a colonel and a commander, and they are all convinced that the Axis powers won't dare a war, since they know they would be crushed. If only they were right.

In a postscript, he adds that he has been notified that the transfer of his "blocked" Viennese bank account can only be withdrawn at a rate of 6 percent, the result of a new Nazi decree. We do not know if any of this money—even 6 percent of it—ever came out of Austria.

My aunt Gretl has settled near Chicago in Winnetka, Illinois, to be near her Strasser in-laws, who had gone there many years earlier. Our parents are now planning to move to the Chicago suburbs themselves. Grandfather sends his next letter to meet them. This one is an uncharacteristically angry tirade, what my mother saw as a genuine bombshell in the midst of his otherwise measured, benevolent communications. I noticed, too, that it was one of the last letters she translated. It's easy to see why she may have wanted—consciously or not—to avoid it, even at 60 years' remove: It rakes her over the coals for complaining about what she has lost. The letter shows the force of Ernst Fürth's presence, the moral severity of which he was capable. Perhaps it also shows that he was only human. Events were beginning to wear him down.

Aug. 23, 1939

My dear Evi!
Received your kind letters of the 10th and 13th and hope that this one will arrive in Winnetka, where you are happily united with Gretl and that her calming influence will keep you from getting so upset about political events. It really makes no sense in your present situation to bemoan the loss of jewelry, household goods, etc. In your lament, don't forget the essentials: You are all far from shooting and in safety; for several years your livelihood is assured; in addition, there is a good chance that the capable Gyuri in the not-too-distant future will be able to earn additionally. Look around a bit and consider how thousands and thousands of people have had to leave their homelands under very sad circumstances and live a terribly precarious life in foreign countries.

And is mine and Ella's fate to be envied? I have lost almost the entire fruits of 50 years of work in Sušice and Vienna, and I don't think you'll find jeremiads in my letters about my sudden fall. And the fact that in your letters you never utter a word of worry about our fate if war does appear—although the first bomb over Nice could hit me—all this fills me sometimes with thoughts that I prefer not to express in my letters.

By the time this reaches you, perhaps everything will have fallen apart, and you may be assured that neither Ella nor I will lose our courage, but will try to the very end to enjoy life, what is left of it.

I greet and kiss you all, your faithful
Father

Even in his outrage, my grandfather's prose is civilized in the extreme. A few days later, the storm of his anger has blown over.

Aug. 27, 1939

I want to express my joy in receiving the group picture and your kind letter by answering immediately. Most of all I find you unchanged, handsome and looking well, which gives me special pleasure. Gyuri's cheeks could still use a little upholstering, but for gaining weight one needs more peace of mind than the troubled times we live in. I see that especially in myself. In spite of excellent cooking and a quiet life, I cannot exceed 70 kilos [154 pounds], but in spite of it feel quite well and can treat myself to swimming daily for 20-25 minutes.

The two girls also look very sweet. Dorli reaches your chest height and Marietta has also grown quite considerably.

During the last days Nice's excess population has rapidly shrunk. In our pension at the beginning of next week, we and Cecile will be the only guests, and we are pondering where we should turn our steps. If everything erupts, we will have to leave Nice without hesitation.

Two days later he writes: "Tonight at the latest we will know what Satan has decided about the fate of mankind." Ernst plans to move his family trio to Arcachon, on the Atlantic coast near Bordeaux, "most likely far enough from the shooting." He says he has received a cable from my parents from Ithaca, then sounds a frugal, admonitory note: "Sending weekly cables makes no sense, when nothing new is to be told. It is not a time for luxury expenses."

Another two days and the world had been transformed. On September 1, 1939, the Nazis invaded Poland, and two days after that, France and England declared war.

On September 1, my parents, with my sister and me, were driving in our brand-new $700 gray Chevy sedan from Ithaca to Evanston, Illinois, where we were to settle for a year and a half. My mother, terribly unhappy in her new life, had agitated to stop in Syracuse and apply for a re-entry visa so that she could visit her father in France. But my father had already put his foot down in opposition. Then, during the drive, they learned on the car radio that Hitler had invaded Poland. The war had begun. Mother never went back to Europe until war's end, and by then Grandfather was dead.

On the same day, Ernst writes with news of his own, making no mention of the events in Poland. He and Ella and his bad-tempered sister-in-law Cecile (she is always with them, a thorn in their side, rarely but always pointedly mentioned) have joined other refugees from Nice and are now in Arcachon.

> Arcachon near Bordeaux
> Sept. 1, 1939
>
> My dear Evi!
> Yesterday the Prefect of Nice posted an edict that anyone not officially "invited" had to leave town within 48 hours, since otherwise there would be no guarantee of transportation. And so we decided in a great hurry to take the train in the evening and arrived here at three in the morning. With the help of all sorts of tricks—baksheesh also playing a role—we managed to get seats, and so the long trip was bearable. We had to bring Cecile along, for better or worse, and she survived without a crisis. Arcachon is a cultivated little place, with a beautiful beach (also a casino) and its greatest advantage is its geographic location: You could not settle down further from the range of bullets. It is about 40 kilometers from Bordeaux, and along the entire railroad track you see only farms and vineyards. For that reason it's uninteresting to aviators. But the prospect of spending several months (or years?) here is not very appealing. I wish we could soon return to the fleshpots of the Villa Brimborion in Nice.

What is remarkable about this card is its verbal energy. These are elderly people, facing a precarious future, and, far from bemoaning his fate—we already know how he feels about this sort of behavior—Ernst is able to keep up an urbane tone, observing, analyzing, even making small jokes. Then, a few days later, he writes gravely about what is happening elsewhere.

Sept. 4, 1939

Yesterday on the radio we heard [French Prime Minister Edouard] Daladier's voice
... announcing the outbreak of war. Although expected for days, the effect of the
reality brings mourning, gloom and somber seriousness to every face. There is no
human being on earth whose fate is not affected by this catastrophe. Lucky are the
children and those of narrowness of mind who do not grasp what this war means.

Today the papers already report that German planes are bombing Poland indis-
criminately, small villages, farmlands. There does not seem to be any barbarism
that cannot be expected. This very moment the radio announces the sinking of a
British boat [the S.S. *Athenia*] by a German submarine with 1,200 people on
board. All we can hope for is that all those "acts of heroism" will rouse the American conscience. Prompt, severe measures might mean a rescue mission. I'm afraid
that overseas mail will have long interruptions and, for that reason, do not worry.
One has to trust one's good star.

Ernst and Ella settle into this small seaside resort town, finding life slow and dreary,
the streets dark at night because of wartime blackouts. "In the evening after dinner,"
writes Ernst a few days later, on September 10, "one takes a walk in the darkened
streets, goes into a cafe for a *pivičko* [Czech: a small beer], listens to the last radio
report and goes to bed at 10:30. Except for Mrs. Steffi Gartenberg (widow), we have
not yet made any acquaintances." He mentions that there are several Americans in
their hotel who do not know how they will get home.

A letter written about a week later reinforces his earlier prediction that, for the
time being, boredom will be their greatest enemy.

Here the season goes slowly to its end. The beach, where up until now jolly
children played their games, is emptying out. The weather is still sunny, but much
cooler, so that yesterday we had to give up our only great pastime, swimming.

The fall and winter in this little town, which at nightfall is totally darkened, will
become very monotonous. One has to try to vegetate. Let us hope the Hitler-
gang will soon be put to an end.

Meanwhile, my parents, my sister and I have arrived in Evanston, nearer to my aunt Gretl. Perhaps my father also thought that there were better opportunities for his farming expertise in the wide-open Midwest than in the teeming Northeast. In the process of everyone's changing places, the mail has become even more unreliable, and Ernst complains about that lack.

Sept. 25, 1939

On Aug. 31st we left Nice and since I've been here, I have not received even the smallest news from you, while from Gretl, four or five letters, partly via Nice, partly directly, the best proof that it's not only the deteriorating postal service that is at the root of the lack of news from you.

For that reason I was very surprised to receive a worried telegram from Vanston [*sic*], which was quite unnecessary since you knew from Gretl that here we are far beyond the range of the bullets. In addition you must have received in the meantime the four or five cards that I wrote from here, but unfortunately sent to Ithaca; you will slowly receive them. For that reason you will understand that I did not wish to spend 180 francs [about $4.50] for a cable.

Up until now we have stayed quite comfortably at the Hotel Victoria, but since most likely we will be staying in Arcachon for many months, we would prefer to have our own house and have food according to our own taste, which would also be cheaper. For this reason we have rented, starting Oct. 1, a little one-floor house, for 1600 francs [$40] a month, 235 Boulevard de la Plage, with a garden, front and back, called La Salutaire. Naturally we will take Cecile along, also a *bonne à tout faire* [all-purpose maid] has been assured, with some knowledge of cooking. I ask you therefore to make use of the new address and write a bit more diligently.

The world may be difficult, Ernst insists, but we can still be reasonable; questions have answers; order is primary; standards must be upheld. The letter that follows gives a sense of the kind of detailed news he wants.

Did you drive in your car from Ithaca to the state of Illinois? What did you do with all the luggage? What are your future intentions? Where will Dorli go to school? Did Imre stay in Ithaca? Or does he plan separately to find a suitable farm?

You write absolutely nothing in your letter about Dorli and Marietta. Did they receive the postcard I sent to them in Ithaca?

But world events roll on: The Soviets move into Poland and sign a Friendship Treaty with the Germans.

Oct. 1, 1939

Just think of all that has happened in these few weeks. Poor Poland destroyed, its inhabitants if not killed or dispossessed of their belongings by the Nazis or the Bolsheviks, then delivered into total slavery. The villainous agreement between Hitler and Stalin shows not only how close Nazism and Bolshevism stand to each other, but should also open the eyes of the Americans to what kind of danger threatens Europe if the Western powers don't succeed in cutting off the heads of this Hydra, a danger against which the U.S.A., with its ten million unemployed won't have the strength to withstand.

The people here show a surprising discipline and calm, yet everybody knows that unfortunately war is unavoidable. Our *bonne à tout faire*, who was supposed to start her job tomorrow morning, came yesterday asking to postpone her arrival so that she can say goodbye to her mobilized son in Bordeaux. For four months she has been without news from her second son. He is doing his service in a submarine. From people like this you must learn forbearance.

As I hear my grandfather's knowing voice, vigorously responding to the events of the war, I am amazed at how well he can describe, interpret and anticipate political events, and yet, simultaneously, how strongly he is weighed down by inertia—that most comforting and deadly of all human impulses. With all his sophistication and information, why can't he see and react to what's coming? What is he waiting for? Along with a disdain for those who complain and feel self-pity, he avoids at all costs the loss of control that goes with panic and sudden movement. But the cost of his measured reasonableness will be confinement, misery and finally death. Why couldn't he have ignored those lessons of forbearance he was learning from the dignified French populace and have chosen instead impatience, impulsiveness, self-preservation? In October of 1939, he could still have acquired a visa to come to America. I could have come to know him in person.

He writes again two days later.

Oct. 3, 1939

The French behave in exemplary fashion, they are serious but calm and one does not hear a word of complaint, not even from those whose fathers or sons have been drafted. The food market is plentiful with beautiful and good things, vegetables, fruit, meat, fish, butter (excellent, and 20 francs per kilo). A good *vin de table* 4 francs per bottle. I cannot imagine that even after several months of war there will be shortages, and I'm told that during the First World War there was no lack of anything.

Your compatriots seem to begin to understand what it is all about, and hopefully Pittman [Senator Key Pittman of Nevada, author of a resolution to rescind the neutrality law and sell arms to "belligerents"] will be able to put down Borah's opposition [Senator William Borah of Idaho, advocate of outlawing war].

Yesterday we moved into the villa, living room, dining room, two verandas, three bedrooms, all appointments in best condition, central heating. Only at night it gets unpleasant. The regulations are very strict: In addition to reducing light in the house, we must glue paper onto any opening or cracks, so that no glimmer is visible from the outside. I walk inside the house with a flashlight. But these are small annoyances to which one gets accustomed in a few days.

Don't worry about me unnecessarily. I'm healthy, Ella cares for me like a baby, and as long as we can live here undisturbed, we have to be content, even though the radiance of a previous beautiful existence and the lack of company and distraction is missing. My great longing for children and grandchildren has to be suppressed and I have to be satisfied with the thought that you are in safety.

This last thought—that he will have to be content with knowing that his family is safe—will be repeated with ever greater poignancy as the war goes on. But he will never again allude to his former life, that "radiance of a previous beautiful existence."

A couple of weeks later, on October 20, Ernst comments on how much this correspondence means to him, "my favorite occupation in these foreign lands," and how speedily he is answering all mail, although delivery at his end is frustratingly slow. He continues to watch and listen to the news—both international and familial—with the greatest attention.

Most likely the only steamships [carrying mail] in circulation are the American ones, for which the German submarines still have some respect. But what will happen if Congress accepts the change in the neutrality act? I wait for that with impatience because I assume that it would have a strong effect in favor of Italian neutrality.

What you write about the little girls gives me great pleasure. Buzli with her natural, lively temperament is born for the American tempo, and her English gibberish must be very amusing.

Even in these Arcachon days we are not letting ourselves be dragged down, we try to put up with and "make the best of it" [writes this in English]. Sometimes I, sometimes Ella each contribute our mite so that our mood does not drop below zero. My appearance has apparently improved during the last three weeks, and I think that thanks to Ella's cooking achievements I am gaining weight again, after losing 5–6 kilos [11–13 pounds] in Nice.

Naturally I'm anxious to hear whether Gyuri and Imre returned successfully from their exploratory trip and were able to bring home concrete plans.

In the next letter, October 26, he perceives an improvement in my father's mood, the return of his "old energy and pluck," the decline of which is mentioned here for the first time. He had worried about my father's state of mind, he suggests, largely because of its effect on my mother.

I had noticed that his depressed condition at times colored your mood, and I always tried to counteract it — as much as I could at a distance. For us too it is not always possible to look into the future and keep our balance, not to speak of cheerful courage. But one cannot let oneself be beaten down and must try to help others in gloomy situations.

Then he refers to an event that my mother no longer remembered, but which sets up an overwhelmingly powerful resonance for me, opening up a whole series of questions about what we call ourselves: "I cannot understand why, when you were searching for living quarters, you did not simply answer 'Gentile.' You have the right to say so. 'Ancestor passports' cannot be necessary over there." This is the only place in the correspondence that Ernst brings up the subject of my family's complex relation to Jewishness. Unlike earlier documents, such as my father's school diplomas, all of which are marked "Isr." for Israelite, the passports with which they entered America say "Roman Catholic" on the line for religion. But although, as my grandfather puts it, they had the right to call themselves Gentiles, my parents were evidently not yet adept at handling anti-Semitism in their new country. As they explored the possibility of new housing, they must have been asked what their religious background was—or more specifically whether they were Jews or Gentiles. In the late '30s, and indeed until the 1964 Civil Rights Act, Jews could legally be denied many rights—home ownership in certain areas, admission to hotels and resorts, not to mention private clubs, prestigious schools and universities. My parents eventually learned to sidestep such questions, to "pass." They were—we really were—Catholics. Weren't they? Weren't we?

One of the houses in Arcachon where my grandfather lived.

9

Adapting to Exile

O N OCTOBER 29, 1939, my grandfather writes with evident satisfaction that two postcards from my mother have reached him from Chicago, and that he recognizes a portrait of Rembrandt's first wife, Saskia, on a card sent from the Chicago Art Institute. He is pleased, too, at the actions of the U.S. Senate, which he is following closely. Congress is about to pass an amendment to the U.S. neutrality act, permitting the shipment of arms on a "cash-and-carry" basis. It is the opening Rooseveltian wedge that will eventually bring America into the war—but not for two long years. "Unfortunately," writes Ernst, "we had no champagne in the house, otherwise I would have celebrated this event."

Two days later, he describes the small-scale harassment he's endured involving a bank deposit.

> In the last four weeks I have had some worrisome days; when I arrived here, I immediately rented a safety deposit box at the local Credit Lyonnais in order to place Ella's jewelry and my cash reserves in safety.

> When four weeks later I wanted to take some money out of the safe in order to pay for our three-monthly rent, I was informed that all safes for foreigners were "blocked" and could only be opened with the permission of the police for foreigners. I was told to supply a certificate from the Czech Embassy in Paris confirming that I always was and still am a loyal and faithful citizen of the Czech Republic. This would speed up the process. After a lengthy, difficult correspondence with Paris, the certificate arrived yesterday, and with this, the difficulties are removed. I would have been in a rather precarious situation if, in the first days of October a "Glarona" [the Swiss account] check had not arrived. It is really

difficult under these circumstances to make the right decision. To keep all your goods and chattels in one drawer seems also very risky. So you have to divide the risks. Anyhow, with the high fees of the Czech embassy and other expenses, this joke finally came to 4,000 French francs [about $100, roughly half their monthly budget]. Evidently our life would be too monotonous without such incidents.

In the same letter he assesses the pluses and minuses of his grandchildren's American education. My sister and I were attending the laboratory school of National Teachers College in Evanston.

> Your report about Dorli's school and the art of education practiced there is of vivid interest to me. There is no question that the aim is to make the children into matter-of-fact human beings, without difference of gender, which nowadays in the hard "struggle of life" [he writes the phrase in English] undoubtedly has its advantages. But the question remains whether the development of their senses for the higher values, beauty, human morality won't be short-changed. Of course with your children I'm not afraid of that. Their spiritual legacy and the house example will certainly prevent them from becoming all-too-sober Americans.

Even as the monotony and attendant isolation wears on a man with such lively social expectations, he seems genuinely glad that his daughter is beginning to make contact with her new compatriots, "through tennis and in roundabout ways via the children." Most of his own pleasures from now on will be vicarious.

> Here it is very difficult to penetrate French society. Apart from our walks and every eight or ten days a movie, there is no possibility for communication. One day I met a former Rotary Club colleague with his wife [Ernst had been a member of Rotary in Vienna, but resigned in 1938 when they began admitting Nazis]. They live with two school-age children in a pension, and although they have been here for two months, we had not met.

> I would love to see your two little American girls, especially Buzli, who must have changed enormously. Dorli was already a finished human being and most likely has remained in her character the same lovable child that I knew.

On November 13, 1939, he describes the new Arcachon household and its difficulties in some detail. But domestic irritants are quickly upstaged in a world where Germany and the Soviet Union have just joined forces.

> Our house is in every respect *prima*. I do my correspondence in a closed-in veranda with a good view of the bay. We have a spacious dining room and living room. Our bedroom is three spaces removed from Cecile, so that except for meals and bridge games, we can separate ourselves. In addition, Ella and I take a daily walk for one to two hours, reducing to a minimum the time we have to spend with Cecile's complaining and bad humor washing over us. We have attained a certain virtuosity at not taking notice. Besides, I must say that Ella offers her more patience and good will than I.

> The weather is becoming more and more rainy and gray, only once in a while a warmer, sunny day shows up and then we try to take as much advantage of it as possible for walks. Quite nearby is a magnificent pine forest mixed with oak, and in the midst of it a mineral spring called les Abatilles, surrounded by baths and therapeutic establishments, everywhere sandy ground so that even after a long rain your feet stay dry.

> The present would be quite bearable, if the war events—especially the threat to the neutral states on one hand by Hitler and on the other by Stalin—didn't mean the possible extension of the war in space and time. In spite of it all, one has to hope for the best. The ferment in Germany reinforces the attempt [on Hitler's life] in Munich. I'm certain more will follow.

Meanwhile harassment over his safe deposit box drags on.

Nov. 16, 1939

> I wrote you a while ago that finally the certificate from the Czech embassy arrived and that with this "sesame" my safe deposit box would be opened. Far from it! The legal document went to the *procureur de la république* [public prosecutor] and seems to be hibernating in Bordeaux, although I was assured by the local police commissioner that the settlement was "une question de quelques jours," which was already a fortnight ago. So one's patience is constantly tested.

In Hungary, he has heard, the anti-Jewish laws are only slowly being enforced, and many Jewish businessmen of his acquaintance still have their jobs. Only his son-in-law Paul Strasser seems to have been singled out, he says. "The poor man is condemned to twiddle his thumbs, while he waits for his quota number to come up. Very sad for him and Gretl."

Sometimes Grandfather seems overwhelmed by the news, especially from Czechoslovakia, whose independence and democratic reforms he had so strongly supported. On November 24, he writes: "The pressures in Czechoslovakia must be dreadful. The brutality with which the Germans entered seems to overshadow all the evils that we have lived through. Will I live to see that country destroyed?" But he never allows himself to stay dramatic for long. He moves on to news of family members in various parts of the world, including his first wife's mother in Budapest — my great-grandmother — known to be impossibly self-centered. Grandmother Roheim's health has improved, he writes, adding, perhaps with a slightly mischievous wink, "It is astonishing how much vital strength that woman has." Then he concerns himself with Christmas presents and with the prediction that I hope this book disproves:

> Eight days ago I sent Dorli and Buzli two little "parcels without value," something for the Christmas tree. I hope the stuff arrives so that the children have a visible sign that their grandfather is thinking of them. For Buzli the memory of me will soon vanish, unless it is possible to renew it in this life.

A letter to my father exemplifies the practical detail in which Ernst is thinking. He also responds with characteristic vigor to a concern raised by my mother: the family tendency to early gray hair.

> Dec. 2, 1939
>
> Dear Gyuri!
> For quite a while I have been expecting a detailed description of your expeditions, inquiries and activities. I see with pleasure that you are forging an existence, just as I expected. It was a happy idea to bring Imre over. The division of labor will lead to quicker success.
>
> Where is Mrs. Blair's farm? Is there a larger town in the vicinity where the children could attend school and kindergarten?

Yesterday I had a good day. After two months of hanging by a thread, the decision of the *procureur de la république* in Bordeaux arrived, which enables me to dispose of my safety deposit box freely. I gave a sigh of relief, for although I had expected a positive answer, I must never forget that the country is at war and a refugee is merely a tolerated person. Cecile for instance received a check of approximately 1,000 f. [about $25] two months ago from her children, which is still blocked at the bank.

Evi should not worry about her gray hair. If you have no other reason to complain about your Fürth pedigree, you have to accept early graying as part of your inheritance. When I was a student of about 23, I was a frequent visitor to a smart young couple in Mödling [a suburb of Vienna], who were active riders. The woman was an excellent coach driver, very snappy indeed. When at the time I made a remark about all my gray hair, she replied laughing, "Don't worry about it Ernsterl, a white horse has the most staying power."

These letters offer a particularly strong sense of my grandfather's deep pragmatism, his belief that the world is controllable, that plans can be carried out, as, for example, in my father's partnership with his brother Imre. And he is graciously indulgent about Ella's hopes about returning home, while also upholding his standards about the company they keep:

Dec. 4, 1939

Ella whiles away the time making plans for the summer of 1940, which is going to be spent, naturally, in the Gregor Mendelstrasse [Vienna] and in Sušice. I can only smile at this, since her Tipperary has a long way to go [writes this phrase in English]. How many neutrals are going to vanish before this wished-for turn of events takes place?

About my French [he sometimes writes in French] that you praise with so much daughterly indulgence, I can only say: *tantum abest ut — ut* [Latin: It is so lacking that...], but I certainly have made some progress, which is not surprising, since I read at least two or three books a week, but without much selection, pell mell, Paleologue, Claude Farrère, Barbusse, etc. up to DeKobra, hoping that something might stick to my somewhat calcified brain. If I were among French company, I would have acquired a better turn of phrase.

Unfortunately a Mrs. von May has broken into our household, and honors us twice a week with a visit. Once very rich, owner of a big chateau, she is a widow now 70 years old, but most likely at 20 was already a stupid goose. Her German has a Moravian-Jewish accent that turns my stomach. In "exile," again and again you make the observation that people stripped of their riches and status show more and more crudely their worth or lack of it.

This last letter first pulls me up short, then makes me smile. Here is my grandfather, elitist warts and all, looking down scornfully on this formerly rich, probably always bad-mannered, ill-spoken woman. Imagine a Boston brahmin having to spend his evenings with a brassy nouveau riche New Jerseyite. I have to admire the comic energy here. This is a man in full possession of his prejudices. My grandfather had inhabited a world where nationality and religion were less important than manners, upbringing, family, profession, talent and merit. He was a snob about people's backgrounds, but even more, perhaps, a rigorous judge of surfaces. Women were supposed to be beautiful or at least attractive. Conversation should be witty and cultivated. The great actors of classical plays in Vienna's Burgtheater—comparable to England's Old Vic—were the models of how German should be spoken. Yiddish, which was not spoken on either side of our family, was used in my grandfather's letters much as many Americans—both Jewish and non—use it now, as a way of adding a little earthy spice to his utterances. Even in the world of exile, where he now found himself, making such distinctions was as natural as breathing. My parents shared these attitudes, which I came to see at one time as maddeningly elitist, snobbish, authoritarian and patriarchal, but which later struck me mostly as quaint. It should come as no surprise, then, to find that my grandfather showed himself in his letters as an authentically elite, snobbish, authoritarian patriarch.

In a subsequent letter, Ernst rejoices in the British and other Allied victories at sea, keeping track, too, of how the family is changing.

Dec. 17, 1939

Thank you for the Buzli photo. I have the impression that she is fatter and sturdier than Dorli at her age and much more a rascal. But perhaps there will be less room for sensitivity for her than for Dorli.

Don't get too upset by the sinking of neutral and British ships; listen rather, if you can, to the 9 o'clock evening reportage from London in German, which I've been doing for a fortnight, ever since I rented an excellent machine for 100 francs [$2.50] a month. Not only do the commentators have a certain dignity, a measured and never boastful way of giving the news, but also you hear interesting people, like members of Parliament, the House of Lords, mostly Labor Party members, professors from Oxford, and you acquire great respect for the British mentality, but also, thank the Lord, their *gewure* [Yiddish: guts]. In spite of Finland and the dangers that threaten other neutrals, you should not abandon hope for a final victory of the Allied forces. The sea-battle at Montevideo was a phenomenal British achievement [the British sank the German *Graf Speë*].

Ella has already bought the Christmas tree; it is not a Böhmerwald [a Czech forest] spruce.

Ernst and Ella spend their second Christmas away from home. He writes on December 26, 1939, to report about it, but also to deliver a sermon about keeping one's spirits up. He wonders if my mother's dental work, "the long-lasting mistreatment of your dental nerves" is to blame for her pessimism. He himself believes that England and France will prevail and that "Germany will one day have its throat cut and be brought to its knees."

A few days later he congratulates my father on his new role in the family, acting now as "paterfamilias" not only to Gretl and Imre, but also to Ella's son. Ernst's words make me realize, as I had not fully done before, the heavy burden on my father, not only to provide financial support, but also to act as the moral fulcrum for the extended family. It was a role he had already assumed in Hungary as the eldest male sibling of four motherless children, but which now took on an entirely different character here in a country where he was himself a stranger.

Two weeks later, a letter to my mother deals with more homely issues, while putting a brave face on any difficulties: the house is cold; the overseas mail is slow; the news from Ella's brother in Vienna is positive but probably unreliable. The next day, January 12, Ernst rejoices in the arrival of mail from the U.S. "As with the game of bridge," he writes, "it helps to complain. An hour after writing a dissatisfied letter about the American mail and throwing it into the mailbox, I received your card of Dec. 8 and your letter of the 16th."

A letter of January 19, 1940, gives a good picture of their all-too-quiet life in Arcachon. It contains, too, the first mention of Frank Wright, an American acquaintance, who will come to be of great help to my parents as the pressure builds on all sides.

I read with pleasure that your Christmas was *gemütlich* and that you have, thanks to the charm of your daughter, enlarged your circle of native acquaintances. It was a good idea to make contact with Mr. Wright in the form of a Christmas card and renew the past memory, although I'm afraid that he does not play as big a role as at the time of his visit to Sušice in 1928. The firm of Lee, Higgins [a Boston banking firm], of which he was a leading partner at the time, has suffered enormously by the Kreuger [Swedish match company] collapse and was forced into bankruptcy. But if he still owns his property on the Hudson, he must have come off with a trifling loss.

We in Arcachon have to give up the hope of making acquaintances, since we do not go anywhere. In Bordeaux, most likely there is a Rotary Club, but the trip back and forth would take three hours, and as a foreigner you cannot leave town without a safe-conduct pass, which you have to get each time from the Commissariat de Police, giving your reason. Since Bordeaux at sunset gets very dark, such an excursion would be neither pleasant nor amusing nor worth the expense.

The British radio fills Ella with such optimism that she is making plans for Vienna and Sušice, which I do not share 100 percent, but I smile in order not to disturb the good atmosphere.

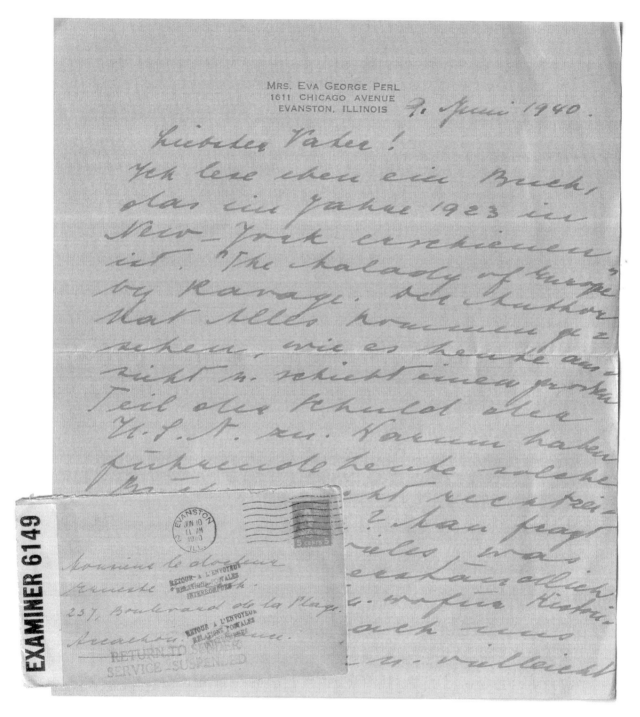

My mother's letter of June 9, 1940, never reached my grandfather. The Germans marched into Paris on June 14.

10

The World Narrows

Ernst is now counting pennies in a way he would never have had to do in his "previous beautiful existence." He writes: "Today is the first time I didn't have to stoke our furnace, a great advantage for my pocket, too, since the heating for the month of January cost more than 1,500 francs [c. $38], a lot of money for a small amount of heat."

On February 13, 1940, he responds to something my mother has said about refugees:

> What you have been told about the treatment of refugees in England is totally wrong. On the contrary, they are much less troubled by official measures than in this country, understandably since there are five times as many here as there, and secondly, France has to protect itself against spying and propaganda. For that reason they watch foreigners intently and keep track of their location. We, too, have to present ourselves once a month at the police station, but this does not constitute a bother since one is treated with great politeness.

My grandfather speaks with apparent calm about the treatment of refugees, even as he recognizes that they are closely watched. I note here with sorrow the change in his attitude: A couple of years earlier, he had decided not to stay in Switzerland—which could have been a safe haven—because he would have had to report regularly to the police. We know, of course, that this "great politeness" with which he was being treated would quickly turn to its opposite as a whole series of increasingly restrictive measures were imposed. France had been inundated with foreign refugees since the disastrous days of the Spanish Civil War. As Michael R. Marrus and Robert O. Paxton write in their invaluable *Vichy France and the Jews:*

> In the climate of the late 1930s, it was not difficult for a French civil servant to become inured to dealing highhandedly with foreign refugees, among whom none were more conspicuous or more defenseless or, evidently, more irritating than were the Jews. The machinery was soon in place to deprive thousands of them of the liberty they had sought in France. [pp. 57–8]

Two days later, Ernst reports that they have found a new place to live, "thanks to chance and a conversation between our loquacious maid Lucie and our grocer." The new apartment on one floor in a neighboring house is just as roomy, but cleaner and a real bargain, "all the more welcome since prices are slowly but steadily rising." They will move in on April 1.

The next letter less than 10 days later is a 33rd birthday message for my mother, who is spending the first of what will be more than 60 birthdays in the New World. It is, ironically, in this world where she will spend two-thirds of her life that she remains an eternal foreigner. She will gain American citizenship, become energetically "Americanized," make good friends among the natives, take part in community life to the extent of being named to the local school board for seven years. Yet she will always be an outsider, sometimes by choice, still talking about American customs as if she were an observant anthropologist from another culture. But sometimes she will imagine easy insiderhood, wishing people would not ask the source of her "charming" accent after she has spoken just a few sentences.

My father's alienation will be greater still. His combination of courtliness, delicacy and a Central European intellectual's ironic humor would make him seem forbidding and strange to all but the most sophisticated, the most naive or the most forgiving. And although he developed business acquaintances through his work on Wall Street and renewed familiar connections among immigrants who settled nearby, he had few real friends in the suburbs where we lived, preferring in the end his books and the always-lively conversation and company of his wife.

And so my grandfather's robust birthday letter to my mother seems particularly sad in retrospect, on the one hand so full of optimism that my parents will overcome all obstacles; on the other hand enjoying his own creature comforts while steadily refusing to accept the possibility that the war might "end badly for us."

> First of all I wish that this first American stage that you have completed—full of homesickness, difficult adaptation to new circumstances, customs and habits, last, but not least work, which up to now was foreign to you and filled your days—will seem like a bad dream that from now on will turn into a friendly reality. Don't let your longing for me cloud your birthday. We must all be thankful to withstand these ugly times of war in comparative safety and hope to live through it to a happy ending. Let's not give up hope, also that here or over there we might celebrate and meet again. I do not wish to consider, even for a moment, the idea that this war might end badly for us. Otherwise it would not be worth continuing in this life.

> For that reason, my dear child, enjoy the good times that you are blessed with, and continue enjoying the great treasure, your children, stay healthy and brave, look with confidence into the future with the help of Gyuri's capabilities. Did I forget anything? Then add it to your list of what you would like.

> Buzli's tendency to be a little gourmand is something she should keep up into her old age. I admit quite openly that an essential part of our daily comfortable life is the excellent cooking that Ella herself prepares, or is done under her strict surveillance, and which fits my old deep-rooted habits. Our *pot au feu* is not different from the old *rindfleisch* with its filling garnishes. *Kalbsgulyás, székély gulyás* and excellent capons appear in lively rounds with *griessnudeln, reisauflauf,* different puddings and even *Salzburger nockerln* at our daily noon meal. And if in the evening I'm especially well-humored, then I permit myself oysters, moistened with a dry Pouilly 1929.

> This will happen on your birthday too, and I hope that my short but tumultuous toast will sound in your ears.

On February 29, 1940, he writes about Ernst Bergmann, a former employee of the match enterprise—the last "non-Aryan" allowed to work there—who has immigrated to the U.S., and he asks my parents to try to help Bergmann find work. Then he comments severely on American drinking habits, about which my mother has reported.

> Prohibition, which I believe lasted for 15 years, has not, according to your writing

about cocktail parties, improved the culture of drinking. Cocktails might have their own charm, but how can such a mixture compete with the noblesse of a wine that is consumed with a matching dish!

In March, my father writes of his efforts on Paul Strasser's behalf, giving also a fuller picture of his own first attempts at earning a living as an agricultural entrepreneur. In fact, pig-breeding for gentleman farmers in the Midwest did not turn out to be viable. Expert as they may have been, my father and his half brother, Imre Guttmann, did not pass muster with the managers of these farms, who most likely didn't want to take instruction from a couple of city slickers with heavy Hungarian accents. As I transcribe my mother's translation of this letter, I hear my father's voice—informed and conscientious, yet at the same time complicated, oblique, ironic, knowing, pessimistic.

> Dear Father,
> Imre and I have just begun to work. We have introduced pig-breeding to the farm of Dr. Muller, a very well-known dentist in Chicago. The farm lies 45 minutes from Evanston by car in a somewhat hilly area, but with good land. Nearby is a pond called Lake Zurich, where there is also a summer resort. The population are mainly German settlers who no longer speak German, but are good, hardworking people.
>
> We have brought breeding animals from the university's farms to this approximately 200-acre farm, and our arrangement is that we can keep our half share until October without having to pay for the use of the buildings. That way we have a certain advantage, and will be in a position to start a good breeding station.
>
> By fall we will decide whether we should rent something in this vicinity or whether it would be better to go somewhere else. I naturally have in mind to get other farms to manage. With two or three more "patients" we could support the family. But we need God's help!
>
> I was in Canada last week, primarily about an entry permit for Paul. It appears that they will give Paul the permit. Let's hope that the decision will not be too late for his crossing.

That country made a very good impression on me in general. The cost of living is about 20 percent less than here, there are many new industries, a certain upswing owing to war needs and a general increase in wealth. Finally, it offers Paul the same chances as in the States, but the "mishpoche" [Yiddish: clan, refers to Strassers, who were seen to be unlucky in business] would not be an active ingredient.

You were kind to inquire about Klári [Svéd, his sister in Budapest]. The Svéds sit on their backsides with their Australian visas in their pockets, and although Klári would gladly leave, I am afraid that we will not meet again until there is peace.

Also Berti [Robert Guttmann, his other half brother], who pursues our interests in Budapest with unheard-of persistence, gives no impression of wanting to leave. He lives in the Andrássy ut [my parents' former apartment], Terese [the housekeeper] takes care of him, and he runs the firm and the agricultural enterprises with great energy. The firm is, as predicted, very passive, so Cserepes [a family farm] appears to provide strong compensation. History will show when and whether we will be able to buy a gulyás at Holub [a fine restaurant in Budapest] from the proceeds.

Berti is as optimistic as Ella; unfortunately I see little difference between what is happening in Budapest and Vienna.

Since this letter will arrive in Arcachon around your birthday, I do not wish to influence the shine of the day with cloudy prophesies. I wish you all the best from my whole heart, and I hope the good Lord will make it possible for you to enjoy your daughter, but especially your grandchildren, in good health.

I also congratulate Ella heartily,
And remain your faithful   Gyuri

Ernst's next letter includes his vivid recollections of a visit to the Chicago stockyards of half a century earlier. Read with the knowledge of the mass murders of humans transported in cattle cars, this passage makes me shudder.

In 1896, the owner of the firm of Armour and Co. took me on a tour of the Chicago stockyards, and even today I can still visualize the procedure. I can see clearly how, for instance, the oxen on a high-lying conveyer belt with their heads fastened upwards rolled along till they reached a spot where a man with a powerful hammer struck a deadly blow at their heads, and so moved about 300–400 animals an hour into the beyond. I wonder whether it is still done the same way?

Winter has lingered in their underheated house, but spring finally arrives and Ernst and Ella are able to take a pleasant excursion to Pilat-Plage, a nearby settlement with splendid villas and spectacular dunes. They keep to their domestic routine, despite the fact that toward the end of April, air raids begin to interrupt their nights. They make a few new contacts among the other refugees in Arcachon, and even manage to get a bridge game going. Ernst follows the news of the war closely and wonders about the fates of acquaintances elsewhere. He responds actively to word from his family in America, applauding and worrying, commenting and advising as always. But although the onrushing train is headed straight at them, he still has no thought of stepping off the tracks. By late May, his letters reflect growing alarm at what "vandalism and bestiality" the Germans are capable of. In early June, along with some health problems of his own, he worries about my mother's condition following gynecological surgery. And meanwhile, the Germans are closing in on France. Paris will be occupied on June 14; the country partitioned June 22.

Ernst is gloomy about the progress of the war, but when he writes on March 19, it is mainly to register his favorable impressions of my American education, based on a close reading of my latest "report card" (I am now three years old).

It is astounding with how much thoroughness and warm understanding a public nursery school can analyze the human traits of each child. No painter could produce a livelier picture than these words of the teacher: "Her excellent English vocabulary is delightfully seasoned with a slight German accent." Also the observation of how they managed to get her to abandon the *noo-noo* [blanket] is precious. I congratulate the parents. You should send a translation to your Helene [Nene, our nursemaid]. She certainly contributed to this educational success.

Are we at a turning point of the events of the war? The interview at the Brenner and the resignation of [French premier Edouard] Daladier seem to point to it. [On March 18, 1940, Hitler and Mussolini met at the Brenner Pass for a session of mutual admiration, and Hitler pushed the reluctant Italians toward war against France.]

It now takes nearly a month for mail to arrive, but it is still moving back and forth regularly between Arcachon and Evanston. Although Ernst surely had many international business connections, this is one of the rare occasions when he suggests that there might be some benefit in pulling strings. He expects, I think, some benefit to my parents, not to himself. Frank Wright, who had visited the Fürths and the match factory in Sušice many years earlier, was now part of FDR's "brain trust" as advisor to the Reconstruction Finance Corporation, and has evidently responded favorably to my parents' testing the waters of an old acquaintance.

March 23, 1940

It is very kind of the Wright family to remember our hospitality from 12 years ago in such lively colors, and to return the favor to children and grandchildren. You made the right move in renewing this friendship. One never knows when the mention of his name could be helpful.

Events in Europe are, as he puts it "very worrisome," and in spite of his confidence in the Allies, he wishes America would learn from Britain's mistake and move quickly against Hitler. But, he adds, "For the time being Ella sees only Easter at the door and is cooking like mad so that I won't miss the traditional striezel and ham. I hope that you too will spend the holidays in a cheerful mood." He writes on March 27 to offer thanks for pictures of the winter landscape of Evanston, commenting that my sister's legs look very slim, but hopes that this is merely the last remnant of a recent illness. Then he goes on ebulliently about my father's pig-breeding efforts and the birth of the first piglets.

When will they celebrate the first *disznótor?* [A Hungarian celebration, hog slaughter and barbecue] It's a pity that I won't be invited to it. Let's hope that Urbana will soon become a wholesale supplier for the packers of Chicago.

We are in the midst of moving. Ella is in her element, with spring cleaning and putting things in place etc. The day after tomorrow we are supposed to dine and sleep in the new place. Naturally I'm not supposed to lift a finger.

My sister has had a recurrence of a persistent bladder infection, and since Ernst himself had had a kidney surgically removed in 1911, he was extremely familiar with the problems connected with this bodily system. He suggests consulting with an immigrant physician, a friend, despite the fact that he is not yet licensed in America. My mother's gynecological troubles prompt other kinds of advice. These worries and Ernst and Ella's own domestic situation momentarily take precedence over the movement of troops.

March 30, 1940

Considering your present style of life, taking care of the children, demands of the household, it is not hard to imagine that your first commandment to take care of your own body is difficult to carry out. You have to make up your mind that your ambition to carry out your duties conscientiously should be reduced, and that you must pay more attention to yourself than you have up to now. How about a young helper, who would take care of the children daily for a couple of hours? That cannot be beyond your means.

Ella wanted to give you lots of medical instructions, but I prefer not to meddle with your physician, and hope that he is at least as competent as Ella with all her experience in this area.

We have been in our new villa for two days and are very pleased with the exchange. Ella worked for two days like a well-trained char from morning to night and today everything is spick and span, in its place, standing, lying or hanging.

A comfortable house and an efficient woman alleviate life enormously in these difficult times. One has to thank the good Lord for them.

A week later:

In our handsome and sunny villa we already feel quite at home. In the afternoon a bunch of children under the tutelage of a nun appear in our garden to play, which does not bother me since I take my siesta at the opposite end of the living room. In order not to let us forget the war, planes arrive in formation from the nearby airfield, but as long as they are decorated with the French tricolor, they do not disturb us.

In April 1940, there might still have been time for Grandfather to leave France for the United States. Again I feel the cold exhalations of dread at the back of my neck as I read these purposefully cheerful, practical letters, my grandfather pushing aside the most important practicality of all—that events could sweep him away too. But his reading of the news still encourages him to hope for a quick Allied victory.

April 15, 1940

The last week was rich in excitement. Just on my birthday [April 8] came the news that the Nazis had invaded Denmark and Norway, and I lost all desire to celebrate. But what a complete change in eight days! Every day brought a new blow against the Germans, the almost entire devastation of their fleet, the complete blockade of the North Sea, the Baltic, and most likely the destruction of their military forces in Norway.

In other words, one sees the future with more confidence and in spite of unexpected ups and downs, I have gained real confidence in the courage of the Allied forces and the hope of our seeing each other in the not-too-distant future.

When he writes to my father, Ernst takes a more hearty, businesslike tone. This is the man he depends upon to see that his daughter—perhaps both daughters—will have the comfortable lives they have been brought up to expect. I confess to an ahistorical twinge of irritation here at the assumption that these two young, intelligent, skilled and healthy women will not contribute to the finances of their households. I'm certain, too, that my father never felt any such irritation, but only pride in being for most of his life a successful breadwinner.

April 17, 1940

My dear Gyuri!
Your nice letter of March 10th brings me friendly details about your first enterprises on American soil. Now I can repeat my congratulations. I see that you have made your agreements with circumspection and care, so that your risk is reduced to a minimum. I'm reminded of the story of a man engaged in an enterprise to start up a new industrial product, who associates himself with an expert. The expert brings his knowhow but no money. After a few years the entrepreneur has the

knowledge and the expert has the money. This is only a joke. Once your knowledge and success as breeders are known, it should bring you more similar business.

It would be a blessing if your efforts in Canada were successful and might enable Paul's crossing before it is too late, before the "mad dog" (as Chamberlain called him yesterday) attacks other victims in the southeast. When Paul arrives in the U.S.A., he should trust you as a guide, and not engage in independent business.

After big victories of the British fleet I hope your pessimism is somewhat reduced; it has increased our confidence. Not even the big snout of Mr. Fritsche [Hans Fritsche, Nazi propagandist] on the German radio can change my opinion.

He thanks him for birthday neckties "chosen exactly to my taste," then praises Ella's kindness toward the always irritating Cecile, who has effectively been abandoned by her own children. And he shakes his head as he recalls his brother Bernard, Cecile's late husband, who had so disapproved of his relationship with Ella: "Blessed Bernard could not have foreseen that Ella, maligned by him, would be the only soul who one day would take care of his widow. Ella's generosity toward Cecile is, in this case, doubly admirable."

Grandfather took letter-writing seriously. It was for him, as for many of his generation on both sides of the Atlantic, an important form of self-presentation. As long as possible, he used fine stationery. The early letters are on heavy, smooth paper with a rough-cut edge. Later in the war, the paper declines in quality. But the handwriting remains elegant to the end. Sometimes, as in the next letter, the Gothic calligraphy, with its large scrolled capitals, its absolutely consistent slant and evenly spaced lines, seems particularly beautiful. Mother told me that it was also harder than usual to translate, because of the specificity and originality of the vocabulary.

April 22, 1940

My dear Evi!
Received your nice and detailed letter of the 30th and am pleased that the capricious mail was in a good mood just on your birthday, and that it assured you by a pile of letters that many people think fondly of you and will continue to do so. The children's birthday ovation must have been a charming performance. But I will have to miss pleasures of that kind for quite a while.

My assumption that Dorli must have had an infection was not entirely stupid. I do not know what *bacterium coli* is, nor do I have an idea how such a damned wretch makes its way into a child's bladder. But the essential part is to get it out of her organism. And how are you? Has the bleeding stopped? and how is your general and local condition?

The two brothers [George and Imre] seem to complement each other well and harmoniously. It reminds me of my relationship with my brother Bernard, which makes me more confident about the work they have started.

Your observation is correct about the changes in Cecile's character. She has discovered that her steady complaints about her situation and the misery that has befallen her have no resonance with us, but on the contrary made us furious, and made living with her unbearable. Ella has found a way to treat her with the right mixture of indulgence and severity. And now Cecile shows that she is aware of it, using an old saying that she doesn't dare not to live happily in our house.

Just so that we don't forget, in our contemplative existence, that the war is on, we recently had our first air raid alert. It was shortly before midnight, we were already in bed reading, but still awake when the sirens began to howl. We waited for an hour, listening to the sirens, turned off the lights and waited until the sirens announced the end of the alert. The next morning we heard that in our region, but not in Arcachon itself, there were overflights, and that the *boches* dropped only propaganda tracts. I did not encounter any of them.

So much for Grandfather's confident earlier prediction about the unlikeliness of enemy planes over Arcachon. Another of his hopeful predictions, the one about my father and his brother Imre's working relationship, remained similarly unfulfilled. Unlike the brothers Ernst and Bernard Fürth, who worked side by side and as best friends their whole lives, my father and Imre Guttmann had an unequal and unsatisfactory connection. The families did not get along, my parents looking down on the weak-willed, childlike Imre and on Lilly, his stagey social-climbing wife, who suffered from various forms of mental illness—or was she just faking to get attention, as my father thought? And although the brothers bought a farm together in upstate New York, where the Guttmann family lived, the association turned contentious and, in the end, bitter.

Written almost exactly two years after her farewell letter in 1938, this next piece of Ella's rare correspondence gives a further firsthand taste of her personality, her managerial powers, and her view of herself as a source of deep commonsense wisdom.

April 25, 1940

Today I am answering three of your kind letters at once. Thursday afternoon is my day of rest, otherwise I'm always occupied. Your letters sound calmer and more balanced, and I see that you have begun to take a bigger part in society. Your charming looks surely help pave the way.

I hear from Ernst that your husband is already working hard, let's hope soon with success. Slowly everything turns to the better. One has to bear up, Evi, is my motto.

Your wishes for our new residence have already been fulfilled, and Father feels well and comfortable. Today he said he feels as if he had lived here for quite a while. He lacks nothing of everyday needs. One needs a bit of luck in life and then should try not to take things too seriously. Grumblers should not even be born.

I hope your two little girls are all right again. Your health seems to be satisfactory, except for those small female illnesses. Don't get too upset over them, Evi, almost every woman has some.

With the coming of warmer weather, you all will be more resistant. When they found blood in Dorli's urine, it might have been caused by her fall in the bathtub. Erich once fell on the ice and had the same symptoms, stayed in bed for two weeks. Since then he never had any further problems. But anyhow, you are a little physician and are well informed. The fear and agony, my child, that we as mothers go through, only we can understand.

Erich and Herbert are working hard. I am only hopeful and do not worry about them. Hard work doesn't do the young ones any harm, but makes them grow up faster. They have success with women — from my point of view too much, since it's distracting.

How differently children are educated in the U.S.A. Certainly better for life; for the intellect, maybe less. What a pity that we cannot share all of this, these are the best years! It must give you immense pleasure, even if you fall into bed dead tired at night.

From home [Vienna] I hear little. It seems that they are well, Fred [her brother] lost his job, because of racial mixing ["versippung": Fred evidently was married to a Jewish woman]. I hope he can find something else.

There is so much misery in the world and so many people don't bother about others. This man Hitler has brought everything evil out of people. Almost everybody has become selfish, out for themselves!

Now enough. All stay well Evi, kiss the little ones for me. Does Dorli still remember Aunt Ella?

On the same date, April 25, 1940, Ernst reports that the air-raid alerts have continued every other night for over an hour. But they are getting used to it, he says. On May 3, he notes a discouraging turn of events in Norway, with more Allied troops being called up. "For a non-strategist," he says, "it is hard to imagine that the Germans can be driven out of Norway."

Then he gives a brief medical report about himself. Although vigorous and basically healthy at 75, Ernst had to keep close watch on his one kidney, upon which his life depended. Now he notes he has begun having headaches, and a urinalysis has revealed slight amounts of albumin, both symptoms of trouble.

I naturally immediately gave up all alcohol, to which I lately most likely paid too much homage. Smoking, which I had already reduced considerably, will be more restricted. And so I hope that with a bland, salt-free diet, with emphasis on milk and desserts, which Ella supervises very strictly, my health soon should be re-established. My appetite, sleep and appearance still seem unchanged. So no reason for the time being to worry. Most likely it is a useful warning signal for the old gentleman not to exceed the bounds.

Also the weather is not May-like—for days gray, rainy, rather cold, which matches the general mood.

On May 7, 1940, he speaks of the valuable diversion that work provides, especially in troubled times:

It is commendable that Gyuri's pigs take no notice of the war, but, as expected, multiply. Gyuri is fortunate to be fully occupied with his business. Is there a better distraction from the unlucky events that affect all of mankind daily? I, too, would be happy not to have all the time for reading newspapers and listening to the radio—a waste of time.

At this moment there might still have been a chance for him to get out of France, but he shows no sign of making such a move. The next letters show that he continues to be a spectator in the drama of his own and other people's lives. Refugees from Belgium are beginning to arrive, and we hear the first ominous mention of internments.

May 12, 1940

Today is the first day of Whitsuntide, and although the sun is laughing, and around us everything is green and blooming, one cannot enjoy all that, since one cannot know or fathom during the last two days how the fury of war on the borders of France will rage on in unimaginable wildness and malice, and whether in the next weeks and months it will claim tens of thousands of victims. But we do not give up hope that this battle of giants will end with the destruction of Hitler. Without this hope, life would not be bearable anymore.

The French radio gives hourly announcements. You can well imagine that we stay glued to this machine until deep into the night. And what does the U.S.A. do in the meantime? Make speeches!

May 17, 1940

The good news about you and the children would have made a cheerful day for me, if other news had not put a strong damper on my mood. But finally it was to be expected that Germany would not quietly submit to a hunger-blockade. So we can expect the next weeks and months to be full of ups and downs and one will need all one's willpower and vigor to hold one's own. Up until now I have managed, thanks to Ella's support, her pluck and sense of reality, and undisturbed by Cecile's whining, which can get on one's nerves.

Yesterday a few private automobiles with Belgian refugees arrived, riddled with machine-gun bullet holes. Unimaginable how those poor people got here.

The big hotels and both casinos prepare themselves for the sheltering of the wounded. I'm afraid they soon will be overcrowded. The official bulletin today says that the situation "est grave mais pas critique." But I would have preferred to hear that report from the German Army.

May 24, 1940

A week full of tension lies behind us. At first we were stunned by the news that the Germans had made "a pocket of about 100 km." into the Allied lines, and penetrated deeply into France. But we see that fortunately from day to day the rebuff is being enforced, and the energy growing on both sides of the Channel gives us hope that [French premier] Paul Reynaud's brave words will prove true.

The vandalism and bestiality of the Boche belligerence — in Rotterdam alone 10,000 civilians lost their lives — seems finally to shake up the conscience of the U.S.A. More and more we hear announcements that leading personalities are saying "America wake up."

If I, an old man, can live to see the destruction of the Nazis, I'm willing to suffer through the troubles of the days and months that lie ahead of us.

Next to the big turmoil this week, there also were smaller disturbing events. All Germans and Austrians of both sexes between the ages of 16 and 56 were sent to a camp in the Pyrenees [probably Le Vernet, 30 miles from the Spanish border]. Among others, the wife of Chairman Strauss, a woman about 48 years old, and her daughter, 17, who was a student at the lycee. A very kind, educated lady from a prominent Viennese Aryan family.

The good news from you that your letter brought me had the effect of the sun's rays in these dreary days.

I hope that you have recovered from your surgery quickly and that the fact that it was benign added greatly to your convalescence and humor. I ask you not to wait for my questions until you report about Dorli and yourself. Don't forget that two months lie between the question and the answer.

On June 3, 1940, Ernst remarks on the high cost of Mother's one-day stay in the hospital, evidently for some sort of gynecological surgery.

These are astronomical figures, and you don't even mention the physician's fee. It is certainly expensive to be, heaven forbid, sick in the U.S.A.

After four weeks my second urinalysis showed some albumin, so I went to a physician, who prescribed a two-week meatless diet, but did not consider my case worrisome, since my subjective condition, sleep, appetite, etc., are perfectly satisfactory. In two weeks another analysis should show whether the diet has worked.

The weather here for days has been magnificent. The bay, gardens, forests breathe peace, but one cannot really enjoy all that when daily and hourly one hears and reads how horribly the battle rages and how difficult it has become to stem the attack. Still we don't want to lose courage.

It is very sad that Paul's permit evidently came too late and that he lost his chance to escape. I hope Gretl will have the strength to bear the inevitable.

What one hears here about the fate of Belgian families exceeds in cruelty all imagination. What might have happened to your beautiful Belgian friend Loulou Cattier?

On June 5, 1940, Ernst writes, on both sides of the same sheet, a letter to my mother and one to my father.

My dear Evi!
I can well believe that you did not celebrate your wedding anniversary, since one cannot get into the right festive mood, then one makes useless comparisons, and with that the present gets grayer.

The liberation of the Allies from the encirclement at Dunkirk and the salvage by boat to England was certainly a masterpiece, but even Churchill was frank enough to tell his compatriots that a war is not won with retreats. For that reason we wait impatiently for the counter-offensive.

The veering round of public opinion in America in favor of intervention seems quite considerable, but the road from speeches to action is long. Also, *bis dat qui cito dat* [Latin: He gives twice who gives quickly] has never been so true as in this case, where Italy's intervention is at the door.

The loss of two piglets is, one hopes, only a single case and will only temporarily influence the end result of the breeding.

The next piece of correspondence in chronological order bears the date June 9, 1940, and was sent from my mother in Evanston to her father. It is the first of a whole series of letters to be returned, a heart-stopping turn of events. The envelope stamped in both French and English reads RETURN TO SENDER, SERVICE SUSPENDED; RETOUR A L'ENVOYEUR, RELATIONS POSTALES INTERROMPUES. My mother had written to her father, as always, in German. Various members of the Perl family are ailing, she reports, but the real news is that Paul Strasser has escaped from Hungary and will be traveling to the east on the Trans-Siberian Railroad and from there by ship to California via Japan.

> Dearest Father,
> I'm just reading a book that appeared in New York in 1923, *The Malady of Europe*, by M. E. Ravage. The author saw it all coming the way it looks today and lays the blame on the U.S.A. Why did leading personalities not read this book in time? One asks oneself many questions. But at the moment we shudder when we read the headlines in the papers. Do you see a great number of refugees in your little town?
>
> Today the Canadian lawyer was here and tomorrow Gretl leaves for Washington D.C., and then it should be possible for Paul to travel via Russia and Japan. All this is raving mad, and the hope that normal times will return is very small.
>
> My Gyuri still does not go out and also the children's temperatures still fluctuate. I think of you more and more often and wish I could spare you this turmoil.

Meanwhile, Ernst begins to lose heart a little, but he puts more passion into complaints about his sister-in-law and her penny-pinching children than about the Germans. Money is becoming a problem for the first time in his life.

June 10, 1940

You can imagine that we are living through days full of tension, but we are keeping our calm and sangfroid, hoping always that it will be possible to stop the German attack. It is only the moodiness of Cecile that makes life a little difficult for us. This hollow face, never softened by the smallest smile, is truly insupportable, and her oldest daughter [Mädy] sends her so little money that I have already had to write her some very strong letters, declaring that I cannot and do not want to have to worry about materially supporting Cecile. It is a matter of only $250 every three months. It's incredible!

June 11, 1940

Yesterday evening the Italian declaration of war was announced. Although we have been prepared for this event for quite a while, it is difficult to deny the impact and momentum of the real thing. Are the neglect and omissions of the last years reparable? Will the Allies have the power to conquer both dictators?

The coming weeks will require from us and all the French steadfastness and a test of nerves. Until now I have not lost my balance, but who knows what awaits us? One lives from one day to the next, the individual is powerless and cannot escape the general fate.

Although Ella oversees my diet strictly, the stress of the last days had a bad effect on my kidney. This also one has to put up with. Health is a precious gift, which enables one to enjoy the pleasures of existence, but when these pleasures disappear, then health loses its importance.

On June 14, Paris is occupied by the German forces. Ernst writes three days later in response to a telegram from his family.

June 17, 1940

My dear children!
I thank you for your kind concerned telegram, but I know even without this written proof that your thoughts in these critical and difficult days are incessantly with us.

While the day before yesterday American newspapers already spoke of an armistice, the just-announced resignation of [premier Paul] Reynaud and the installation of a military government show that the battle will continue. One can only hope that it will be more successful than up to now.

Naturally we cannot do anything, but stay put and await the fate of France and ourselves. For the time being one has to be glad to have a roof over one's head. Since millions have fled from the north, you can imagine how overcrowded the not-yet-endangered provinces are. Here, too, every garret is filled. A week ago we had to take in Mrs. von May, who was forced to leave her hotel. Yesterday a member of the Czech legation called and asked us to give shelter to his two daughters, 13 and 17 years old, which we could not disregard; and in the late evening the convent sent an abbé to be kept in safety.

We could more than gladly accept these small inconveniences if we knew that with this or even greater sacrifices the situation would be settled. But whatever happens, we must keep our heads and face our more-or-less benevolent fate with composure. You would not believe it, but last night we slept very well from 11:15 to 7:30.

Tomorrow it will be two years since we left Vienna. They have not been pleasant, heaven knows, but evidently we have not reached or surpassed the height of the evil.

I'm glad in the knowledge that you are safe and in God's keeping.

And another letter the next day.

June 18, 1940

My dear children,
Now the catastrophe has broken over us to an unforeseeable extent. There is no way to think of escaping. We must wait patiently for what is going to happen to France and to us, and mainly whether a human existence will be possible.

I'm not resilient enough to set out on a flight to Spain or Portugal, and cannot make up my mind to leave with a rucksack and lead a beggar's existence. For a few months I'm supplied with money, although I have Cecile around my neck, who gets so little from her children that she soon will be completely dried up. A cabled transfer sent 10 days ago did not materialize until now.

On this occasion I would recommend, dear Gyuri, that the management of the "Glarona" be transferred as quickly as possible from Switzerland to America. Under the present circumstances a Swiss deposit is not safe from seizure by the Germans.

The next letter, mailed June 21, 1940, has been opened and rubber-stamped "ouvert par l'autorité militaire." The resealing strip on edge reads "Contrôle Postal Militaire." The military regime is in full swing. The battle itself is coming closer too:

Last night and in the morning we had two alerts. Bordeaux was bombarded, but Arcachon was spared. Just now I hear that the Germans are 200 kilometers from Bordeaux. But the armistice discussions started yesterday—what are they going to mean for the poor French and for us?

The next communication is a telegram in French via Mackayradio to my parents at the North Shore Hotel, dated June 29–July 1, 1940. It reads:

WE ARE WELL THREE AIRLETTERS EN ROUTE YOU CAN'T DO ANYTHING HAVE TO WAIT
PEPE FURT. [*sic*]

[*ALLONS BIEN TROIS CLIPPERS EN ROUTE POUVEZ RIEN FAIRE FAUT ATTENDRE*]

A letter dated June 30, 1940, brings the news that Arcachon is now part of the occupied zone. At this point, the tone of my grandfather's writing changes, as if he were speaking through clenched jaws. For the first time in what had been his transparent writing, I feel the presence of riddles, and from here until the end of his life, I am on the lookout for coded messages. At the very least, he is concealing his real thoughts. Still, one perfectly clear and heartbreaking request comes through: He has finally decided that he would like to come to America. I have returned again and again with sorrow to read and reread this next letter.

My dear children,

I have just received your telegram, and regret very much that you are worrying over our health, but as I have written you many letters via air last week I hope that they will arrive little by little and take away your worries.

For three days we have been in the occupied zone, but up to now normal life continues. The German soldiers circulate in the streets, they make their purchases in the stores, but they are polite and behave as they should. One hopes that they will not get involved in civil administration.

Nevertheless we would very much like to come and see you. Do you think it might be possible to get a visitor's visa? For the moment all communications, whether by road or railroad—even to Bordeaux—are closed, but if one could get to Bordeaux, I would like to inform myself at the American consulate of the possibilities of a voyage.

The next five letters are the last my family will receive from Ernst and Ella for more than a year.

July 1, 1940

My dear children,

It is only three days since I wrote you, but knowing that you are uneasy, I am sending you our news as often as possible. Happily, I can assure you that up until now nothing has changed with us and that we are well. In the past days the number of troops occupying the city and the surroundings has greatly increased, and one cannot tell whether our apartment will be requisitioned, which would be troublesome. Life has not become easy.

I'd like you to send all my letters to Gretl because I am not writing her separately.

I embrace you with my whole aching heart.

July 3, 1940

... I hope that with my telegrams and frequent letters you are reassured about our fate. Until now, touch wood, we have been lucky. What the Belgian refugees and those from the north of France have experienced was at the limit of their strength. To survive that would probably have been beyond my strength. And since until now we have not had to leave our house, have our daily bread, I'm not allowed to complain. Since the "repatriation" of the refugees is supported by both the French and the German side (refugees are even being awarded certain quantities of gasoline), Arcachon is being vacated. I hope it won't come to requisitioning of inhabited apartments.

Everything you write about the children gives me great pleasure. Will I ever have the chance to see them and embrace them again? One barely dares hope for such happy moments.

The weather here is absolutely wonderful—beautiful, cloudless days, always bearable temperatures and a cool breeze from the ocean. Two years ago it would have been a precious summer vacation.

I can barely imagine the outcome of Paul's traveling plans via the USSR, Yokohama, California. But what is not possible these days?

July 8, 1940

[He has not heard from them in several weeks.] ... Most likely it will still take quite a while until the postal service turns halfway round. Also my letters, if they arrive at all, will be late, since the English have confiscated air mail in Bermuda—according to a newspaper report. One has to put up with all this and be content that one can continue one's daily life. Also the possibility of going to a place in the "*zone non occupée*" no longer exists as of today. I just read the new decree, wherein any "*déplacement*" for foreigners is prohibited. I have been the one in our circle, when plans like that had been discussed, who was opposed to it, since then, less than ever are you the master of your fate.

July 18, 1940

My dear Gretl!
I laughed at the top of my voice when I received your air letter from Vermont with its reminiscences of Stubenbach [a place] and Martin [the coachman in Sušice]. While I read it, I could readily believe that in those surroundings, full of

memories of your native place, you only geographically belong in the U.S.A. But what a pity that by the time you receive this letter, the idyll is over and you are back at work in your gray everyday life.

Since the major part of Belgian and French refugees have left, Arcachon should have become quieter than usual, but the street scene is enlivened by the presence of the German soldiers. They behave properly and with discipline and even the French admit that, and gracious females begin to make friends with them. The beach, which, because of recent cool weather is not very populated, offers a favorable opportunity for them.

We are well provided with food. Ella returns daily with two heavy shopping bags from the market, and if I did not have to watch my diet, I could live the life of a gourmand. But the cigarette situation is bad. *Le tabac blond* has vanished, and what you can buy for smoking is good for breaking the habit. My consumption is reduced to six to eight cigarettes and even those I discard halfway through. I think of you while I smoke. [Gretl was a heavy smoker.]

July 27, 1940

My dear Evi!
About our quiet—one could almost say monotonous—life there is not much to report, but I know every sign of life is welcome and so I dispatch a rather uninteresting bulletin.

The day before yesterday I went again to see my physician, showed him my analysis of albumin, which had declined from 0.06 to 0.04. He examined my heart and found a slight change and besides the diet prescribed small amounts of digitalis and recommended "*eviter des marches rapides et du vent*" [avoid fast walking and wind]. With that he confirmed my own observation that fast walking, mainly uphill, has become more difficult. I knew that it was not caused by overwhelming weight. I do not want to complain, since for such a long time I have been spared the infirmities of age, but slowly and surely I am turning into an old man.

The street scene including cafes and restaurants are taken over by German troops. In the morning they already stream singing through the streets. On the beach you can see them exercising, and their cars are almost the only ones that still circulate. The population grits its teeth and is silent. They have the feeling that worse is to come.

Then the family received two telegrams, one on September 12, one on October 9.

Sept. 12, 1940

All in good health remain here. Tell Redlich Siebert [Cecile's and Ella's children] eager for news of you and Paul. Cable. Furth

Oct. 9, 1940

My cable Sept. 12 announcing our good health, asking news of you all and Paul without reply. Waiting impatiently. Furth

My parents' communications were not reaching Ernst. And his were about to end; after this, there was silence for a full year.

Early days in America: My mother and I enjoy a picnic on the running board of our 1939 Chevrolet.

11

Puzzles—Life in the U.S.

T HERE WAS A TIME, earlier in my life, when I loved doing jigsaw puzzles. On a card table in our playroom, on the wicker tables of rented summer houses, the tiny precut pieces with their perfectly defined interlocking or straight edges promised what few other human endeavors do—clear and unambiguous completion. Puzzles were one of the only activities that could utterly absorb my mind, keep my thoughts from chattering. The earliest puzzle I can remember is from my early childhood: 48 thick wooden pieces in different pastel colors and frankly educational. When you finished, you had the map of the United States, a good thing, on the whole, for an immigrant child to be getting under her hands, into her head. Later puzzles gave back images of glowing scenery or historic events—autumn in New England, Napoleon at Waterloo, Washington crossing the Delaware. Still later there were maddeningly subtle works of art, Monet waterlilies or Vasarely squares. I got so that I couldn't pass through a room where a puzzle sat unfinished without trying to add a few pieces. At some point, I stopped doing them. My life, I decided, was too short for jigsaw puzzles.

As my mother and I translated and transcribed my grandfather's letters, I was back in the puzzle mode. But the picture on the box that we were working from was imperfect; bits of detail were blurred; colors failed to match perfectly. Pieces were missing. The images melted and morphed—a fish becoming a bird. Yet though I knew we would never produce a single, unified image, I found the process as absorbing as ever. I'd look up from my work and several hours would have passed without my noticing.

It was a good thing for my mother and me. Often in open conflict during my adolescent years, we maintained an improved—because more detached—relationship after my marriage. Though I was only 20 when I married, I was immediately treated as an adult, left alone to make my own decisions, my own mistakes. My parents were intensely interested in our lives, but they were pleased also to be able to keep a safe distance, have their own lives, their privacy. They wanted to know about the activities and accomplishments of their daughter, son-in-law and grandchildren, and liked to have occasional decorous visits with us, but they preferred not to get their hands dirty, psychologically or physically. They did not offer to babysit, nor did they want to know too many details about the messy facts of all of our growings up. I was still, after all, the designated happy, cheerful second child. We kept up this fiction.

When I reached my late middle years and my mother was old, we forged a new connection around my interest in the family's history. And because my father was no longer around, she was able to narrate the events her own way and we could do our work without another voice to interpret the clues, to tell us where the pieces belong. The work we did in assembling and translating and exploring her father's letters was important for her too. It gave her an opportunity to revisit, to make peace with a past that was in many ways too painful for her to come to terms with at the time. "You know," she had said to me when she gave me the first of those letters from France, "I never had a chance to bury my father." Together we were able to offer her some sort of conclusion.

Still, as we worked, I sometimes wondered if my mother were holding on to these letters—doling them out only in small increments—because she worried that she would die when they were all translated. Dragging out the process to make sure it never ends. It wasn't exactly Penelope undoing the weaving, just slight delaying tactics. We were learning together, but she was controlling the pace, quietly resisting my efforts to speed things up. Yet she was unbelievably generous with her time, her energy.

One day, a few months short of the end of our translating, I asked if we might look through the box of letters, so that I could simply list by date the ones that hadn't yet been translated. She agreed, and so we sat in our accustomed places opposite each other at the counter of her little kitchen pass-through. Instead of my usual pad of white, lined paper, I had brought my laptop computer so that I could more easily make a chronological list, while taking a few notes. There were, it turned out, about

75 pieces of correspondence still to go. She would read aloud from some of them, commenting as she went. When she had finished reading one aloud and we'd talked a bit about it, I'd say, "Are you done with that one? Do you want to hand it over?" And she'd think, and mostly decide to keep them. She let me have a few, a couple of them—for my sins, since my German is so inferior to my French—typed in German. It was quite a little dance, a psychic tug of war. She was not to be hurried, would hand them over when she was done with them, when she was good and ready. We were traveling together, but she was firmly in charge of this part of the journey.

It is the journey that matters and not the arrival, so the saying goes. The search is as exciting as the discovery. In the process of trying to get to know my grandfather, I have had to learn many things—about the history of the war, about the process of match manufacturing, about the history of my family, about the society and culture of prewar Austria and Hungary, about my mother and her sister, about my father and his siblings, about myself and my sister. The fuzzy picture on the puzzle box is not a map I can follow. But most of the time the pleasure of uncovering new areas to explore is satisfaction enough. An example: I want to follow up a couple of remarks in my grandfather's letters: one (May 27, 1939), about how he could live better in France on $200 a month than he could have done in the States; the other, a few months later (October 3, 1939), about a proposal to the U.S. Congress by someone named Pittman. I go to the library and take out the *New York Times* microfilm for October 1, 1939. I learn that Key Pittman, a senator from Nevada, wanted to repeal the neutrality law. And in the course of several riveting hours scrolling the microfilm through an immense *Sunday Times*, I also make note of ads for clothes—a Harris tweed topcoat at Rogers Peet for $25.95; wingtip shoes for $7.95. I check out real estate and furniture prices: a four-and-a-half-room apartment in Forest Hills for $79 a month; a maple dinette set with four chairs at Wanamaker's for $39.50.

You could have lived here, perhaps not quite as cheaply as in France, but you could have easily managed, I say to my grandfather, who looks at me kindly, but with the all-knowing indulgent nod of a wise, elder male of that generation of Middle Europeans. I know this look well. It says: You are a lively young woman and not unattractive, though a little sloppily dressed and in need of a manicure. You are intelligent and have some accurate information, perhaps even some good ideas. But there are too many things you do not know, do not understand, and which I could not possibly begin to explain to you. I will be all right where I am.

As I hear his words and watch his confident manner, my heart sinks. He turns and goes back into his modest but comfortable house overlooking the sea in Arcachon. My fists pound on a door that is muffled with the soundproof padding of events already past. He cannot hear me; his fate is sealed. It is useless to try to rewrite the past. And so I settle back into my role as researcher, reporter, detective looking for clues, puzzle solver. I search and snoop, and as I work, write, copy, transcribe, translate and ask questions, a picture begins to solidify—this complex interlocking network of people, places and events. And once in a while I am rewarded by the puzzle worker's success, the small sound of something falling neatly into place, the burglar's prize as the combination lock's tumblers signal their readiness to open. The journey, the search, is surely a reward in itself, but do not underestimate also the pleasures of arrival, of discovery.

Following the July 27, 1940, letter from Ernst, the next letters chronologically are all from my parents in the United States, and the reason we have them is that they were all returned. Mail from the States was no longer being delivered within Occupied France. Then, except for those two telegrams from my grandfather, there was no contact for over a year. For me, the sadness of knowing that my parents' letters never reached Ernst and Ella is somewhat lessened by the pleasure of seeing the rich picture the letters paint of these particular immigrants at this moment in their lives. My family was passing its second summer in the United States, and had left the broiling heat of Chicago for one of Michigan's vacation spots, Shadow Trails Inn on Walloon Lake. My sister, Doris, was eight; I was three and a half. Mother writes on August 2, 1940:

> My dearest Father!
> Here we have a float and I think frequently about bygone Brioni days [an island in the Adriatic where the Fürth family went on vacation]. Never since then have I been able to swim as much or as easily. Here the lake is in front of the house

and you need, so to speak, nothing but a bathing suit all day. In other respects there is no similarity with Brioni. We sleep in small cottages, and there's certainly no lobster on the menu, nor does anyone drink chianti. In spite of that, it is an ideal spot for my present expectations. The children are happy and outdoors all day long. They have found young playmates in the vicinity; they are taken along on motorboat rides; people play children's records for them. They chat with everybody in the inn. The owners are very nice people who introduce us to every newcomer and take us along to their neighbors. This way we collect new connections with General Motors and other large Detroit enterprises. It is interesting to observe how wealthy Americans choose a very simple life for their vacations, even simpler than was customary in the Salzkammergut [Austrian vacation spot].

Everybody is asked the question of conscience: Which church do you go to on Sunday? Gyuri is already looking very well, and eats pancakes for breakfast — a Negro relative of *palatschinken*. I feel very ladylike in that I don't have to cook, I can read, take a little nap after lunch, as if nothing in our lives had changed. I wish we could share all these delights with you. We just received a wire from the Wittmans [old Hungarian friends] saying that they left Lisbon on the *Excalibur* and expect to arrive in New York next Thursday. I wish Paul were already on this route. From Budapest we get comforting news. Klári is spending the summer vacation in Visegrád [in Hungary] and is much braver under pressure than when times were favorable. Here politics are fervently discussed, but basically everybody wants the status quo ante in order not to be drafted. The battle of Willkie-Roosevelt is going to be very interesting.

I have had no news from you in ten days. Will we see each other again in the near future? For this question there is no answer yet.

I embrace you from the bottom of my heart.
Your faithful   Evi

Aug. 12, 1940

Dearest Father!
Gretl fortunately found a furnished house in the vicinity of the school in Winnetka and can move in on Sept. 1st. I do not know whether we mentioned to you that Professor Blum [Ernst's former doctor] lives in Chicago. For our own

peace of mind I'd like you to send us your urinalysis, so that Blum, who knows your kidney so well, can make a comparison. But in any case I'm glad that you now sleep well and don't have headaches anymore. I wish you could see the Buzlein, she sits next to me on a little stool and looks at her picture books. This child radiates peace, is sunny, cheerful, finds friends without difficulty, loves humor. She herself tells very dramatic jokes, and even has one about Abraham Lincoln in her repertoire. Here the children are so popular that I'm really quite proud of them. Dorli has a special patron, who occasionally takes her on small automobile trips and who yesterday told me the following: Dorli told him in a perfectly coherent fashion about Sušice, about you, the two factories and the way matches are manufactured, which impressed this rather dry American. Mr. Quaintance told me: "From all she told me, I now have a very good picture of that little town." From all these details, I felt that Dorli remembers much more than I imagined, and talks about it so rarely only out of tact, to avoid hurting me.

I can quite truthfully say that the two children make our life sunny. Dorli swims extremely well and Buzi, moved by ambition, lies on her life-preserver without fear and paddles into the lake.

Today we start our trip home, for which we will take several days. Gyuri recently made an enormous entomological mistake. He extinguished the spiders in our cabins, which up until now had kept the ants captive, and now all of us — the children and I too — are full of disgusting ant bites. In spite of it we had a good time in this nice place.

The answer from Washington about your visa was unfavorable. For this reason right after our arrival in Evanston, we will look for other possibilities. There are so many islands with a good climate in the vicinity of this continent, which perhaps would not be bad for a transition.

You and Ella are a thousand times embraced
by your faithful Evi

Next is an undated carbon of a letter from my father to Ernst, picking up on the subject of obtaining a visa to go someplace besides the United States. Those islands with a good climate that my mother has mentioned refer, presumably, to Cuba or elsewhere in the Caribbean. My father also provides the address of a distant cousin in Spain, guessing that Ernst and Ella might have to travel to Spain and thence to

Portugal to find passage out of Europe, as some refugees from France had been doing. Despite all the anxiety and uncertainty of trying to make these arrangements, my parents manage, remarkably, to keep up the forms of ordinary, conversational exchange with my grandfather. Here is my father's letter to Ernst:

Dear Father!
We have returned again to our adopted home, Evanston, and continue our normal life. The pictures Evi sent you prove that we had a really good summer, where the children could swim and we had the chance to encounter new people and surroundings. There are two changes in our present circumstances that might influence our mode of life. The one is that Imre has accepted a job as a chemist in a sugar factory. As a result, I will be able to devote more time to the farm operation, and it is possible that this will make a difference in our plans. This job assures them a minimum standard of living, security that especially appeals to [Imre's wife] Lilly.

The other change might be brought about by the arrival of our friend Ernö Wittmann in New York. He is here with an introduction to some wealthy people, and he hopes for their cooperation. We will meet next week and I will listen to his proposals. With his help we have made inquiries about the possibilities for your immigration. Visitors' visas for the U.S. are issued autonomously by local consuls, who also have the right of denial. In your case it can only be carried out with local connections in Bordeaux.

Possibilities exist for immigration to Cuba, Mexico or other South American states. But if I see what the outskirts of large American cities look like, especially during heat waves, I would discourage anyone who is close to me from making that choice. Canada offers a possibility that is appealing in all respects, and I presume that in the not-too-distant future we could be successful in this direction. I ask you to supply me with information about the type of travel documents that you have, and send me photocopies of both yours and Ella's. I will have them legalized immediately. If the U.S. consul in Bordeaux assures you that an affidavit from your children is of value, we will send it right away. The address of my cousin in Spain (she is my mother's cousin) is: Elena Lövy, General Oraa 64m., Madrid, España.

I just received her address and will write her simultaneously. I hope your health is satisfactory and that the dreary fall days do not affect your mood.

I embrace you
your faithful Gyuri

Back in their apartment, Mother gives a full account of the return trip from their vacation.

Aug. 18, 1940

Dearest Papitsch!
Now I'm sitting again at my old, rugged typewriter in the North Shore Hotel. They were nice enough to paint and clean our apartment during our absence, and if the temperature were not tropical, we would not miss our cool Walloon Lake. We had a beautiful return trip. If you happen to have a map nearby, then trace our travel around Lake Michigan. We went north to Mackinaw City and from there on a large steamship—which absorbs any number of automobiles without difficulty—we crossed the lake at a point where Lake Michigan and Lake Huron touch. We spent the night on the opposite shore at St. Ignaz. Dorli is perfectly at home with the Touring Club Book, knows every abbreviation, and chose the proper accommodations with common sense according to the number of beds and baths. The drive the next day through the incredibly beautiful mixed forests of the Upper Peninsula was very impressive. This part of the world is sparsely settled and, compared to other parts of the U.S.A., has very rough roads. Two hundred miles of it are like Winterberg-Bergreichenstein [beautiful mountainous country near Sušice]. We arrived at Manitowoc—the names are all Indian. There you see the ideal, prosperous, modern American city with 200,000 inhabitants. In the north a very groomed residential section, in the south, big modern factories: aluminum mines, cardboard box factories, shipbuilding yards, breweries—I got homesick for a high smokestack. On the third day we got the usual tropical climate of Wisconsin and Illinois—the Middle West!

Back here, I found three very kind letters of yours. I'm glad that you have gotten rid of your symptoms. Our physician friend Dr. Anday [a Hungarian] tells us that you are in the hands of a good doctor, who prescribed Digitalin, according to him the best digitalis product—made by Prince, isn't it? Dorli again needed Urotropin today, but I hope it's just a small flare-up of an old complaint.

I kiss you a thousand times, your faithful Evi
P.S. Buzi, à la Grandfather on the trip, is able to have a nap in all situations.

The next letter is one of the few where my mother allows herself to express the depth of her sadness, her sense of loss, and some of the emotional demands of the new life.

Aug. 24, 1940

Dearest father,
Yesterday I thought a great deal about you, partly in tears. We saw a movie, the story of a Lippizan stallion, after a short story by Felix Salten called "Florian." It showed performances in the Spanish Riding School, and I remembered that we had been there together and that you knew the different equestrian paces by name. In general we rarely go to the movies, except when something special is shown in one of our provincial, inexpensive movie theaters. Then it's all right to cry profusely for 25 cents, since the rest of the time one pushes away feelings that would only be in one's way in the new life.

Dorli told me today that most of the time when it is nice and quiet before going to sleep, she thinks of you. Both girls have finished their dental work and when I have lengthened their dresses considerably, school can start.

Still keeping up her hopeful tone, despite the ominous news from Europe, Mother keeps writing, although she is now not getting any letters back from her father. And the good news that she reports about her brother-in-law, Paul Strasser, will turn out to be a phantom. He was not able to sail from Greece, but had to wait many more months in Budapest before he was able to travel across Siberia by train.

Aug. 30, 1940

My dearest Papitsch!
Two weeks have gone by since I got your last letter and since I know that physically you are not 100 percent, I await your news with much impatience. I read frequently that Bordeaux is being bombarded by the British—there are scarcely any places left in Europe where it is possible to sleep peacefully. Gretl has had an exciting day. She got a cable from Paul, who is supposed to get his U.S. visa tomorrow, and plans to sail via Piraeus with a Greek ship to the U.S.A. I hope

My sister, Doris, age eight, in some shots by a professional photographer.

that nothing happens in between—everything hangs on a hair. Gretl anyhow is very unhappy to have to move house again alone. Moving is always the moment when our existence manifests itself as most gypsy-like.

Fredi was just here, had known nothing about his father's departure and it was quite moving to see his joy. Fredi is taller than I, and I think camp did a great deal for his social skills.

This week we expect our friends the Wittmanns, who promised to visit us. He arrived in the States with four great trunks and seems to be very busy. If he can't get away, I'll join Gyuri, who wants very much to talk to him, in New York. My young woman from Munich [a babysitter] seems to be up to the mark, the children are fond of her and I believe that I can leave with good conscience.

Today we were all fingerprinted, the new form of registering foreigners. I could not quite rid myself of memories of my social work with prisoners, but the children thought it was great fun. If this is it [no worse harassment than this] and Roosevelt remains, we must be content.

In the hope that no news is good news, I remain with many, many hugs your Evi

Meanwhile, back in their former apartment in Budapest, my father's half brother Robert ("Berti") Guttmann has made room for two older relatives, Paula and Richard Steiner, who have fled from Vienna. Their fate was not happy. Although the Hungarians did not begin a systematic roundup of Jews until 1944, the country was officially

From the same session; I am three, and wearing a matching outfit.

closed to foreigners. And although the Steiners tried to remain undercover, they were denounced by someone, deported, and perished in the camps.

Sept. 4, 1940

Dear Father,

Unfortunately there is a complete stoppage of mail service. For more than three weeks no letter has arrived from you. One has the feeling that the contact is completely interrupted. I'm afraid that you find yourself in the same situation. In any case I continue to write twice or three times a week and alternately by regular mail and airmail, since we know that there are still Export U.S. Lines and Greek boats that deliver mail.

Ernö and Rozsi Wittmann spent four days with us and were able to tell us what they saw and lived through during the last four months. In February they still had dinner with Berti in our old apartment [in Budapest], and since then have traveled all over Europe. After all the hardships, they seem amazingly steady. One probably tries to forget the painful situations as quickly as possible and is thankful to be in a peaceful part of the globe. Their American connections from older days seem to function well, so that Ernö already has some prospects for earning money.

On the occasion of the Wittmann visit, Dorli and Buzi suffered from the "grandparent complex." They were so affectionate and sweet with them, and I'm convinced it was meant for you and Ella. Dorli cried when they left.

Next is a letter from my mother to Ella.

Sept. 16, 1940

My dear Ella!
Yesterday to our surprise your son Erich, who was on a business trip here, came
to see us. We all ate together and he helped put the babies to bed. Finally Gretl
also came for a drink. Erich looks unchanged, handsome and healthy, but what is
much more important, he has gained confidence without losing his pleasant
unpretentiousness. His English is really very good, although with a strong Viennese accent. He seems to have gotten to know the country well in these two years.
Gyuri and I had a good feeling about our get-together. Also he doesn't seem to
be disliked by the local girls!

Marietta tried to understand how Erich is related to her. After long explanations,
she finally asked: "Why did he not bring Opi [grandfather] along?" And Marietta was right. School for the children starts on Wednesday, and for that occasion
both girls got very cute new red and white polka-dotted dresses, of which they
are very proud.

I hope to get mail from you again soon. Otherwise I don't want to see the mail
carrier.

After this come the two final telegrams from Ernst and Ella, September 12 and
October 9, 1940.

Naturally my parents had been replying to all of Ernst's communications, but the
next letter from my mother is the last of those that were returned. At this point they
evidently gave up the futile effort of trying to reach Ernst by mail.

Oct. 10, 1940

Dearest Papitsch!
Your cable which arrived today was a great disappointment for us. We naturally
had responded in September by telegram, but were simultaneously warned by
Western Union that they could not guarantee its fate. It must be grim for you to
be without mail from us. In New York I saw Cecile's telegram at Mädy's and
am glad to know that you are well. Naturally it is impossible to grasp how the
connection works only in one direction. Gretl and I continue to write to you
alternately by airletter and by boat. We are told that after the First World War,

millions of letters got lost, but maybe one of them will slip through and reach you before this nasty war is over.

We are back in Evanston, after Gyuri returned from New York full of new business possibilities. As a matter of fact he is drawn to New York, and it is foreseeable that we will make another attempt to relocate [*unkrempeln*, Viennese word for a messy decamping]. We have become more flexible, the luggage gets less and less, and so I would not hesitate to make another move. These, at the moment, are only very, very vague plans, but they are connected with an epidemic among the pigs. This fact has reduced Gyuri's enthusiasm for agriculture. With the death of nine sows (all were pregnant), the result is a great financial loss for the work of this year.

Gyuri now regularly attends the university [Northwestern] and tries to familiarize himself with commercial law and other particulars of American business methods.

The children are obsessed with their school life. Dorli learns French and really has a very good accent. The little one, unfortunately, is not a baby anymore. She grows, is independent, not only in her activities but also her way of thinking.

You can well imagine with what impatience Gretl waits for Paul. The real danger for him starts when he gets on the boat.

I hope, Papitch, that you will have a chance to decipher this letter and to read how unbelievably we all miss you.

Then followed the long silence on both sides.

As soon as my parents received my grandfather's request for a visa to come to this country, they naturally began to do all they could to make it happen. They contacted Frank C. Wright, the American businessman and Roosevelt advisor with whom they'd had a friendly exchange of Christmas cards the previous year. Wright replied to their request, offering to help in any way possible. The main thing, he said, was to demonstrate that my family had enough money to support my grandfather.

RECONSTRUCTION FINANCE CORPORATION

WASHINGTON

FRANK C. WRIGHT
SPECIAL ASSISTANT
TO THE BOARD OF DIRECTORS

April 2, 1941.

Mrs. Eva Perl,
1611 Chicago Avenue,
Evanston, Illinois.

My dear Eva:

      I submitted both affidavits of support today to Mr. H. L. Troutman of the State Department, Room 216 Winder Building, Washington, D. C. Mr. Troutman said these affidavits would be satisfactory, with the following corrections made:

      Bank statements, now dated October 15, 1940, Guaranty Trust Company, and November 25, 1940, First National Bank of Chicago, should be brought up to date;

      Certified copies of income tax return for 1940 should be certified by the Collector to whom the return was made. If this is not feasible, send a photostat of the check for the March 15, 1941, payment of income taxes.

      Dr. Perl should join in the application with you, as he is a joint owner of the bank account.

      These changes, plus the information you said would be forwarded from Chicago, covering the number of your naturalization certificate, should be made, and all papers sent to me at 20 Exchange Place, New York City.

      It was very pleasant to see you and the Doctor at my home last Sunday. Of course, we will all join you in the effort to get your father out of occupied France.

      With regards, I am,

Very truly yours,

Frank C. Wright.

Enclosures.

Despite the efforts of a powerful friend, Grandfather was never granted a U.S. visa.

Nov. 13, 1940

Dear Eva:

I can tell you, after thorough investigation with the State Department, that our Government would offer no objection to your father entering and residing in this country, if official assurance was received that he or his relatives possessed sufficient means to keep him from being a public charge.

Of course, this will not be hard for you to establish, I am sure. The State Dept. advises that the U.S. Consul in Bordeaux has complete authority to issue a visa if your father will make affidavit there. If there is any difficulty, have him write or cable me at this address, and I will ask the State Department to cable the Consul at Bordeaux.

He goes on to recommend that they get one of the large banks in Chicago, preferably the one where they have an account, to verify their financial independence. Since the Czech quota is still open, it should be easy for Ernst to come to the States. (Ernst had chosen Czech citizenship when the country became a republic in 1918.) If they have any problems, Wright offers to contact a friend, who is the head of Chicago's largest bank.

Wright's next letter, about 10 days later, concurs with my mother's concern about the unreliability of ordinary postal services, and offers to have their letters sent via diplomatic pouch directly to the consulate in Bordeaux. As the situation in France worsened, various affidavits and letters were made available to the authorities to show that my parents were, indeed, able to support my grandfather. Meanwhile the silence from my grandfather gaped like an open wound. Despite Frank Wright's intervention, bureaucratic wheels turned with excruciating slowness. It was even true, according to other observers of the time, that American consulates in France were making life unnecessarily difficult for refugees by rigidly adhering to regulations imposed under the Nazi occupation, when they—the consuls—could just as easily have looked the other way.

Despite these worries, my parents could not hang suspended here in the New World. They needed to move forward with their own lives, and had decided to leave the Midwest, which, although it had been hospitable to them in many ways, felt all too foreign. My mother remembers being unable to get any news of Europe on the local radio or in the isolationist *Chicago Tribune*. And although there were the Strasser relatives and some developing connections in the Chicago area, my family saw few recent European immigrants there because most of them were settling in New York. The Midwest was too provincial, too narrow-minded, too Republican—and most of all, too far from Europe. They were thinking about moving to the New York area, to the town of Scarsdale, which, they had been told, had one of the best public school systems in the country. In late March, my parents traveled east and paid a visit to Frank Wright in his home in Tarrytown, N.Y. The tone of his letter the following week is kind, but four months have passed and the State Department is still asking for more documents.

> April 2, 1941
>
> My dear Eva:
> I submitted both affidavits of support today to Mr. H.L. Troutman of the State Department. . . . Mr. Troutman said these affidavits would be satisfactory, with the following corrections made. . . .

Troutman wants the bank statements sent in October to be updated; he wants their income tax return for 1940, the numbers of their naturalization certificates, and so on. Wright adds: "It was very pleasant to see you at my home last Sunday. Of course, we will all join you in the effort to get your father out of occupied France."

Next is a stiff, bureaucratic letter to Frank Wright (postage of 11 cents was due from Wright, it notes) from an official in the visa division of the State Department a month later and forwarded to my parents.

> May 26, 1941
>
> In reply refer to VD 811.111 Fürth, E.
>
> My dear Mr. Wright:
> I refer to your letter of May 7, 1941, with enclosures, concerning the immigration case of Dr. Ernst Fürth.
>
> Recent information received in the Department indicates that exit permits are being denied all persons desiring to leave occupied France, and until there is

some relaxation in this respect our consular officers cannot accord consideration to the visa applications of persons in that territory. However, the documents enclosed with your letter are being forwarded by official pouch to the American Consular Officer at Bordeaux, in an envelope to which the sum of 11 cents in postage has been affixed. I feel sure that at such time as Dr. Fürth may obtain permission to depart from occupied France, our consular officer will examine his case sympathetically and will extend him every consideration consistent with our immigration laws.

Sincerely yours,
A. M. Warren
Chief, Visa Division

This was the last official mention of a visa for my grandfather. In fact, the American consulate at Bordeaux was about to be closed down. In the 11 months since Ernst had asked—at long last—for a visitor's visa, France had become a prison.

The house in Angers from which Ernst Fürth was taken to the camp at Drancy.

12

Guardian Angels

THE CONTACT BETWEEN MY GRANDFATHER and his children was broken for more than a year, until September 1941. The man who restored this invaluable link was Frederic Reyfer, a Frenchman living in Switzerland. But the story of how Reyfer came to be in touch with Ernst and Ella remains one of our puzzle's missing pieces. Our first evidence of contact is a postcard from Ernst to Reyfer dated July 19, 1941. It is possible that my grandfather had met Reyfer at some earlier time in his life. There could have been a business connection, since Reyfer worked for a firm that put advertising labels on matchboxes and matchbooks. Indeed my father, in a letter to the U.S. Treasury Department a year later, asserts that Reyfer had been the Swiss representative for Solo matches. But it is clear, in any case, that Frederic Reyfer and Ernst Fürth were not well acquainted, since in his first postcard to him, my otherwise meticulous grandfather gets his correspondent's name wrong, addressing him as *Arnold Renfer.*

This card was the only type of correspondence permitted within France's "free" and occupied zones. It was the only way for Ernst and Ella to communicate their news. The card itself is a daunting object, bristling with heavy censor's markings in black ink, with peremptory printed warnings that read:

ATTENTION
Card reserved exclusively for family correspondence.
It is permitted to write here seven lines of correspondence of a familial nature,
but it is strictly forbidden to write between the lines or to give news that is not of

this nature. It is indispensable to write very legibly to facilitate examination by the German authorities. Any card that is irregular in form or in subject matter will not be sent; its purchase value will not be reimbursed.

Ernst writes in French to Reyfer—oh so carefully—with no mention of names or places, and nothing physically between the lines, but whole volumes behind the words:

> I thank you infinitely for your kind card which gave me great pleasure in bring-ing me such good news of my relatives, which I appreciated even more since it has become very rare. Have you left your former home for good, and your business? We are pretty well, must not be too hard to please in these times. Cordial salutations EFürth [a formal signature]

Reyfer, it turned out, was able to provide a route for mail, provisions and eventually money from my parents to my grandfather. And through this same route, Ernst's correspondence could reach his family in America. That family now also included my uncle, Paul Strasser, who finally arrived in San Francisco in January 1941. In the summer of that year, the Perl family moved to Scarsdale, N.Y.

Mail from German-occupied France traveled only within "Greater Germany," which now included Austria, Czechoslovakia and the other occupied countries. But it could not legally go to neutral Switzerland, and certainly not to the United States. The Reyfers lived in Geneva, but also kept an office just a few miles away in the French border town of Annemasse. Annemasse was in the so-called free zone, that portion of France administered by the puppet Vichy government. Ernst and Ella could "legally" write to the Annemasse address, from where their cards were smuggled across the border to Switzerland. My parents, in exchange, could write to the Reyfers in Geneva, and their mail would be carried into France at Annemasse, from where it was "legally" sent to Ernst.

On September 12, 1941, Reyfer writes to my mother, sending her a full explana-tion of how the triangular correspondence could be made to work. The letter, like most of his communications, is typed on onionskin airmail paper, whose semitrans-parency and crinkly sound bring back a whole era to me. It was the paper my father preferred to write letters on, especially when he was at any distance or writing more

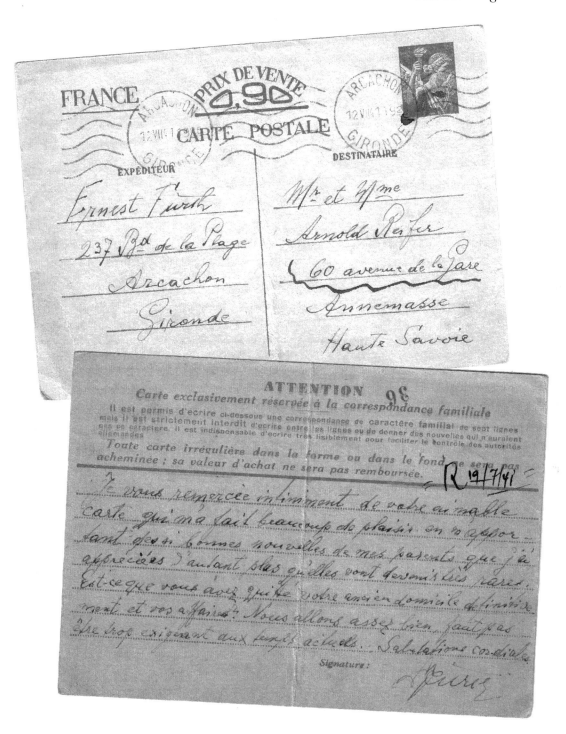

Front and back of one of the first cards Grandfather sent to Frederic Reyfer.

than a short note. I have many of them in his often-hard-to-decipher hand. Reyfer's letter has a Geneva return address; and as in all of his correspondence over the next year and a half, it includes a reference number. This one is Ref. No. 1257. Most of his letters are in French, but this one is in German. Perhaps he did not yet know that my mother wrote and spoke perfect French. I include this one in full to show the kind of details Reyfer was attending to. Emphases are Reyfer's.

Dear Honored Lady!
I received your correspondence of Aug. 18 through Sept. 3 and have immediately forwarded the enclosed cards to your father. The postal connection takes 10–12 days (and so send and return, 20–24 days); I would expect a reply around Sept. 25. As soon as I get a reply, I will foward it to you. Your father and Mme. Cecile are, since the middle of August, no longer in Arcachon, but in TOURS (Dept. Indre & Loire) Pension DUVIELLA, 31, Rue de l'Archeveche.

In regard to your question about food *from Switzerland*, it is at present unfortunately impossible to send any kind of food or useful articles (soap etc.) from here to foreign countries. All these goods are carefully rationed and export is strictly forbidden. My wife had left behind a variety of food in our Paris residence (which we left on June 10). In the past few days we have given instructions that these items should be sent to your father and your aunt (Mme. Cecile F.). In France also most foods are strictly rationed, and are therefore very hard to get and very expensive. If you get something from abroad, as I understand it, you can be sure that normal rations will somehow be shortened. The difficulty is, however, to manage to get these foods abroad and then get them to their destination.

I have absolutely no idea of whether and how your father has been managing financially. I have written him in any case that he should tell me frankly whether he has anything that we could help him with in case of need. When I receive his reply, I won't hesitate to write you immediately. I am also in the process of gathering enquiries into how food could be sent from Portugal (Lisbon) to France. I will send all this information to Mr. Paul Fürth [Cecile's son, currently in England].

I take the liberty of enclosing two of the official "inter-zone" correspondence cards. I remain always at your disposal and will do my best to forward the correspondence between you and your father, and to be of service. I ask without reservation that you tell me what you might possibly want, and I will do whatever possible to reply and give you satisfaction.

My wife and I send you our best wishes.
I remain your faithful
F Reyfer

This meticulous letter is full of useful information. One important fact is omitted, however, which would have explained why Ernst and Cecile had moved to Tours: On July 15, Ella had been interned in a camp at Monts, not far from Tours, and so Ernst and Cecile had left their "home" in Arcachon to be nearer to the camp. Why was she interned? Who can say? She was not Jewish, but she was married to a Jew, and in any case, foreigners were being arbitrarily interned all over France, as Ernst had noted in one of his pre-occupation letters. In his memoir of the time, Arthur Koestler, who was himself interned, remarks bitterly that "if there were any spontaneous popular feeling left in the apathetic masses of France, it was the feeling of hatred for foreigners."

Nine weeks later, after acquiring an "Aryan" certificate, Ella was released. The Aryan certificate was a new document, invented by the collaborationist French government. Its real name was *certificat de non-appartenance à la race juive*, a certificate of nonmembership in the Jewish race. A card from Ernst to Gretl on September 12, 1941, his most unhappy yet, shows that he expects Ella back the following week. All of his correspondence from now on is in French and written in a tightly controlled, cryptic manner on these official postcards.

My dear Gretl,
What a pleasure to see your writing again after long months, and to learn that Paul is already hard at work at his new job with good hopes for the future.

In my current life, the good news about your children was likewise like a ray of sunlight, of which I have more need than ever. It has been several weeks since Ella was obliged to show herself at Monts—15 kilometers from here, separated from me, but happily she will return next week. We have left Arcachon for good, but we do not know yet whether we will stay here. Why do I have no news from Evi? Write to me as often as possible. All my love to you all Ernst.

The Reyfers quickly begin to have a positive effect on Ernst's life. He writes them from Tours, grateful for a package they have sent, but insisting that they must not think of him as a charity case.

> Sept. 17, 1941
>
> Dear Madame and Monsieur,
> We have just received a large package containing delicious things that give us very keen pleasure, and we thank you sincerely. But the more we appreciate these precious and almost unavailable things, the less we can accept them as a gift. Please let me know the price of this shipment and allow me to reimburse you. This way I will also dare to accept a new packet after an appropriate interval. You have shown us so much friendship during these last days that I cannot describe my gratitude.

Frederic Reyfer, the man we meet through the ensuing correspondence, is painstaking, humane, courteous and eminently practical. He sets high standards for himself as my grandfather's protector, and he expects the rest of the family to perform with comparable energy and efficiency. He does not hesitate to encourage, correct and, occasionally, scold. It is as if a guardian angel in the person of an extremely orderly, upright, bourgeois Frenchman had suddenly emerged from the miasma of war. We have no photographs of Reyfer, but I imagine him as a small man with a neatly trimmed moustache and the points of a well-ironed white linen pocket handkerchief in the breast pocket of a well-tailored but slightly shabby dark suit. He was endlessly resourceful, but alas, like all guardian angels, he lacked omnipotence. He was able to protect my grandfather up to a point, but he could not persuade him to make the risky move toward possible freedom. He could not, in the end, rescue him from the collapse of civilization.

This new triangular correspondence mainly takes the form of Reyfer's own typed letters, along with Reyfer's typed copies of Ernst's writing to his children. At the same time, Reyfer also sends the original cards written by Ernst, as well as tiny photocopies of them under separate cover. Reyfer's thoroughness is almost beyond belief: He sends every piece of correspondence in duplicate carbon copies to my mother and her sister Gretl, and avails himself of both air and regular mail for each piece. He is taking no chances.

As the months go by, Reyfer begins to establish an independent relationship with my mother and her sister, to get to know all of us through our photos, through our illnesses, through our larger and smaller successes and disappointments. He becomes a treasured friend.

The next card from Ernst is dated September 20, 1941.

> Dear Mr. Reyfer,
> Finally yesterday morning, our separation from Mme. F. came to an end, and you can imagine that we are happy to be reunited. Tuesday morning [September 23], we will all leave for Angers where we will find an apartment that good friends have rented in advance for us, hoping that we can stay there as long as possible. Please note our new address: ANGERS, 13 rue Louis Leroy. Please inform our children of the new address.

The next letter contains a small mystery: Although the return address is Geneva, the wording suggests that the Reyfers have been "here in Paris." So I wonder: Were they able to slip themselves back and forth across the border as easily as they did the mail? Postwar accounts of French Resistance activities suggest that this was probably the case. The Annemasse-Geneva region was evidently a location for lively crossings of all kinds, with border guards conveniently looking the other way. Reyfer writes to Ernst:

> I immediately sent your latest cards along to Madame Gretl. We were likewise very happy to be able to send you the few useful articles in these times of restrictions. A good number of them still are to be found here in Paris. Do not worry about the financial accounts; I will not fail to settle them with you when we have the happiness of meeting again! You may be sure that we will do our very best to send you similar useful things from time to time. We hope, according to your last cards, that Mme. F. is now near you. Give her my respectful greeting.

Copies of the next communication from Reyfer are sent to all members of the Fürth family, including Cecile's children, Paul and Mädy. Reyfer takes a severe tone toward their silence, and their neglect of their mother. He asks them what they are going to do about sending her money. This question, which Ernst had indignantly been asking from the beginning of their odyssey, was never to be answered satisfactorily. Indeed, after Cecile's death in late August 1942, Ernst refers—in a rare flash of anger—to her daughter Mädy's "shameful avarice." But for now, Reyfer has arranged for a payment to Cecile of 20,000 francs, about $500, more than enough for her to live on for several months.

The family trio now settles in Angers, thanks to the help of some old friends, also refugees. We have no details about Ella's internment or her release, and Ernst does not—probably cannot because of the censors—dwell on what must have been an ordeal for all of them. Rather, he takes his pleasure where he finds it.

> Oct. 3, 1941
> Angers
>
> My dear children,
> After a painful interregnum lasting more than two months, we have settled ourselves here, where we hope to live tranquilly all three. We inhabit a small maisonette with two bedrooms, small living room, small dining room, all very clean and well furnished, veranda and a kitchen garden, which will provide us with a certain quantity of vegetables, something not without importance these days. Here we have found the two sisters of Lisa Reitler with their aged mother, who have been living in Angers for 14 months, and a bank director with his wife whom I have known for a long time. They concern themselves very kindly with us, and a party of bridge is assured from now on. I hope that you all are well and that I will soon receive your news. I embrace you all Ernst

On the same sheet is a note from Reyfer to my mother, with information about Grandfather. He encloses two blank cards for my parents to use. In what looks like a glance at the watchful censors, Reyfer tells the American families to write only to Switzerland, not to France, emphasizing considerations of convenience and speed, while carefully avoiding any mention of illegality or danger.

Ten days later, on October 25, 1941, Reyfer sends along some words from Ernst:

> Please tell Eva that we are very content in our new domicile, that here there are fewer shortages of essentials, heating, etc. than at Arcachon and that we have the well-founded hope of living here tranquilly, since Mme. Ella has received formal authorization from the military authorities to take up residence in Angers.

What is not even hinted at in these descriptions of life in Angers is the fact that Ernst was required to put in an appearance every week at police headquarters, as we learn from a postwar letter. This was part of the highly efficient registration and tracking of all foreigners, especially Jews, making their eventual roundup and deportation that much easier. At the police station, the postwar letter goes on to say, my grandfather "was received with deference, and in fact an officer of the French police had promised to inform him in advance if he knew of any special measure taken by the Germans concerning M. Fürth."

On October 25, 1941, Reyfer mentions for the first time his hope that Ernst might relocate to the unoccupied zone. For the moment, he says, it is impossible, although he suggests that if the Fürths were able to move closer, he might be able to "do much more" for them. I take this to be a hint that they might even have been able to smuggle them to safety in Switzerland. Indeed, this is proposed to Ernst at a later date, but he refuses to take the risk. Reyfer writes that they have been sending the Fürths various hard-to-get supplies, including Nestlé powdered milk, chocolate, boxed cheese and Nestrovit (a fortified concentrated vitamin food). Medications, he writes, are mainly available at the moment in France. But, he adds, ever resourceful: "The export of food from Switzerland is presently strictly forbidden. So I have turned toward Portugal. I have ordered a trial package for delivery to Annemasse. If this trial package arrives, I'll let you know."

Finally, the connections are completed, and my grandfather receives news directly from my parents, who have by now rented the modest brick house in Scarsdale that they would eventually buy, and where they would live for the next 43 years. My father is enrolled in an economics seminar on business cycles at Columbia, in preparation for his future occupation as an investment counselor with a Wall Street firm. My sister and I are going to the local public school, an easy walk from our house. It is early November. Grandfather's delight in resuming contact with his daughter seems to surpass all else.

> My dear Evi,
> What joy finally after 18 months [since July 1940] to receive your writing and to learn from your card that everything is well with you, that the dear children are developing as one might wish, and that they have not yet forgotten their grand-papa. And your health? Is it still satisfactory? What is the nature of George's

relation with the university? Does he have a paid position? Our life has been quite tormented. On July 15, Ella was forced to leave us, and had to spend nine long weeks before this torture came to an end. This experience has not been without effect on our state of health. I have lost weight to 59 kg. (130 lbs.) and Ella had to have a hernia operation a week ago. Happily she is recovering very quickly, and will be able to leave the clinic in a few days. You see that our current life is so full of cares that one can only make plans for a better future. Let us hope that we will see it. I embrace you all a thousand times and with all my heart. Father

On November 7, 1941, Reyfer again refers to the goal of bringing Ernst out of the occupied zone, this time rather pointedly mentioning—in a parenthesis—how easily transportation can be arranged from Annemasse to Geneva. He also mentions for the first time the friend who will visit the Fürths in Angers, and who will become the second bright angel in this dark story. His full name, which Reyfer is careful not to commit to paper until after the war, is Pierre Lelièvre. Every sentence in this next letter seems freighted with extra meaning.

I think the best thing we can do is to try to bring your father and the two ladies into the free zone, and also, necessarily for the moment, without attracting attention. I have occasion fairly often to make trips into the free zone of France. From what one hears, the conditions of life, from a purely material point of view (food, heat, etc.) are generally better in the occupied zone; but from the point of view of "general ambiance," life in the free zone would be, understandably, preferable. If we could settle your relatives, for example, in Annemasse (where one can get by tram from Geneva), we could certainly do plenty of things to make their stay more agreeable.

At the end of November or in December, I will perhaps have detailed news of your father from a friend who will no doubt have a chance to go to Angers. This friend should return to see us in four to six weeks. I am beginning to get information on the subject of the possibilities of change of residence for foreigners, but I am proceeding very prudently. You mention a visa for Cuba: A foreign voyage cannot be contemplated before your relatives are in the free zone.

On November 25, 1941, Reyfer sends word from Ernst to my mother, reporting that he has gained over three kilos since Ella's return, and inquiring avidly after news of his daughters and their families. In an indication that he is still concerned with keeping the family unit intact, he hopes that, in spite of their geographical separation, his daughters will continue their "intimate and cordial relations."

Reyfer promises my parents that he will take care of all of Ernst and Ella's needs through the agency of his "Parisian representative."

Dec. 27, 1941

The same middleman in Paris in September 1941 — when the monthly payment was delayed — twice took care of the transfer. In any case you should not worry. Your father will not be in difficulty because of money, even if a transfer from you is delayed or becomes impossible.

I can also put your concerns about provisions to rest, since in the last weeks I have been able to get your father and your relatives quite a lot of very good and essential food. The export restrictions are becoming sharper and stricter every day, but I hope to find ways around them. The only thing that I can unfortunately not send is heating materials!! But until now, we have not had too severe a winter. I received the photos that you sent me. Your wish that they should reach grandfather by Christmas is unfortunately entirely impossible. But I am expecting a friend from Paris around January 10–15, who will take the photos to Paris and will send them from there to your father.

Mme. Cecile F. constantly writes that she is longing for news from her children. Would you have the kindness to write your cousins that they should make the old lady happy and write as often as possible.

My wife and I thank you for your kind Christmas wishes and also we wish you and your family a happy and lucky New Year.

A card from Ernst on December 28 shows that he has been apprised that the Perl family has settled in the suburb of Scarsdale, which he refers to approvingly as "the country." It shows, too, that the flow of mail orchestrated by Frederic Reyfer continues to move well. The next letter in chronological sequence is a draft copy of a letter my father wrote to Reyfer. It introduces a problem that will become serious over the next months: how to get money to my grandfather. We do not know exactly

Madame Marguerite STRASSER ,　　　　　　　Réf. No. 2639 / le 10 Juin 42.
79,Abbottsford Road , WINNETKA (Ill.)　　=============== : ============
- - - - - - - - - - - - - - - -　　　　　　　　　　::: Gve:29,Q.Mt-Blc
Madame Evy PERL , SCARSDALE(New-York)　　- - - - - - - - - - - -
　　10, Hadden Road ,　　　　　　　　　　　　Chère Madame Marguerite ,
======= = = ＊ = = ＝ = ============:　　　　Chère Madame Evy ,
J'ai reçu il y a 2 jours : la carte postale - écrite à la main par MmeEvy -
datée du 9 Mai et la lettre de MmeMarguerite du 19 Mai .- Toutes ces communications ont été transmises à Monsieur v/père.-(Attention : Utilisez
s.v.p. seulement les cartes postales nouveau modèle avec timbre rouge à 1.20
Les anciennes cartes brunes avec timbre 0.80 ne sont plus valables !!!! -
= : = Par ailleurs j'ai reçu ces jours derniers différentes cartes de M.votre
père, que vous trouverez reproduites sur la *PHOTO-COPIE*que j'adresse à
Madame Evy:(Prière de la transmettre à Mme.Marguerite après lecture): i.e.:
pour Madame Marguerite:　　　　　　à:pour Madame Evy :
R-2594　du　26 Mai　　　　　　　　::R-2619　du　4 Juin (2 cartes)
R-2605　du　29 Mai　　　　　　　　::　　et également
　　　　　et également　　　　　　　::R-2522　du 3 Mai et R-2523 du 5 Mai
R-2515　du 2 Mai (copie déjà envoyé /:::(copie envoyé par R-2524 le 16 Mai):
　/ par R-2524 le 16 Mai):　　　　::R-2585　du 21 Mai　(copie déjà en-
　　　　　　　　　　　　　　　　　　　::　　/voyé par R-2586 le 30 Mai).
　　= : = : = : =　　　　　　　======　　　= : = : = : =
Les cartes originales suivront la semaine prochaine .-
　　　　　　　　　= : = : = : = : =
Nous étions très contents et heureux pour vous d'apprendre par la carte de
Mme. Evy(du 9 Mai) que la petite Marietta a pu quitter le lit et se trouve
en bonne convalescence.- - - - -
Nous avons eu la visite de notre ami qui est allé rendre visite à M.v/père
il y a une quinzaine de jours.- Il nous a dit qu'ila trouvé M.votre père
ayant très bonne mine et très courageux (malgré les ennuis qu'ils ont main-
/tenant, à cause de l'Insigne que l'on impose !).-Madame Ella est toujours
de bonne humeur et un grand soutien pour M.v/père.-Ils vont démenager au
1er Juillet, car leur propriétaire désire occuper la villa.Mais - il parait-
que le nouvel appartement dans une petite villa qu'ils ont loué est encore
plus confortable que l'actuel et plus dans le centre de la ville.(leur
/adresse sera : 109, Rue Bressigny).-
　　　　= : = : = : = : = : =
Nous serons toujours contents d'avoir de vos bonnes nouvelles.- C'est un
grand plaisir pour nous et une très grande joie pour M.votre père.-
　　　　　　　　　= : = : = : =
Ma femme et moi-même , nous vous envoyons à vous et à vos maris toutes
　　　　　nos meilleures amitiés.-　　　　Votre très dévoué :

GENÈVE (Suisse)
29, Quai du Mont-Blanc
Téléphone: 2.23.23　　　　　　　　　　　　　Fred. Reyfer :

The letter of June 10, 1942 (above), from Frederic Reyfer to my mother and aunt, never reached them until 1946, as the envelope (opposite) shows. It is one of the only places that Reyfer mentions the "insigne," the yellow star that Jews were made to wear.

how much money Ernst was able to take with him when he left Vienna in 1938, but we know that it had to be a small fraction of his total wealth. He had named my father co-owner of his Swiss bank account, referred to occasionally as "Glarona," and had made use of that money until he could no longer get access to it, after France was occupied. Since that time, my parents had been making the transfer from the Swiss account via the States, using the services of their Chicago bank.

But now, at the end of 1941, these monthly transfers have been declared illegal by the U.S. Treasury Department. Following the Japanese attack on Pearl Harbor in December, the U.S. declared war on both Japan and Germany. Because Hungary was allied with Germany, my family were now designated as "enemy aliens." My father does not come out and say that he hopes Reyfer will be able to help out financially, but there is an implied request in his last sentence, asking him to continue his "understanding attitude toward the Fürth family."

Jan. 1, 1942

Dear M. Reyfer,
I received your letter of Nov. 25. We are happy to know that our father is in good health.

Our holidays were peaceful and we spent all our free time with our little girls who had 10 days of vacation. Next week my wife will resume her work at the Red Cross.

We have just been informed by the bank that the monthly transfer for my father-in-law, legal up until now, has been suspended. The monthly payment for December could not be transmitted. It is to be feared that this situation will cause financial difficulties for our father.

Wishing Mme. Reyfer and you a Happy New Year, I ask you to continue your understanding attitude toward the Fürth family.
Your devoted, George Perl

Meanwhile, the Fürth family in France has undergone a loss. Cecile has died after a severe heart attack. Ernst's sorrow, which can be described as distinctly finite, quickly yields to practical considerations. Cecile was never anyone's favorite companion, but they had, after all, gotten used to having her around. Noticeably greater energy in a card to Gretl and in a subsequent one to Mother is devoted to responding to the family photos. In the absence of other contact, these pictures play a major role in keeping Grandfather up to date about his children and grandchildren. He reads them carefully, joyfully, with an undimmed sense of the importance of physical appearance—especially for females. And the transfers from the Swiss account via Chicago—those made prior to the declaration of war—we hear with relief, are still making it through.

Jan. 19, 1942

My dear Gretl,
A whole series of pretty photos, from which only yours is missing, arrived yesterday and gave me enormous pleasure. I see from them how Erna has changed greatly to her advantage. With her frank and free appearance, she has bloomed into a

truly pretty girl. Doris by turns smiling and serious is adorable, and Marietta entirely mischievous; at the same time I haven't forgotten to contemplate the vigorous Fredi. May they continue to give pleasure to their parents!

Poor Cecile has left a great gap in our little house. You know that she was never very amusing and even less gay, but all the same we miss her a great deal, and perhaps Mimi Stern will come to live with us. She is agreeable company and could help Ella do the cooking.

A note from Reyfer confirms that the Fürths are "relatively well," based on the visit of his Parisian friend. Life, as Ernst puts it in his next card, "runs along monotonously enough." But by now they have lowered their expectations so that even monotony seems preferable to the alternative. He has no special news, except to continue praising the Reyfers, who have made even this minimal existence bearable. The austerity of Ernst's writing during this period is in notable contrast to the expressiveness of his earlier letters. Of course, he is under severe formal restrictions: On these officially provided postcards, which will certainly be read by the censors, he no longer mentions international events, nor does he ever refer to what he is reading or hearing on the radio, nor what is going on around them. He confines himself to reporting on domestic matters, on his and Ella's health, on the weather; and he responds vigorously to news from his children. His chief pleasures come from the knowledge that his American family is well, happy, comfortable and safe. In what seems to me a remarkable display of decorum, he rarely permits himself the dreary tones of self-pity. Quite the contrary, his writing sometimes even shows some of the vibrancy that characterized his earlier correspondence.

Feb. 7, 1942

My dear Evi,
Since the card of Nov. 28, I have been deprived of your news, which I miss a great deal, but that does not prevent my thoughts from being with you always. As the mail works so irregularly, I am already hurrying to write you today for your birthday [March 29], even though it is quite far away, my deepest and warmest wishes, also from Ella. Our life runs along monotonously enough, but we are happy to be in good health, to live tranquilly and relatively well provided, thanks

to the help of our friends from Annemasse who heap us up with concern and un-precedented friendship. It was also they who did more for poor Cecile than her own children, and in a truly touching manner. We must remember them forever! I embrace you my dear Evi with my whole heart, give some good kisses to the little ones and my best regards to Gyuri. Your faithful Ernst

The winter has been quite hard and alas! it still continues.

Ernst's last sentence lamenting the hardness of the winter seems ambiguous: Does it refer to the weather or to the political situation?

The next card reports the death in Budapest of his first wife's mother, Grand-mother Roheim, the lady famous in the family for her fine voice and her insatiable appetite.

March 2, 1942

My dear Evi! It is today, after long weeks of a hard frost, passed in an apartment barely half heated, the first day that one feels a bit relieved and can believe that spring is approaching at last. Also your monthly payment has just arrived. From Budapest, Alfred Roheim [his first wife's brother] informed me that poor grand-mother died Jan. 18. As she had been in a deplorable state for a long time, her death is a deliverance for herself and her entourage. Ella and I are well, the cold, happily, has not altered our state of health.

Then comes a draft of a letter in French from my father. Although there is no date, it must be about now, sometime during the spring of 1942. The letter addresses the increasingly urgent problem of how to get money to Ernst, and its crossed-out phrases show how my father struggled with asking Reyfer for outright financial assistance.

Dear M. Reyfer,
You probably remember that we transmitted to my father-in-law a monthly amount of $100, representing about 4,000 francs. This transaction was made possible by the First National Bank of Chicago, using the permission of the

Federal Reserve Bank. The permit expired in the month of February of this year, and renewal was no longer possible. Under the prevailing circumstances, there is no choice but to ask you to replace this sum. [Sentence crossed out here: *We are convinced that it is vitally necessary that our father be provided with this sum.*] Perhaps you could make him believe that the monthly deposits come from us. [Words crossed out: *Whether we would be able to repay you only when …*] It is understood that this matter will be put in order as soon as the monetary restrictions are abolished.

Your extraordinary kindness has encouraged us to make these proposals.

A letter from Reyfer dated March 21, 1942, shows that he and his wife are beginning to see themselves as family friends, enjoying photos of growing children and anticipating Ernst's pleasure in receiving them. The tone of Reyfer's letters is now sometimes more personal, less purely businesslike. In this letter he introduces in greater detail the person of his Parisian friend, who has already visited Ernst.

Your father will surely be very happy with this avalanche of missives. We also feel with you the pleasure that you have of seeing your children develop in good health and make progress in their studies. We are very happy to see that your situations in your new country begin to consolidate themselves.

The little photos that Mme. Evi and Dr. Perl had the charming thought to send us for Christmas have given us great pleasure, and my wife has put them, framed, into her dressing room. I will immediately let your father know that a monthly payment was approved at the end of January.

I have asked one of my faithful friends in Paris to keep in touch with your father. He is a tradesman in Paris, an old fighter in the other war, a great Catholic with a heart of gold who is very devoted to me. I went with him to see your father at the end of January, and the two were delighted to meet each other. Your father now has someone nearby in whom he can confide, and who has already rendered him confidential services.

In the next couple of communications from Ernst, I hear the return of a stronger, fuller voice. This may have to do with his pleasure at the "avalanche" of news that Reyfer has been forwarding to him. It may also have to do with the presence of a new and trusted friend, with the advent of spring and the loosening grip of a very hard winter. It may even — dare I suggest it? — have to do with the departure of his sister-in-law Cecile. Despite his declaration that she had left a "great gap in our little house," his most convincing emotion in connection with her death is his fury at the neglectful behavior of her children. By contrast, he praises the Reyfers' generosity and offers some wisdom on the subject of age.

March 27, 1942

My dear Gretl,
Deprived of your news for more than five long weeks, my joy in receiving your "chat" of Dec. 14 is that much stronger, since all you tell me is completely satisfying, and the fact that it arrived a month after your card of Jan. 1 does not diminish my pleasure. First I am very happy to learn that your headaches [Gretl suffered from these all her life], for whatever reason, only torment you rarely and are bearable. But especially, I advise you, do not regret your "lost youth." For I have had the experience — and you will have it too, I hope — that ripe age is often richer in a lasting happiness that youth is unable to understand.

Erna independent and resourceful! What a change of character has been produced by the new conditions of your life. It's almost unimaginable, but I congratulate her for it. With the same pleasure I learn that Fredi also gives you every satisfaction; he has enough time to choose a career.

Up until now the monthly payments have arrived quite regularly, the last at the beginning of March; let's hope that it will continue. My state of health is satisfactory; also Ella is well, indefatigable. She works from morning to evening to keep the household running just right and so that I will lack for nothing. Only she is very disturbed to be without news of her two sons for long months.

March 29, 1942

My dear Gretl,
I must tell you a few words about our friends M. and Mme. R. in Annemasse. From the moment they were able to get in touch with us about seven or eight months ago right up until the present, they have not ceased to overwhelm us with their kindness and generosity. Without being asked they very often send us

packages of all sorts of precious things, for which they refuse even our thanks. Poor Cecile profited right up until her death from their good services, since the payments from Mädy became so rare (they were always insufficient), that without our friends' help, she would have remained without a penny. They would have done even more for Cecile if Mädy, in her shameful avarice, had not prevented them. I do not have room on this card to enumerate the heaps of other good services that we owe these unexpected friends, and I ask you, my children, *never* to forget how much gratitude you owe—you too—to these friends who have shown us a nobility as rare as it is perfect. Today, another birthday [my mother's 35th] that I am spending far from you. Will I ever have the happiness of celebrating one with you?

The next letter, of which we have a pencil draft, is a chatty and informative piece of correspondence from my mother. Her garden is blooming and my father and his half brother Imre Guttmann have purchased a farm in upstate New York, where the Guttmann family is living, and where the pig-breeding enterprise is once more under way. Life is moving forward, as members of the younger generation begin to settle in on this side of the Atlantic. My mother writes:

> Dear M. Reyfer,
> We spent Easter week with Doris and Marietta at the farm with the family of my brother-in-law, who sent cordial greetings to Ernst and Ella. Even though there was a lot of snow, it was a ravishing excursion for us all. It is a strange corner of this country, where one finds old families with noble traditions and many interests. For the children, the 100 newborn pigs were a continual source of pleasure.
>
> During the past weeks George has traveled a great deal with friends who are interested in another agricultural enterprise in the vicinity of the capital [Albany]. In a few weeks perhaps I will be able to give some details.
>
> At the moment the countryside is all in flower, and we all have the hobby of working in our little garden.
>
> On April 2, Doris celebrated her tenth birthday with eight little girls. Marietta has two friends, with whom she plays every day, and makes an enormous racket.
>
> I hope that Ella does not worry about [her sons] Eric and Herbert, who are both

truly in good health. As for me, I have passed my second exam with the Red Cross, work which interests me a great deal.

Please accept, dear Monsieur, our cordial greetings.
Yours Eva Perl

The letter's tone is chipper, positive, with no mention of the conflict between my father and his brother over the management of the farm (site of the 100 newborn pigs). And I know that although my mother passed her exams to do Red Cross volunteer work—rolling bandages—she was finally, humiliatingly, denied permission to do even this menial work because of her status as an "enemy alien." Yet these are small irritants compared with the mortal dangers facing my grandfather. The Nazi noose is tightening.

My garden in Amherst, Massachusetts.

13

The Noose Tightens

L AST FALL, as I worked in my garden in Amherst, Massachusetts, I thought about that letter from my mother to Frederic Reyfer in which she mentions her "hobby" of gardening. I was cutting down the faded stalks of my perennials—tiny brittle coreopsis, sturdy peonies, hollow-stemmed bee balm with its fragrant leaves. I had left standing the purple globe thistle, which was still blooming, and of course the dark red chrysanthemums, the only spot of real color in an otherwise browned and yellowed bed. I was wondering what kind of gardening my mother had been doing in the spring of 1942 when she wrote: "At the moment the countryside is all in flower, and we all have the hobby of working in our little garden." I have a few plants from her garden, mainly indestructible sedums and ferns. But, I wonder, were they already there in 1942, our first spring in that house where my parents were to live for 43 years?

Although my mother's letter is undated, I know that it must be shortly after April 2, 1942, because it mentions my sister's 10th birthday. By late October, by the time my mother's garden had faded the way mine just had, her father had been interned in the Nazi "transit" camp at Drancy, a way station for Auschwitz. I want to be able to picture what kind of gardening my mother was doing, and I want to know what she was wearing, what she looked like and what she was thinking about, what she was feeling. My mother was 35 that spring; my sister was 10; I was 5½; my father, 47. My grandfather had passed his 77th birthday on April 8. He and Ella had left Vienna four years earlier. For him, there were to be no further birthdays.

Time is such a strange enterprise, always out of joint, with its reels, like some avant-garde movie, running both backward and forward at once. At 73, I am now closer to my grandfather's age in 1942 than to my mother's at that time. Yet I was closer to the events in her life than to my grandfather's. I might have been playing with a friend in the yard of our red-brick house while Mother worked in the garden. Oddly, I can't remember her working in the garden. Maybe she always did it when we were somewhere else, me in kindergarten, my sister in fourth grade. Maybe she liked the privacy, preferring to work alone with her thoughts, so that if she wanted to cry while she was digging in the dirt, she wouldn't have to explain it to anyone.

Spring and summer of 1942 were frightening times in France. In Occupied France, the anti-Semitic measures instituted in October of 1940 were ratcheted up, and the pace of internments and deportations increased. In May 1942, Reyfer refers to the fact that Jews must now wear the yellow star. What he does not mention is that Jews were now also prohibited from using most public places, including restaurants, parks, cinemas, museums and libraries. Shopping hours for Jews were restricted to after-noons, by when most scarce items were already bought out. Ella's Aryan certificate most likely eased the conditions of their daily lives somewhat, since as a non-Jew, she would have been allowed ordinary freedoms denied to Ernst. He never mentions any of this in his cards, but I imagine him sitting indoors or taking the pale springtime sun in their narrow walled garden, barely able to leave a house that was just a few blocks away from the police station.

By the spring of 1942, the time of my mother's last letter, America had already been in the war for five months. Most newspapers of the time focus on American losses in the Pacific. On April 9, in the Philippines, Bataan fell to the Japanese, and the conquerors forced their prisoners onto a grisly death march. In May, the Germans attacked the Russians in the Crimea; but by the end of the month, the news was improving for the Allies: The British had launched crushing air strikes against the German city of Cologne. And in October, the Russians began turning the Germans back at Stalingrad.

Meanwhile in France, the horrors mounted. On July 16 and 17 in the Vélodrome d'Hiver, a sports arena in Paris, some 13,000 Jews were rounded up and sent to camps in France. Then, as the result of extremely efficient work on the part of the

French police during the summer and autumn, some 42,500 Jews were deported from France to die in the Nazi death camps in Poland.

During these months, although he is never able to mention what is going on around them, my grandfather's communiqués begin to show the strain of living under such pressure, with the words "monotonous existence" taking on special weight. And although he continues to respond in a remarkably focused way to the family's news from overseas, he also refers to himself as a grizzled elder, a "*greiser vater*," a man with no future. Despite Reyfer's attempts to shield him, he worries, quite rightly, about money. And still, and yet, he expresses his fierce longing and love for his children and grandchildren.

April 11, 1942

My dear Evi,
What a nice surprise to have received the very day of my birthday your card of March 4 with your good news. I thank you for your congratulations and for the prayers that the little ones address to the good Lord in my behalf. If only a small part of your good wishes could come true, I could picture the future with a light heart. But for the moment let us be content with a bearable present. Although I am surrounded by the tireless care of my good Ella, I do not want to lose the wish for happier days. But while we wait, the expression *greiser vater* that I so often joked about has become a sad reality. Yesterday Ella finally received good news from her two boys, and so she is happy.

Reyfer continues in his role as the perfect intermediary, transmitting and commenting on the news, even taking the liberty to tease my Aunt Gretl a little about her devotion to cigarettes.

April 24, 1942

Dear Mme. Gretl, dear Mme. Evi,
We regret to learn from the letter of Mme. Gretl that she had to undergo a little operation on her tonsils; but we are happy to be able to send to your father at the same time the news that at the moment of writing her letter of March 28, she already felt entirely recovered (since she had already started smoking again!!). I will send your father all the news that you give me in your letters. It is particularly

pleasant to be able to send him a handwritten card, since such news inevitably gives him even more pleasure.

His unnamed Parisian friend, he reports, has visited the Fürth household in Angers, and finds that they appeared well, have enough provisions, and are comfortably set up in a little house outside the city. Reyfer has sent along an enlargement of the photo of the Perl children, which Mother had sent with her Christmas greetings. Reyfer says he has not yet told Ernst about the problems with the monthly payments, although he has already told him that he could count on Reyfer for any monetary needs. But, as you know, he says, "your father is, above all, very reserved about accepting money."

A few weeks later, Ernst writes, admonishing his daughter to rejoice in her freedom despite whatever restrictions she may be experiencing in the U.S.A.—which country, of course, he never mentions by name.

> May 3, 1942
>
> My dear Evi,
> . . . I understand very well that for you too life has had to conform to new conditions, but be content that the restrictions do not become any sharper. I'm glad to hear that George's farm prospers and am convinced that pigs will be a good business these days.

In looking for clues, trying to read between the lines, I wonder if there is some black humor in his comment about pigs. A card from Ella soon afterwards expresses her happiness at hearing from her sons (indirectly through Mother), but with the always dissatisfied backbeat that they do not contact her directly. A detail in this card strikes me as significant and a little sinister, only because I know the history of Ella's financial demands on my family after the war. Perhaps I am working too hard to find clues: Ella, who has never before referred to herself by any other name, now signs her name "Elsa." Still later, she begins to sign herself "Elza." She becomes not *Ella Fürth* but *Elza Fürth*, the name of my extravagant and self-destructive grandmother, my grandfather's first wife who had died 11 years earlier.

May 11, 1942

My dear Evi!
. . . Do not worry about your father, I am doing my best to see that he survives these bad times and to keep him for our reunion. All my tenderness and a thousand kisses to you all Elsa

On May 16, Reyfer writes that he expects a visit in June from his Parisian friend, who will be able to give him "fresh and direct news from your father." Meanwhile, the mail moves even more slowly. On May 21, Ernst gently laments this fact, while mentioning also his much more practical concern that the monthly payments appear to have stopped for good as of March—as indeed they have.

Reyfer's next letter was one of several that my father sent to the U.S. Treasury Department a few months later, in September, when the department was threatening him and my mother with unnamed action for forwarding funds and addressing correspondence "through an intermediary to an individual in enemy-occupied territory." My parents worried—among other things—that they might lose their green cards. Reyfer also mentions a source of further anxiety to my parents: I had contracted scarlet fever. But Reyfer is withholding this fact from my grandfather for the time being.

May 30, 1942

(R. 2586)
Dear Mme. Evi,
I await your news to know whether you have been able to achieve a better result for the "MONTHLY PAYMENTS." Up until now I have told your father on this subject only that you are having *difficulties*, but that you are taking steps in view of being able to *continue the payments*.

I hope to receive by the next mail your good news and the confirmation that your little girl is completely recovered from her scarlet fever. I have not said anything about it to your father so as not to upset him.

The next card from Ernst responds to my mother's description of my sister's 10th birthday.

June 4, 1942

If my dear Doris has had her 10th birthday without my good wishes arriving on time, tell her that nevertheless my thoughts full of tenderness were hers and that I pursue from a distance with much joy her physical and intellectual progress. Were the exams for the Red Cross those of a nurse? And can you perform your service on the spot? Ella's health and mine too are satisfactory and our daily life goes by regularly, but since the cares do not disappear from the horizon, that is all one can report from us. What you write me about George's enterprises interests me greatly and I hope you will keep me up to date. It is more than three months since the last monthly deposit came to me. Will we be able to count on it in the future?

A letter two weeks later from Reyfer contains the promised report from Reyfer's friend on how the Fürths are doing. The envelope in which this letter came to my parents is covered with postmarks and stamps and stickers. The first postmark is Annemasse, where Reyfer mailed the letter. The next, two weeks later, is from Lyon. There is a strip of white paper glued over the lefthand edge of the thin blue envelope where the censor opened and then resealed it. That paper strip is marked in English: OPENED BY EXAMINER 510. And there is a purple rubber stamp on the front of the envelope above the address of my parents in Scarsdale, which reads: HELD BY BRITISH CENSOR, RELEASED JANUARY 1946. It draws me up short, reminding me again that reassembling this puzzle with pieces from the past is quite a different experience from what it was like to try to make sense of it as it happened. My parents never got this news about my grandfather until a year after the war had ended in Europe, three years after his death.

June 10, 1942

Dear Madame Gretl, Dear Madame Evi,
We were very pleased and happy for you to learn from the card of Mme. Evi (of May 9) that little Marietta was able to leave her bed and is having a good convalescence.

We had a visit from our friend who visited your father two weeks ago. He tells us that he found your father looking well and very courageous (despite the troubles they have now because of the Insignia [yellow star] that is being imposed). Mme. Ella is always in good humor and a great support for your father. They will be moving out on July 1, since their landlord wants to occupy the villa. But it seems that the new apartment in a small villa that they have rented is even more comfortable than the present one, and more in the center of the city.

When Ernst finally hears of my illness, he is reminded that my mother also had scarlet fever at about the same age. For my mother, as she and I work together, that reminder brings back a sense of having been abandoned by her own mother, who had left for Munich after young Eva fell ill. Elza Fürth was not about to interrupt a vacation merely because of a sick child. As compensation, she had brought back a doll, a "Münchener kinderl." But the medical wisdom of the time required that anything potentially contaminated by this serious disease had to be destroyed — the new doll along with the little girl's other belongings.

UNITED STATES CENSORSHIP REGULATIONS DO NOT PERMIT CORRESPONDENCE WITH PERSONS IN ENEMY OR ENEMY-OCCUPIED COUNTRIES. THE USE OF THE ENCLOSED CARD FOR COMMUNICATING WITH OCCUPIED FRANCE IS, THEREFORE, NOT PERMITTED. PERSONAL MESSAGES OF NOT MORE THAN 25 WORDS MAY BE SENT THROUGH THE AMERICAN RED CROSS. INFORMATION MAY BE OBTAINED FROM THE NEAREST RED CROSS OFFICE.

FORM No. 245   3 M. 7-42.

The date of this warning is July 1942.

14

Time Runs Out

DURING MY CHILDHOOD, except for polio, scarlet fever was considered the worst of the childhood diseases. It was the worst, that is, compared with the more ordinary ones—mumps, measles, chicken pox—most of which my sister and I eventually had. Penicillin, the first drug effective against scarlet fever's streptococcal bacterium, had recently been invented, but did not become generally available until after the war. Some of my earliest coherent memories are connected with this illness.

I was five years old and attending kindergarten at the local public school. My teacher was a large, benign, sensible woman named Miss Hayes, generally covered in the silky, flowered dresses that most elementary school teachers wore in those days. In my memory, she was old and soft and shapeless, with white doughy arms. She was kind but firm. Most of the discipline was conducted by persuasion and precept: "Gently, gently," Miss Hayes was always saying, and "We don't hit." For those who stepped outside the bounds of acceptable behavior, there were special chairs, representing different degrees of reprimand. A child would have to sit, removed from the rest of the group, in the Little Chair for minor infractions, in the Big Chair for major ones. Memory may play me false here, but I do not remember ever sitting in either of these chairs. I was a lively child, but also an obedient one, eager to stay within the group and enjoying the warmth of adult approval.

I loved kindergarten, as I did most of my schooling. It was not until junior high school that I was ever sent to the principal's office for making trouble—in that case, talking back to a teacher. And even after that, even during my small-scale forays into social rebelliousness, I continued to enjoy the formal limits of the eight-period day, with its clear demarcations and explicit academic expectations. The kindergarten classroom was large and bright and sunny, with an entrance and a playground of its own, which meant that we kindergarteners didn't have to share a jungle gym with the enormous sixth graders. There were cork-covered floors where even falling towers of blocks didn't make much of a clatter. There was regularity and order, well-kept toys, colorful smocks to wear while we painted at easels, puzzles and games and trucks and books, interesting things to do and learn. There were plenty of other kids to play with, and grown-ups who behaved in predictable ways. We had graham crackers and milk in the middle of the morning and little multicolored rag rugs on which we took our naps.

In May, when I came down with scarlet fever, I had to miss four weeks of school. The whole thing was treated with enormous seriousness by my parents, acting, I presume, under instructions from our pediatrician, another figure of benevolent authority. Except for a favorite stuffed animal, a gray-flowered Eeyore, which I was allowed to keep, my toys and clothes—like my mother's 30 years earlier—were destroyed. I have an image of my belongings being thrown out the front second-floor window. My sister had to go to live with friends on the other side of town for the duration of my quarantine. And I was moved into my sister's room, presumably because it was larger, sunnier, and nearer to the bathroom than the small, shady room that looked out on woods in the back, my room until I left home to marry at 20.

Of the illness itself I remember little, except that my backside was terribly sore from four huge shots of gamma globulin. Since sitting in bed was the rule of the day for a sick child, that sensation is particularly vivid. Otherwise, I remember life much as it was during other childhood illnesses: sponge baths rather than tubs until the crisis was over; simple meals in bed on attractively prepared trays; plenty of fluids in the form of ginger ale and juices between meals; lots of sleeping and daydreaming and listening to the radio, interrupted occasionally by my mother worriedly taking my temperature or looking at my throat. At the convalescent end of things, I remember sitting in the sun in the front yard in a lawn chair, wrapped in a blanket like some older invalid in a deck chair on a therapeutic ocean cruise. Now that I was no longer contagious, my friends were allowed to come and visit me there, but I could not get up and run around with them.

The main dangers from the disease were its secondary aftereffects. One of these, a slight heart murmur, was detected in the office of the infamous Scarsdale cardiologist Herman Tarnower, inventor of the Scarsdale Diet and victim of a bullet at the hands of Jeanne Harris, his spurned lover. I remember Tarnower as terrifying, as was the experience of the cardiogram itself, which was conducted on a cold, slablike table with what seemed to a five-year-old as huge, menacing machinery. The experience infected my imagination as the prototype of the evil doctor conducting dreadful medical experiments on helpless innocent victims.

But that unpleasantness stands out in especially strong relief from what I mainly remember as a happy childhood. As I work my way through my grandfather's letters and try to imagine what my parents had to contend with at the time, my sense of a secure and benign childhood world seems all the more remarkable. The credit for this, I think, goes largely to my father, who, as much as he could, absorbed the responsibility for keeping things on an even keel. He was, as before, the stability my mother could count on. By contrast, she was much more fragile psychologically, much more volatile. Her level of distress at having to cope with the menial details of house and children was enormous. Meanwhile, in addition to my grandfather in France, my father was also keeping track of and trying to help a number of others in Europe: his sister Klári Svéd, who was still in Budapest; his other half brother, Robert "Berti" Guttmann, also in Budapest; as well as several other relatives and close friends who had not had the combination of foresight and luck to be able to leave in time. And all this was going on as my father was trying to establish himself in his new profession as an investment counselor, while keeping an eye on the new family farming enterprise in upstate New York. So a child's scarlet fever was taken seriously, but it was also just one more blip on an extremely complicated chart.

On June 14, 1942, my father wrote to Reyfer, in French, as usual. The official English translation of this letter, which appears below, was another of the documents submitted to the U.S. Treasury Department in September, when they were investigating my parents for sending money into enemy-occupied territory.

Dear Mr. Reyfer:
We have just received your letter No. R2585 dated May 30, 1942 with all enclosures. I would like to answer at once the question, which seems to us of utmost importance: the monthly payments. Unfortunately they have become impossible.

Despite our efforts this situation must be considered as final. In other words, our father, since March of this year, has not received the monthly payments of $100–$120, which had been paid to him in francs at the official rate.

Nothing remains but to ask you as a real friend of our family, to replace that amount, if it is not too difficult and there are no legal obstacles.

It will be necessary to make our father believe that your payments are a direct continuation of our former remittances. As you mentioned yourself in your letter of April 24, one has to respect our father's feelings.

For the time being we are not allowed to carry on any transaction whatsoever with any foreign country, but please be assured, that with God's help, the time will come when it will be possible to return what we owe you.
Sincerely yours,
George Perl

The next card from my grandfather to Reyfer again contains a puzzle. When Ernst refers to a hoped-for event, "our rendezvous," does he mean that he has agreed to leave the occupied zone and try to escape to Switzerland? If true, he must have soon afterwards changed his mind. Ernst writes:

June 17, 1942

Dear Friends,
It goes without saying that we share your hopes, only we must not put our patience to such a hard test and put off our rendezvous to days too far away, since an old man like me does not have much time to lose. For the moment we are occupied with preparations for our next house move. To be sure, we will give you below our new address once again, hoping to receive there your recent and good news.

In a postwar letter, June 25, 1945, Reyfer looks back to describe the situation that this previous card only hints at:

In the summer of 1942, I sent my friend, M. Pierre Lelièvre, with the mission of speaking with your father and Mme. Ella, to urge them to come from Angers into the "free zone," since from there I had the possibility of bringing them secretly into Switzerland. I even informed them that there would be no worries about financial matters, since I was taking care of all of it. Unhappily your father replied to me that they were very well at Angers and that he did not want to move. Materially they did not effectively lack for anything. They had everything they needed for daily life.

With everything else that is going on, Ernst's politeness in his next card seems almost beyond belief as he voices his regret at Mme. Reyfer's hay fever. It is hard to imagine that this is not a code for some other message, but anything, I suppose, is possible for a gentleman of the old school. In any case, in the next two cards, one to the Reyfers, one to Gretl, I feel some renewal of spirit, perhaps corresponding to a revival of hope. Ernst is once again responding vigorously to family news, expressing, as before, his high expectations for his grandchildren, especially for Fredi Strasser, the only male.

> June 23, 1942
>
> It is with much regret, dear Madame Angèle, that we have learned that you are suffering from hay fever, which we know, is an illness not only overwhelming and stubborn, but also hard to combat, but we hope that you will succeed in getting rid of it as soon as possible.

> June 25, 1942
>
> My dear Gretl,
> It is with great joy that I learn of the probable renewal of Erna's scholarship, and I congratulate her heartily. It is too bad that Fredi is not reaching the good results of which he is capable. One must encourage his ambition; with a boy, one can ask more effort than of a girl.

Ernst and Ella move to their new place and find even more evidence of their friends' attentions. Ernst writes to the Reyfers, amazed at the welcoming display — a package, flowers and letters both from the Reyfers and Pierre.

My sister, Doris, age 10, at camp in Michigan in the summer of 1942.

July 3, 1942

Dear friends,
Truly we do not know how to acknowledge all the kindness and generosity with which you overwhelm us on the occasion of our moving house. It seems as though you want to make us forget that we are separated from our dear ones and from so many friends and that you want to replace them all yourselves.

Writing to my mother on July 12, 1942, Ernst sings his wife's praises for her hard work during their latest move. He mentions that he has been in touch with an old friend of my parents in Hungary and with my father's sister, Klári, in Budapest. The letter from my father that follows is another of the ones submitted to the Treasury

Department in September to substantiate the assertion that their correspondence with Reyfer consisted mainly of family news. My father writes:

> July 12, 1942
>
> Dear Mr. Reyfer:
> It is six weeks since we have had news from you. Your last letter was dated May 30 and bears No. R2586. We are happy to inform you that there is no change in our situation. Doris visited her Aunt Gretl, making the long trip all by herself on the train. Now she is at the same girls' camp as last year, where she can swim and learn all the sports suitable to her age. We get charming letters from her almost every day. She is a smart little person.
>
> Eva, Marietta and I are leaving for the farm. The little one has completely recovered. The crops were good and our hog breeding is developing satisfactorily.
>
> I am busy with different plans to develop farm enterprises for friends on a larger scale.
>
> We hope father and Ella are all right and continue to be protected by your friendship.
> Devotedly yours,
> George Perl

On July 30, 1942, Ernst writes to Mother that he has not had news from her for over two months. He hopes that this is because the family is having a summer vacation. He and Ella are satisfied with their new apartment. Then he speaks briefly of money and other things that are missing from their lives. "As for the deposits, George's proceedings have not yet produced any visible results. Also Ella's desire to have news of her sons remains unfulfilled; it has been months since she has had any. Sometimes life is also sad."

Ten days later, Ella—now signing herself Elsa—thanks Angèle Reyfer for a gift, a "sweet souvenir from Chambéry." Then, a few days later, Ernst tells his daughter that she might not recognize the somber person he has become:

It is nice that you have kept such a faithful memory of my voice, but you would be rudely disappointed if you looked for the tone that you had known in the past, moments of gaiety having become quite rare in recent times.

In a card to his son-in-law, Paul Strasser, Ernst says he has received some family photos and gently teases him and Gretl about their outward signs of aging:

The six photos show to my lively satisfaction the same smile of well-being and contentment on all of your faces, which God keep you in! Neither your slightly more advanced baldness nor Gretl's slightly whiter head can diminish my pleasure in contemplating these photos.

The form in which I have this card is a tiny photocopy about 3 x 4 inches, one of eight reproduced on a normal letter-sized sheet. These early photocopies, which have the stiff feel and shiny surface of a photograph, were another means by which Reyfer sent cards to the U.S. I had to use a magnifying glass to make out the words.

A few days later, Reyfer writes at length to my mother and Gretl, concerned that their mail has taken almost two months to reach Switzerland. More importantly, he mentions again the enforcement of the yellow star, and, for the first time uses the word "deportation," a matter about which they have asked him. News of these dreadful events has evidently begun to reach the States. Reyfer writes to Eva and Gretl:

Aug. 17, 1942

You asked me what is the reaction of your father on the subject of the decree about the yellow insignia. I cannot answer that, because I have not had a verbal report since our friend Pierre visited him in May. In the cards I avoid talking about it. What you say about the "deportations" has also been one of our great sorrows in these last weeks. From what we have heard from different sides, the deportations, carried out by the occupation authorities since June 17, only affect men of up to 60 years and women up to 45 years. We also have a good friend in the same situation in Paris—where the measures are even more severe than in the provinces—who has not been bothered until now. In the cards that your father writes us, he says only that he is well, that they are peaceful, and that they hope it continues this way. In any case, we are continually in correspondence with him and we are doing our best to encourage him.

When he says that he and Pierre are doing their best to "encourage" Ernst, it is not clear to me whether this refers to some kind of general effort to keep up his morale, or whether they are still hoping to get him out of France. Reyfer speaks with rare passion and palpable frustration about the impossibility of sending money, and then about "political measures"—internment and deportation—"in the face of which we are absolutely powerless."

Aug. 19, 1942
[stamped on envelope: Held by British Censor, Released January 1946, so not received by my parents until after the war.]

My dear Doctor,
I have made inquiries here at the U.S. Consulate. They confirmed that *payments* from you to the *occupied zone* are not authorized (not even to the address of *American citizens* who may find themselves in the *occupied zone*). I made this inquiry to be able to demonstrate to your father-in-law that you have come up against a regulation that is absolutely definite. I have written to Mr. E. F. the 13th of August on this subject as follows:

"I would like therefore to ask you immediately to be willing to accept the services of Pierre. I will arrange with Mr. George afterwards. We rely on your friendship to tell Pierre what you wish."

As I have already written, we have already told Mr. E. F. on several occasions that we are entirely at his disposal for all that might be necessary for him. Up until now, he has always declined. The very last time, in a card of July 29, he wrote word-for-word as follows:

"I have just received a very friendly letter from our friend Pierre in which he offers me his good services, of which I have no need at the moment, since he cannot rid me of my other sorrows, alas! Let us hope that everything will calm down."

In any case, I can assure you that we will watch to see that your father-in-law has no material troubles! The great worry that we have, and that they have there too are the measures of a political nature, in the face of which we are *absolutely powerless*. Up until now—thank God—they are peaceful. We offer up our prayers that it will stay that way!

The next card from Ernst sounds some familiar themes, while alluding obliquely to the severe restrictions under which they live.

Aug. 24, 1942

My dear Gretl,
I learn with pleasure that you are well and that the children are enjoying their vacations, Erna on the family hearth and Fredi at camp. Their photos show me that Erna has become a very pretty girl and Fredi a giant with features that are still a little boyish. The summer at Angers was ideal in terms of the weather, we had very little rain and no excessive heat, but all the same we didn't take much advantage of it, since we go out very little. Ella is very busy with the household, and I have to be content with little walks of short range, 40 to 50 minutes a day is enough for me. And although we lead in general a very retiring and mostly solitary life, we don't lack upsets that remind us from time to time that we are still at war. Ella finally had good news of her sons a few days ago, which has calmed her for the moment. Cecile's gravestone will be laid at the end of the month and will be paid for by the remains of her fortune. Without being authorized by her children, I have taken responsibility for it myself.

In his next communication, Reyfer includes a copy of a card from my mother, which he has already sent on to Ernst. The Perls have had no news from France in two months. Mother's card reads as follows:

Aug. 26, 1942

My dear father,
We were happy to receive your cards of May 21 and June 4. But unhappily, since then many weeks have passed and I have not had your news; and what one learns from the newspapers is not reassuring, quite the contrary. I say prayers and form wishes that you will continue to be in good health and that your life will not be troubled.

So often it seems to me that life is unjust, giving us beautiful vacations, a little trip and everything that one needs for daily life, while denying the same things to those who are so close to our affections.

I wait with impatience for your next news.
We embrace you both:
Eva

Ernst and Ella await Pierre's arrival, and write to the Reyfers expressing their gratitude once again. But now the mail seems to have stopped again in both directions. Ernst complains of having had no news since June. There is considerable forcefulness in his next three cards, and even a note of the old indignation that his children are not living up to their obligations. Evidently Ernst has not yet had Reyfer's letter explaining about the end of financial transfers. In the card to Gretl, he expresses his pleasure combined with some high bourgeois qualms about the fact that his granddaughter is working as a babysitter.

Sept. 11, 1942

My dear Eve,
I wrote ten days ago, whereas your last news is only dated from the month of June, so one cannot pretend that I am spoiled in regard to your mail. To my regret I have just learned that our old Jane [Miss Jane Canitz, Eva's former governess] died from a brain tumor a few days ago, but without having suffered much. Up until the end she was invited every week for dinner by Ella's brother in the Gregor Mendelstrasse [Ernst's former villa in Vienna]. Also she had received a little pension from me. She was a faithful soul! It is a very long time since I had news from our brave Glarona. Has he preserved or again expanded his old vigor?

Sept. 11, 1942

My dear Eve,
Since your card of June 9, I have been deprived of the pleasure of your news, whereas during the same period four cards from Gretl have reached me and it is also from her that I learn that Doris has made a trip to camp all alone, which proves that she has become very resourceful. Is it your work with the Red Cross that prevents you from writing me more often? How are you and George? Is his business going well? And the harvest? And Marietta, I hope, perfectly recovered and cheerful as always? Aside from a few upsets, we have spent the summer tranquilly and we are in good health, but life is far from gay.

Sept. 15, 1942

My dear Gretl,

Your cards of July 26 gave me a great deal of pleasure and even more since I have been deprived of news from Eva for more than two months, which is incomprehensible to me. I hope there is no situation so serious in her family that it would prevent them from writing me more frequently. The fact that my dear Erna has accepted a place working with children in order to earn a little money for her pleasure, filled me if not with pleasure, then at least with satisfaction to see her firm will to familiarize herself with the new conditions of your life. I hope that this first meeting with practical life will not be too hard an experience. For a long time I have had the impression that Paul's position has not developed as he had hoped in the beginning.

Ella and I are in good health and we are well, but you are right: One needs to be armed with a good dose of stoicism to keep oneself up and not lose courage and morale. But up until now we haven't lost hope of seeing better times again, and we will try to keep that hope.

In a long letter on September 22, 1942, Reyfer reports on some firsthand news of Ernst and Ella transmitted by Pierre, who has been to visit them. An interesting detail here is Reyfer's mention of information in one of Gretl's cards, which he has decided to suppress. But mainly, the news is that Ernst and Ella continue to be safe, although conditions in general are much worse. Reyfer writes:

I suppressed only (for prudence, because the cards pass a censor at the line of demarcation of the occupied zone) the passage where you say that Mr. Paul has, for the third time, given blood for the wounded. Do not be surprised if the reply from your father doesn't speak of it.

Before coming to the free zone, Pierre went to see your father so that he could give me completely fresh news.

Since July 1, '42, they have been renting a little private apartment of two storeys (for 1,000 francs a month). This little apartment is very comfortably furnished: downstairs: salon-office, dining room and kitchen; on the second floor: two big rooms with bathrooms (about 7 meters by 5 meters with three windows); the other is occupied by their friend, Mme. Stern. Behind the house is a garden, half vegetable, half pleasure, with shade for resting. During his stay, my friend slept in a room also very spacious on the third floor. Every morning, Mr. Ernst takes a little promenade of half an hour. The two ladies divide the shopping for groceries. They have a maid, Alsatian, very, very devoted, and their life runs along without too much disturbance, embellished, adorned by the cheerful and energetic character of Madame Ella. They were, perforce, very troubled these past weeks by the different measures enacted against foreigners. But now everything seems to have subsided. They had envisaged coming closer to us here, but that presented too many risks, so that they finally decided to stay where they are. They have agreed to entrust to our friend a certain amount of their baggage (about 300 kilos), which he has stored in his office. They have also entrusted to him certain valuable objects, which they did not want to keep with them. In sum, they have passed several very painful and troubling weeks; but at present their life has once again become quite calm and tranquil and almost normal—if one can call it that!

Ernst wants my father to know that his current financial needs are being taken care of by Pierre, who had also proved himself the "guardian angel of poor Cecile." Obstacles to maintaining anything like regular contact have multiplied on all sides. Around this time, some of the correspondence contains a small slip of onionskin paper, an official form, about 3 x 5 inches, with a printed date of July 1942, and the following message in English:

> United States censorship regulations do not permit correspondence with persons in enemy or enemy-occupied countries. The use of the enclosed card for communicating with occupied France, is therefore, not permitted. Personal messages of not more than 25 words may be sent through the American Red Cross. Information may be obtained from the nearest Red Cross office.

On September 28, 1942, Reyfer writes, enclosing a card from Ernst, which had reached Geneva a few days before Pierre's visit. Reyfer says: "We have the impression that this card shows a certain calming of the spirit and satisfaction to know a devoted friend is in the vicinity." Then Ernst writes to the Reyfers on October 2, 1942. This communication contains a sentence that I still cannot work out. What is the "proposition" to which he refers, and who are the "interested parties"?

Dear friends,
It is with sincere satisfaction that we learn from the report of our friend [Pierre] that you are well and that you have approved his proposition and hope that all the interested parties are happy with it. At the same time there arrived from our friend a big package that was received with much joy and gratitude! I was happy finally to have a word from Eve, the reply to which I allowed myself to send to you yesterday, even though the card from Gretl you announced has not yet arrived.

What follows is Ernst's last card from Angers. I may be imagining things here, but the handwriting seems to me rather irregular and weak compared to its firm appearance, even in the recent past. I am not much of a believer in premonitions, but if I were, I would say that Ernst feels the cold wind of something coming.

Oct. 5, 1942

Dear M. Reyfer,
I hasten to acknowledge receipt of your cards containing news of Gretl, for which I thank you greatly; I will send you the response in the next days. In the meantime I would be very grateful to you if you would give her a little report about our daily life, better than I can do myself.

The weather has turned fine and mild and we hope that it will remain so for several weeks. I hope that you are both well, I ask you to offer my very warm respects to Mme. Angèle and to accept for yourself my good wishes.

Four days later the blow fell. Unprotected by age, by the promises of the local police official or by the human decency shown by the Reyfers and Pierre Lelièvre, unprotected by the great democratic powers, by civilized tradition or by anyone's God, Ernst was swept into the Nazis' cauldron of misery and death. On October 9, 1942, he was taken to the Nazi camp at Drancy.

This card from Ella, who now signs herself Elsa, dated Oct. 10, 1942, informs Reyfer of Ernst's arrest and removal to the concentration camp at Drancy—though without using those words. She asks if there is anything she can do, and notes that the last letters from his daughters had brought Ernst great joy.

15

Drancy and After

D RANCY IS A SUBURB OF PARIS, a stop on the Métro. On September 30, 1997, the eve of Rosh Hashanah, the Jewish New Year, French archbishop Olivier de Berranger stood on the grounds of the former camp and made public apology for the French Church's silence in the face of French collaboration with the Holocaust. "Conscience," said Archbishop Berranger, "is formed by memory, and no society can live in peace with itself on the basis of a false or repressed past, any more than an individual can."

The archbishop had chosen a place heavy with guilt and grief to make an act of contrition. It was from Drancy that 76,000 French and foreign Jews were deported to the death camps in the east. Conditions at Drancy were appalling. Food was barely above starvation levels; sanitary essentials were nonexistent and dysentery was rampant. A French intelligence report described the wretched state of internees there and concluded: "It is said that the notorious camp of Dachau is nothing in comparison with Drancy." On December 7, 1942, after three months of imprisonment, and through the efforts of Ella Fürth and Pierre Lelièvre—someone was surely bribed—my grandfather Ernst Fürth was freed. Already near death, he lived only a few more weeks, but at least he was not deported to Auschwitz. He was, at least, able to die in relative peace, surrounded once again by people who cared for him.

Some of the saddest yet most uplifting communications from my grandfather are the cards he was allowed to send to his wife from Drancy. I find in them an unfathomable courage and a deep human affirmation. Ernst was 77, separated from his homeland, from his children and grandchildren. He was an old man with only one kidney, which had already been causing him trouble. He had also begun to have the painful and debilitating symptoms of angina pectoris, and while in the camp he developed pleurisy. Yet in these cards, even under the most degrading circumstances, he does not disintegrate nor lose his essential dignity. He was not a religious man in any conventional sense of the word, but he had a surpassing spirit, a vital energy that pulses through these small pieces of paper. For reasons that I can't explain, the words that rise to my mind as I read them are from the Book of Job, and I hear them in Handel's setting for soprano in Messiah, an aria that I have sometimes tried to sing:

> I know that my Redeemer liveth, and that He shall stand at
>   the latter day upon the earth.
> And though worms destroy this body, yet in my flesh shall I
>   see God.

Ernst Fürth was a believer in the things of this world. It was on the earth and in his flesh — if anywhere — that he would find salvation. In his last written communications, he battles with despair, but he does not give up hope. He retains his characteristic turn of phrase, his consciousness of personal worth. He does not become a saint, able to give up his sense of rank and merge his sufferings with those around him. Rather he is appalled to find himself thrown together with with the coarsest of humans — an educated gentleman imprisoned with the uncouth. He asks his wife to send him nourishing foods, jam and butter and canned goods, and he asks, touchingly, for his slippers and for shoe polish. He hopes for truth in the rumors that he might be sent to the Rothschild Hospital, France's largest Jewish hospital. He worries, in the end, not so much about pain or death as about returning filthy and unrecognizable, an object of disgust to his beloved Ella. Because he was released from Drancy, not sent to Auschwitz as were 76,000 others from France, one could say he was spared the worst of the horrors. Still, all such judgments are comparative. The horrors of Auschwitz cause the mind to go blank. The horrors of Drancy merely cause indescribable pain. Here, without further comment, is my grandfather's entire correspondence from Drancy.

Oct. 20, 1942
[card, but no address nor postage, in French, in pencil from Ernst to Ella]

My dearest,

It is four days since we arrived here after a very tiring trip of 24 hours, and what awaited us here was not very reassuring. Seventy-six men, women and children in a room without any furniture, neither benches nor chairs nor tables, but only the straw mats on which we sleep. Your huts at Merignac and Monts [where Ella was interned in July 1941] were real deluxe hotels. As for provisions, the bread ration is enough for me, but everything else is not worth much, some cabbage, leeks, cooked carrots, hardly any potatoes. As an old man I had once a small bowl of good milk. At the medical visit I asked to be transferred to the infirmary, but the doctor did not find me sick enough. I probably won't have to wait very long before I'm in bad enough condition to be favored. Perhaps you will be able to send me packages of three kilos every 8 or 15 days: forbidden to send chocolate and tobacco. Try to send biscuits, cheese and butter and canned food, but nothing that needs to be cooked. ∧ [insert] and pencils and paper. You need to send as quickly as possible the registered copy or photograph of your Aryan certificate, addressed to the commandant of the Drancy camp. That way I will at least be sure that they will not deport me, and that I will be able to stay here. Now I can tell you that I am very unhappy, . . . [rest of sentence covered by a censor's red crayon]. Whether I have the strength to undergo all these privations in the long run, I do not know. Don't be too unhappy and try to remain safe and sound. I embrace you my love forever your Ernst

Oct. 23, 1942

[regular postcard with postage, in French, in pencil, police rubber stamp: Internment Camp of Drancy, Bureau of Censorship, Prefecture of Police; addressed to Ella in Angers; return address: M. Ernest Fürth, Camp de Drancy, Staircase 5, Room 19]

My dearest,

I have already asked you to send as quickly as possible to the address of the commandant of the Camp of D. a copy of your Aryan certificate, because with that I will not be deported. For the husbands of an Aryan there are exceptions . . . [four lines covered by purple crayon] They claim that with my 77 years I could be transferred into an old people's home where one is much better than here, but I can't do anything about it! What are you doing? I think of you day and night! Will we see each other again? And in what state will I return to you?

I embrace you, I love you with my whole heart Ernst

This card was sent by Ernst to Ella from Drancy. The censors were at work even here.

Oct. 31, 1942
[postcard with postage to Ella, in French, written in pencil, stamped: Internment Camp of Drancy, Bureau of Censorship, Prefecture of Police; return address has changed, different stair, room, Ernest Fürth, Staircase XXII, Room 18, Camp de Drancy]

My dearest,
I have received your Aryan certificate, but they asked again for our last marriage certificate dated from Paris and I ask you to send it to me as quickly as possible. With this document I will be entirely in order, and they say that I could not be deported, which already says something.

I embrace you Your Ernst
I miss my slippers very much. I wish you would send me them in the next package of clothing.

Oct. 31, 1942
[card, not postcard, no postage, in French, in pencil]

My dearest,
Everyone has received a food package, some even two, but until today I have not received anything! You must make a claim at the post office. My provisions that I brought from Angers are almost exhausted, there only remains a bit of chocolate and some sugar and the three cans of sardines. What they give us here is not much: 200 grams of a pretty bad bread, in the morning a bowl of a blackish liquid that has nothing in common with coffee, and noon and evening the soup, which you need to be very hungry to swallow, a mixture of all kinds of nameless vegetables. With your Aryan certificate and the marriage license which I asked you for, I will be nearly certain that they will not deport me, but there is only a rumor that the old people will be transferred to the Rothschild Hospital, and I have before me terrible weeks. Try to send me all and packages as often as possible. I have abandoned indefinitely the hope of being freed, and I do not know how long I will be able to stand this life with its lack of freedom, the entourage of 50 strangers where one feels so alone with one's sad thoughts without being able to do anything, stretched out for hours and hours on my straw mat.

One sees walking around in the big courtyard 4,000 or 5,000 men who endure the same fate, but that doesn't console me. Your news is the only ray of sun that gives me a little courage. Tell me what you are doing, if you are well! Remain safe and sound and do everything to comfort your life, which also is sad enough.
I embrace you a thousand times your unhappy Ernst

Drancy Nov. 14, 1942
[small card, no stamp, in ink]

My dearest,
The two first packages reached me the 4th and 12th of November, but the other three all at once today, so for the moment I am very well provisioned! Everything arrived in a perfect state except for the meat, which was spoiled. The packages are very necessary for me since I am always disgusted by the soup twice a day and I only eat a part, also the quality of the bread leaves a great deal to be desired. So to sustain me I need butter, jam and biscuits and canned food. My state of health is relatively good, but I tire very quickly, after 20 minutes of walking my back hurts and I have to come back in. As for my morale, I do my best to stay upright, but there are moments when I lose my composure. For example, last week two old people in my room, but less elderly than I, were transferred to the Rothschild Hospital because they were French, but I, as a foreigner had to stay. That was a blow. But then I doubt whether different measures would lead to a better outcome. The Rothschild Hospital would already be paradise! Here I need all my energy . . . [part of a line blacked out] the lack of the most primitive and almost indispensable commodities. But you spoke the truth: Always think about seeing my dear Ella again and that will make me bear the unbearable. Let's hope that my patience and my strength are not put to too long and hard proof. Next time you could send me a pound of pasta. I could have it cooked.

I received all your cards and the marriage license. Write me as often as possible. [underlined in red ink, then inserted below] /\ The internees have the right to receive mail every 15 days. /\ [insert] and a box of shoe polish.
I embrace you with a thousand kisses.
Your poor Ernst

Nov. 29, 1942
[small card, no stamps, in ink]

My dearest,

On the 19th of November my thoughts were busy with you and if my wishes for your birthday come late they are nevertheless warmer than ever. Unhappily I cannot give you any good news from me. Three days ago at 2 in the morning I was awakened by a violent cardiac crisis which left me gasping. They called a doctor who had me transported on a stretcher to the infirmary where I find myself at the limits of my strength. One is much better here than in the room, one has a real bed, there are only ten in the room, a nurse-doctor is always present, but the food is absolutely the same. I remain in bed almost all day, but even so the crisis repeated itself last night, but it was not so vehement.

I thank you for the packages which are arriving very regularly. I wish you would send me my slippers. You can wrap something with them. The butter which I received is sufficient, but since it is the most important nourishment, it is necessary to continue, also with the pasta. Try again to send some meat. Very well cooked, with plenty of fat and well wrapped, it should arrive in good condition in this cold weather. Some eggs, a little coffee and tea would also be accepted with pleasure. /\ [insert] and a good piece of sausage and some [bouillon] cubes. Send my greetings to everyone, Fred, Angèle, Steffi, Mimi Steiner [means Stern?] and above all to the children! Although I am sick I have not lost hope. It is my firm will to see you again that sustains me.

I embrace you with my whole heart
A thousand times Ernst

Drancy, Nov. 29, 1942
[small card, no stamps, written in pen]

My dearest, your card arrived very fast, although the impatiently awaited package has not yet arrived, but the service is very irregular. I hope that the next will come faster. A half-kilo of good bread, and some jam and butter would be very welcome. Yesterday I changed stairways. Until now I had been surrounded by 90 percent of Poles of the lowest class. How happy I was to leave them, and I am now among French people without women and children and there are so-to-speak beds, and

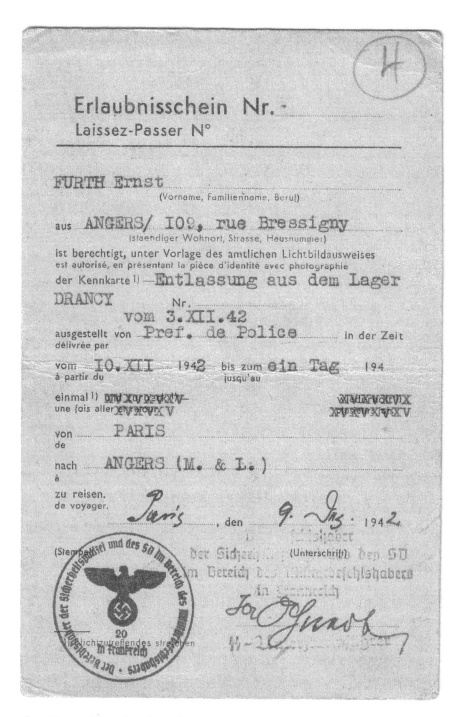

Certificate of Ernst's release from Drancy. He died within a few weeks.

instead of 92, we are only 50 in the room. To balance these advantages one is devoured by the bugs and the fleas, but my sleep happily resists. . . . [rest of page—three lines—erased] . . . people who don't interest you and whose fate is always the same with only a few differences. Is Mimi already with you? Or when is she coming? Have you informed Reyfer and his friend Pierre? Have you any news from Fred and from our children? I am so thirsty to hear something about you and our families. If this lasts much longer I will become a pig and you will reject me if I return one fine day! O, how I would like to begin a normal life with you again!

Without this hope this life would be intolerable to me.
I embrace you with my whole heart Ernst

Ernst was never to begin a normal life again, but on December 7, 1942—my sixth birthday—he was released from Drancy. We know little about how this was accomplished, except for a couple of sentences in a letter from Reyfer after the war: "Mme. Ella and M. Lelièvre did their utmost to bring your father out of the camp. After huge difficulties, Mme. Ella, with the complicity of a guard, succeeded in bringing him out. . . ." Two days later, on December 9, 1942, Pierre Lelièvre writes from Paris to Reyfer in cool, uninflected, coded language, concealing much, leaving out much, and mentioning a person named Soucin, with whom they are also evidently dealing. He speaks of plans to return Ernst to Angers, but this never happened. He was too frail to travel. He stayed with the Lelièvres for a few days, then was moved to the clinic where he died. Pierre writes to Reyfer, telling him of "Uncle Ernest's" release:

> Very good friends,
> I confirm my letter of day before yesterday. As promised, I am now communicating the good news that Uncle Ernest has been in the house since day before yesterday, Monday evening. He arrived quite tired, and the doctor whom we called yesterday morning declared that he needs a little rest before leaving again for Angers. Yesterday he had a good day, and for my part I ran all around to arrange the formalities of his return. If all goes well as I hope, we expect to depart tomorrow, Thursday afternoon. Of course I will accompany him to his house and return Friday morning to Paris.

I hope you are both in good health; as for us, it's not bad, we haven't yet had a troublesome frost, let's hope it lasts. No news from Soucin. I can't make any other observations concerning his silence, I think he is a little unreliable.

I look forward to your good news and while we wait, Marguerite and I send you our best friendship. Pierre

[Postscript in a shaky hand:]
After such hard weeks I am happy to find myself under this friendly roof surrounded by all the possible solicitude of Mme. Marguerite and M. Pierre. All my friendship to you. Ernst

Ernst Fürth died four weeks later, on January 4, 1943. His death certificate, issued the next day, gives the barest data, including the fact that during his life in exile, he had, to his sorrow, "no profession."

On the fourth of January, 1943, at 2:15, died in the rue du Texel 7, Ernest Jacob Fürth, residing at Angers (Maine and Loire), born in Sušice (Czechoslovakia) April 8, 1865, no profession, son of Fürth, no other information known from the informant, widower in his first marriage of Elsa Roheim. Spouse in second marriage of Elsa Edwige Melanie Polak. Drawn up the fifth of January following by us, Jean Maury, deputy mayor of the 14th arrondissement of Paris.

On January 29, 1943, more than three weeks after Grandfather's death, I remember hearing the phone ring, followed by my mother's wail of pain from the kitchen. It was the telegram she had been dreading. She scrawled the telegram's words on a piece of yellow lined paper that had the beginnings of a grocery list. "Eating apples" is written neatly at the top in Mother's hand. The message from Reyfer, written crosswise, reads: "Profondement attristés apprenons décés Erneste Fürth sincères condolences." [Profoundly saddened, we learn of the death of Ernst Fürth. Sincere condolences.]

My sister, who was 10 at the time, remembers that my mother heated up canned potatoes with our dinner that night, an unheard-of relinquishment of culinary standards.

We have other communications that followed Ernst's death. Ella writes thanking the Reyfers for their help. My parents write to Ella thanking her for taking care of Ernst. In a letter to my parents of June 1945, Reyfer remarks that he has not heard from Ella since spring of 1943. My mother rolled her eyes as she and I read this sentence together in 1998. This was Ella all over, ever the opportunist. The Reyfers were no longer useful to her, so what was the point of writing to them? She had stayed in Angers for a time, then left for Austria, where she took up residence with her brother. She died there in 1967.

The most informative and touching of the postwar correspondence comes from Marguerite Lelièvre, Pierre's wife. Reyfer describes his friends at one point as "very well-bred people of modest circumstances, with hearts of gold, and . . . who did their utmost for your father." The letter that follows surely demonstrates many of these qualities, while offering up a summary of events along with an affectionate benediction. It was written to my mother from Paris on October 1, 1945, just a few months after the end of the war and almost exactly three years after Ernst's arrest.

> Dear Madame,
> We received your kind letter of September 14 and were very touched by the sentiments that you express. You write in French in a very clear manner, and your handwriting very much resembles Monsieur Fürth's.
>
> You ask us for details about his last moments, and I think you would also like to know about the history of all our relations with him.
>
> Our friends, Mme. and M. Reyfer, even though they lived in Switzerland during the war, remained in constant contact with us, and my husband had occasion to see them several times at Annemasse, a border town. They had often spoken to us of your dear Papa, about his troubles with the Germans, and had asked us several times to bring him packages containing sweets that we could not get in France, but that they were still able to get in Switzerland. At the end of 1941, they asked my husband to go to Angers. In addition we had an exchange of correspondence with M. Fürth for several months, but because of censorship, we could write only in very vague terms.
>
> In January 1942, my husband went to visit M. and Mme. Fürth, and we discussed their fate at length, and the possibilities for easing it. We even thought about bringing M. and Mme. Fürth to the southern zone of France, a zone called "free"

because it was not occupied by the Germans; but because of the measures taken by the Vichy government with respect to the Israelites at the request of the Germans, we gave up this project.

After this first visit to Angers, my husband, having established the best relations with M. Fürth, considered sending him things that were scarce in Angers, helped in this by our friends in Geneva. He renewed his visits in May and in September 1942, and each time he confirmed that your Papa endured his trials with great courage. Life itself at Angers flowed along pretty calmly for him; he had enough comforts, good food and comfortable enough living quarters. He had to present himself every week at police headquarters, but there he was received with deference, and in fact an officer of the French police had promised to inform him in advance if he knew of any special measure taken by the Germans concerning M. Fürth. One must understand that this measure was taken so rapidly that it was impossible to do anything at all, for on Oct. 9 in the morning, the German Gestapo presented themselves at your Papa's, asking him to follow them immediately, and that was the departure for Drancy.

Alerted by a letter from Madame Fürth, my husband, despite the difficulties that such a course presented, went to Drancy to visit Monsieur Fürth, but despite his insistence, he wasn't able to see him.

What can I tell you about life at Drancy? Your dear Papa, who never complained of his fate, however sad, told us that he did not go through actual bad treatment, but that he suffered mainly morally from the promiscuity in this camp, being mixed in with people who were unclean and uneducated. And along with that, he suffered physically, from the lack of comfort to which he had always been accustomed. He slept on the floor with only the covers that he had brought. The food was bad and insufficient. Several times my husband succeeded in getting money through to him via a cooperative French guard, and he used it to have his laundry washed by a co-detainee, and other small things of the same kind. Madame Fürth, for her part, had tried various measures to have her husband released, and finally, through the intervention of a German officer, she got your Papa released on Monday, Dec. 7, 1942. And so he arrived at our place the same evening, happy to have come out of that hell, but unfortunately in a deplorable state of health. Knowing that he was to come that evening, I had prepared a dinner to revive him. I am still moved at the joy he expressed about it that evening.

The last days that he was at Drancy, he had been transferred to the infirmary and was only sustained by injections to control his frequent attacks of angina. During the last days at Angers, Monsieur Fürth had already had some mild attacks, but at Drancy his condition became aggravated by the lack of care and the moral and physical suffering, so that at his release, he was irretrievably condemned.

He spent three days at our house, happy to find himself with us, not knowing which kindness to speak of, so happy was he to find himself free. We spoiled him as much as possible, but his condition was truly too serious. We immediately brought in a doctor who had recommended injections to sustain his heart, injections that I gave him according to the doctor's directions, but the nights were terrible, he was suffocating, it was painful to see him suffer in this way.

The last night that he spent with us was the most dreadful. The doctor had prescribed a shot every two hours, but little by little the relief this shot gave had only a very short effect, and your Papa insisted that I give it more frequently. I refused at first, but seeing his condition, I agreed to do as he wished, and I managed to keep him this whole long night that I spent at his bedside. Your dear Papa was very affectionate to me and I returned it; he treated me as his daughter. All that night he held my hand, saying: "Give me your little hand, perhaps it will have the power to bring me back to life," for he knew he was very ill, and believed that his last hour had arrived. All that long night, he never stopped speaking to me between the spasms that overtook him, speaking of his life and of his children and saying how much he loved you.

All the same that anguished night came to an end, and the next day we succeeded in getting him into the nursing home Leopold Bellau, 7 rue de Texel, Paris 14e. There he was very well taken care of, and Madame Fürth, whom we had preceded, arrived from Angers and stayed near him. My role as nurse was to go and visit him. Every day I went to see him, and despite his great weakness, he always welcomed me with open arms — until the day of his death.

What more is there to tell you, dear Madame? Your poor Papa is one of the too-numerous victims of the war. The heart ailment (angina pectoris) that felled him was certainly provoked by the worries that he had about his situation and of the impossibility of getting out of it, whereas in the rest of his life he had been able to conquer all difficulties. This illness was terribly aggravated during his stay in Drancy, and he was mortally afflicted by the time he came out.

He talked to us often of his children, of his grandchildren and was so happy when my husband sent him from Angers the photographs that you had sent via Monsieur and Madame Reyfer.

The last month of his existence, after the sufferings endured at Drancy, was sweet for him. He had a moment when he hoped he might recover and return to Angers, but this hope was short-lived; even so, he expired gently, happy to be surrounded by the affection of his wife and to have found in us two friends who did our utmost to soften his last moments.

Here you have, dear Madame, the particulars of our relations with your dear Papa. We would be very happy, my husband and I, if, as a result, we might make your acquaintance. Be assured, in any case, that we have a great esteem for your dear departed one, and that we preserve the best memories of him. It was a great heart whom we have greatly missed.

Please accept, dear Madame, our best wishes.
Marguérite Lelièvre

A lost world. Grandfather with my sister, Doris, in Sušice.

16

Tears and Afterthoughts

I DO NOT CRY EASILY ANYMORE. There was a time when tears of hurt and disappointment and anger and self-pity flowed freely—when I was a child, when I was an adolescent, when I was a young wife and mother. But somewhere along the way I hardened my heart, turned off the fountains, found a way to be, or learned at least to *appear* less vulnerable, less reachable, less movable to quick, exhausting, ego-dissolving tears. It was the women's movement of the 1970s that helped me see those tears as a defeat, as a traditional weapon that didn't work. Even worse, I began to see, it was a weapon that inflicted the most grievous wounds on the one who wielded it. In the battle of the sexes and all the other important battles, when you wept, the flag of surrender immediately shot to the top of the pole. I retreat, it said; I give up; I am a child, a weak person. Don't hurt me; take care of me. I saw my mother's tears as a cruel evasion, a way of tormenting us with what we were not responsible for: her own unhappiness, the death of her father, the loss of everything she had believed was due to her, her own displacement to a life lived among strangers.

It was about the time I was confronting the difficult adolescence of my own eldest son that I finally learned to keep back my tears, scarcely even giving them a chance to take hold. "You must cry a lot," someone said to me when I spoke of the ways in which I felt this talented boy had retreated from life. "Not anymore," I replied, realizing only then, only as I spoke, that I had, at last, put down my mother's weapon. And then, some years later, I saw that it had become almost an inability, a loss, something only too successfully suppressed. I barely wept after my father's death. I sat at his deathbed, heard him breathe his labored last and did not cry. At his memorial service in the Episcopal church, I was able to read aloud from his memoir without losing my composure. Only at home when I turned on a recording of the Fauré *Requiem* and sang with it at the top of my lungs was I able to weep, to find expression for my sorrow. It was art, film, and especially music that still allowed me to weep. Sometimes it was really powerful sex, sometimes the most banal television ads about happy families.

About halfway through the movie *Schindler's List*, I began to sob uncontrollably. I had sat through the depictions of Nazi cruelty, of humiliation, of children hiding in the ordure of a latrine. These I could stand, evidently. What reached the center of my sorrow was the moment when the list itself was read off, the list of those who were to be saved. I wept for the saved, as Primo Levi would have it, not for the drowned. I wept for myself, for my children, whose very lives were an expression of my father's stubborn choice.

I had wept too less than a year earlier in Budapest's Jewish Museum. There was nothing special about the displays there, nothing that anyone who has been around for the past 40 years has not seen many times. I had seen similar exhibits in Amsterdam a couple of years earlier, at the New York Public Library only a few months before, so often in books, and as a child after the war, as they emerged and were published in *Life* or in the movie newsreels: Here were the railroad stations with well-dressed people being herded into boxcars while jackbooted soldiers stood around looking smug and implacable. Here were the pictures of emaciated prisoners in striped garments being released from concentration camps at the end of the war; here were the piles of bodies that had been shoveled into mass graves. Some of the pictures here in Budapest were new to me: groups of young, still-healthy workers in Hungarian forced-labor camps, lined up for the camera to show how happy they were to help their German allies in the war effort.

And new to me was this particular batch of anti-Semitic propaganda: prewar posters and cartoons with captions in Hungarian showing fat, rich, huge-nosed, bejeweled Jews disporting themselves in heedless luxury while ordinary (Christian) Hungarians huddled together in the misery of economic want and winter cold. There was a copy of the fascist edict of May 10, 1944, that defined the limits of Budapest's ghetto. There was a photo of a dignified-looking gentleman, seen from the back, standing on the street reading one of those edicts. He was gray-haired and wore a dark wool overcoat, a muffler, a brimmed hat. (Why was he so warmly dressed? Had

A poster in Budapest's Jewish Museum titled "Hungarian Christmas 1937" depicts rich, heedless Jews and desperate, poor Christians.

it been a cold spring?) He could have been my grandfather. He could have been my father. We could have been the people on that railroad platform, in those striped prisoners' uniforms, in those mass graves. I don't remember consciously thinking any of those things, but suddenly the tears were streaming down my face. It was almost as though it was someone else weeping, someone else's feelings. I remember thinking: "I am weeping. Why am I suddenly doing this?" But I had to weep for those people, for the ones who were left behind. I had to weep for myself, for escaping all that.

My father did not want to talk about it. He did not want other people to talk about it. Talk about anything else—art, music, literature, philosophy, history, science, agriculture, technology, food, fashion, manners, sports. But don't talk about the destruction of a whole population, about the destruction of a small country in the center of Europe. No wailing, no keening, no vulgar displays of emotion.

Some years ago, when I told a friend with strongly mystical inclinations that

My father with my sister and me, Budapest, 1937.

I wanted to write about my family, she asked, about my father who had just died: "Do you talk to him?" Well, I said, maybe not exactly in the way you mean, but I often feel in touch with him, have a sense of his presence. This is a relatively easy matter, because I knew my father in person. I knew the way his hands trembled in his later years. I knew the sound of his voice, a little gravelly and heavily accented with his native Hungarian. I remember the smell of his Yardley shaving soap. I know that he would not eat a meal without bread, and that he tolerated green vegetables mainly as a health measure and that he liked to put apricot jam on his cornflakes. I know that he did the bridge and chess puzzles in the daily papers, and I can see his unorthodox but annoyingly effective tennis serve. I know the sorts of books he liked to read, the kinds of unmannerly behavior that irritated him and the sorts of things that made him laugh.

But how well can we know even the people we know best? Who are these people — our best friends, our spouses, our children, our parents? And what would it mean to know them fully? Many years ago, when I used to try to figure out why my children were doing what they did, another friend said about her own children: "These people are a complete mystery to me." At the time I thought she was being perverse or merely whimsical, but now I see that she was onto something important. She refused to claim an explanation even for the people she knew best. Yet she had all the novelist's material: the physical detail, the memories, the face-to-face encounters. When I try to imagine my grandfather, I can never surmount the fact that I never knew him in chronological time or tangible space. No matter how thoroughly I have studied his letters or quizzed my mother and others about him, I will never know him the way we know those we have lived with. I will never know him "in my flesh," the way the believer expects to see God.

Still, in getting to know my grandfather's letters, I have succeeded in breaking through one sort of barrier. I know how he addressed his children and a few others during his last years in exile. I know his handwriting, and the care he took with words in several languages. Letters, it's true, provide just one angle on a person. In letters, you can, to some extent, choose how to present yourself. And unless you are an utterly intemperate and passionate letter writer, you can show more wisdom, humor or forbearance than you might do in person. You can select your words more carefully than you might in the heat of anger, in the grip of fear. Yet, because few letter writers are also novelists, you probably leave out dramatic detail or dialogue. When, for example, my grandfather says, in a letter of November 13, 1939, speaking about his annoying sister-in-law, Cecile, that "Ella offers her more patience and good will than I," my curiosity is aroused: I want to know the particular forms my grandfather's impatience might have taken. I want a transcription of a conversation with Cecile. But then, because of some of my mother's recollections, I can reconstruct a little of that side of him too. Mother, unlike others in the family, was never a happy or skilled bridge player. Even so, sometimes, when there was no one else around to fill out a foursome, she found herself drafted to play. Then, she remembers, her father would say to her as she hesitated over her next move: "Make your mistake, but make it quickly!" Of course, this humorous scolding was directed at his beloved daughter; most likely the whiny Cecile was treated to something much more severe.

Pictures help too, in the absence of living memory. We have no photos of my grandfather as a young man, but I have several of him as a vigorous older man. There is a formal portrait that sat in a frame on the bureau in my mother's bedroom and now in mine, made probably about 1920, when he was in his mid-50s. It is the conventional official portrait of a European, British or American businessman of that era, the suit jacket open to show a gold watch chain traversing the vest underneath. My grandfather has a large head, with the characteristic square Fürth jaw. What remains of his hair is white, and he wears a neatly trimmed moustache. He looks directly at the camera, giving the impression of firmness, reliability, solidity. The match industry had brought prosperity to the Fürths and to Sušice for several generations, and there was no reason why it should not continue to do so. He does not smile, but there is a hint of a twinkle in his eye: "Make your mistake, but make it quickly."

There are other, more informal photos that give me a sense of this man's presence. There is one from August 1935, when he was 70 and my sister was 3. They sit together on a bench near the family tennis court in Sušice. My sister has her black hair cropped short and she sits up very straight in her flowered summer dress with its white collar. My grandfather relaxes at ease next to her, dressed in his tennis whites, short-sleeved shirt and long flannel trousers, a racket in his hand. In tennis, as in everything else he did, my mother tells me, he played to win. And although his form was imperfect because self-taught, he often won by sheer determination and tactics, making clever, well-placed, unreachable shots.

Another picture, two years later, shows Ernst and my sister, again in Sušice. This time they are striding up a long hill together. Behind them is a misty view of the valley and the mountains beyond. Sušice, with a climate much like northern New England, could be chilly even in August. Perhaps they are returning from some social event, because both of them are dressed up. Grandfather wears a suit, hat and overcoat; Dodo, her hair now longer and in pigtails tied with bows, wears a white, smocked dress with a double-breasted coat over it. She has on high-laced shoes and white socks, and she carries a bouquet of wildflowers picked on their walk. They stride along perfectly in step with each other, deep in conversation. Both of them are smiling, their coats blowing open behind them. A year later, this world was lost forever.

1998. We study inscriptions on the gravestones in the Jewish cemetery in Sušice.

17

Among Strangers

THE WEATHER WAS SO SUMMERY when my sister and I arrived in Prague on a Thursday in early September 1998 that we wondered if we'd brought enough short-sleeved T-shirts with us. A day later, when we got off the train in our mother's family homestead of Sušice, south and west of Prague, it had turned to more normal Czech weather, cool and damp. By Sunday, when we visited Sušice's two Jewish cemeteries, it was chilly and raw with a steady rain falling. We had come to this small town to pay our respects to Ernst Fürth, who is not buried in either cemetery, although his father and grandfather and their wives and children are. The visit to the cemeteries was purely private, not part of the official celebration, which had taken place the previous day in the match factory founded by Ernst's grandfather.

There were five of us: my cousins, Erna and Fredi, and Fredi's wife, Laurie Wilson, and my sister, Dodo, and me. If the skies were effusive, we were not. As befits middle-aged pilgrims, we were restrained and low-keyed. We did not weep or gnash our teeth or rend our clothing or cry out to heaven, even though there was sorrow enough behind our visit to justify such extravagant expressiveness. But if we thought about the terrible end to a life here in this wet, autumnal place, there was no talk about quieting a restless spirit or bringing peace to a wandering soul. If we were moved, we kept it to ourselves. We were serious, respectful, well behaved—people from another world, another life. We could have passed for a group of conscientious tourists from almost anywhere. Dressed sensibly for the weather with our umbrellas, raincoats, bright turquoise and green parkas and sturdy shoes, we walked through the fallen leaves and climbed up the grassy steps, calling out family names as we found them. "Look," said Erna, whose voice was still rich with the emphatic vowels and consonants of Hungarian, "Here's Marie Kaufried Fürth, Ernst's mother." Marie had died when Ernst, the youngest of her eight children, was only 11. As we wandered about these precincts—remarkable in that they had survived the official anti-Semitism of both the Nazi and Communist eras—we consulted each other about the translation of German verses inscribed on the stones, calculated the ages and relation to us of the long-dead, noted with pleasure that the cemeteries were better tended than on previous visits. All of us had been here before, but never together.

Over the gate of the older cemetery, in the semicircular space beneath the entrance arch, is an inscription on polished dark stone put there in 1992. In Czech, Hebrew, and English, it tells some of the history of the town's Jewish community. This Jewish cemetery was founded in 1626; the newer one in 1876. The last synagogue, founded in 1850, was demolished in 1964, during the Communist era. The final sentence is the most chilling: "On November 27th, 1942, the Jews of Sušice were deported to Terezin [Teresienstadt]. Almost all of them were exterminated in concentration camps." A memorial stone in the newer cemetery tells us that some of the murdered were distant relatives of ours.

Shortly after the war, our parents had visited Ernst Fürth's grave in Angers, France, but on a more recent trip there, our cousin Fredi had found that the grave was no longer marked, that it had been removed to make room for more recent remains. It was this disturbing discovery that had spurred Fredi to initiate the celebration here in Sušice. He and his sister, Erna, had arranged for a commemorative medallion of Ernst to be made into two bronze plaques, one for the museum, one for the factory. Ernst Fürth, as Fredi had said in his talk, now lies in French soil, un-acknowledged and "among strangers." It was time, he said, to bring him home. This factory, which Ernst had directed—as had his father and grandfather before him—was the right place for him to be remembered. My mother had solidly endorsed our celebration, even though, at 91, she could not travel with us. There would now be a chance for her to bury her father.

The Saturday morning event was held at the long table in the factory's conference room, adorned with Czech and American flags. The factory's directors had fully co-operated with our efforts, helping us to make contact with essential people, helping to make the scene a festive one. The table was decked out with food and drink—

open-faced sandwiches of ham and salami and cheese prettily garnished with roasted peppers and pickles, bowls of peanuts, bottles of beer and water. All the participants were properly attired for the occasion, women in dresses and suits, men in coats and ties. In brief speeches by the four grandchildren, and one sent by our mother, we honored Ernst's accomplishments as a humane and progressive industrialist and businessman, as a man who believed in the newborn Czech democracy of 1918, as a classically educated patrician who valued education for everyone—including his two daughters, mothers of the four cousins. We stood up in turn, delivering our talks a few sentences at a time so the translator, a Czech engineer friend of Fredi's, could do his work.

Also present at the event were representatives of the factory, of the town's museum and of the local secondary school, the town's young ponytailed mayor and two elderly archivists. Absent were representatives of any religious affiliation. This was a strictly secular event. No powers higher than humanity, democracy, material progress, loyalty, education or generosity were called upon. There was no priest or rabbi. The word *God* was not spoken. The word *Jewish* was not mentioned. When family members finished our speechmaking and had presented a scholarship in Ernst's name to the local secondary school, we went out into the factory's main entrance for the unveiling of a bronze plaque bearing Ernst's portrait along with a brief inscription. We toasted him with sweet, fizzy white Czech wine, and then the assembled group of about 15 proceeded to a hearty lunch in the town's best restaurant.

It was a rare convergence of the four American cousins, and we congratulated ourselves and each other on the success of the occasion and on the cordiality of the local people. Before the official celebration, the two archivists had addressed us. One spoke about the factory, one about our family's history. The director of match production, an indefatigable, wiry man, fluent in English, gave us a tour of the factory's still-profitable match-making division. Away from the official events, we returned to our roles as knowlegeable tourists, driving about the countryside in Fredi's rented car, visiting a friend's picturesque property dotted with fruit trees in the mist-covered hills, stopping at the region's oldest Romanesque church, a handsome white-washed building, in whose churchyard parishioners were tending their neatly kept family plots. Fredi and Erna, who had spent their childhood summers here, recalled riding their bikes, hiking and picnicking to some of the places we passed in the open, rolling countryside.

Next morning we went to the local museum with its displays of the history of the town's match industry. There we struggled to generate a meaningful exchange with the museum director, a round, bespectacled young woman who spoke only Czech. We took a rainy walk up to Angela Strazte, the Chapel of the Guardian Angel, which overlooks the town, and my sister and I went up Svatobor Mountain in the other direction, a hike our grandmother was said to have taken every day as part of her lifelong battle to stay slim. After my sister and I left on the train back to Prague, the other family members were given tours of the factory's outmoded, unprofitable pressed-wood fabrication works and of the well-run secondary school. The school, we agreed, had a better chance of surviving than the factory, which had been taken over by efficiency-minded owners with offices in Brno, some 200 miles away.

Business or pleasure? the immigration officials always ask as you cross the border. Pleasure, I said. I know enough not to get complicated in my answers at border crossings, an early lesson learned from my immigrant parents. But how do you define a pilgrimage of this sort? Family business, I guess you'd call it, though nothing of any economic value was transacted. And pleasure—however you define that—was really beside the point, although surely there was considerable satisfaction. We'd done our work as members of the Fürth family. We'd been dignified but not pompous. At the ceremony itself, we'd dressed elegantly but not ostentatiously. None of us had worn any of the showier pieces of the inherited family jewels. We'd worked hard with our various non-Czech languages—German, French, English—to make contact with these bright, energetic people. We'd made little jokes and proposed toasts at lunch. We wrote thank-you notes afterwards and asked the archivists for more information. We said we'd be back to hike and cross-country ski in the beautiful mountain country. No one could deny that we knew how to behave among strangers.

When we arrived back in Prague for a whirlwind day and a half to see the city, I mentioned to my sister that on our last visit there, in 1991, we had missed going into Prague's ancient and picturesque Jewish cemetery. Might we include that on our tour? "Absolutely not," was her unhesitating reply. "No more cemeteries." Time to live in the here and now. Or even make some plans for the future, visit places we've never been, where no one in our family has set foot. She has a point. Spending all that time looking over my shoulder at the past may have given me a serious crick in the neck, psychologically speaking. But obsessions are hard to shake. Something, some irrevocable need to know, some inescapable sense of loss has driven me on, has driven me back. It is terribly hard to walk away from a puzzle that still has missing pieces. For instance, I have tried to learn more about the two generous French couples who helped our grandfather survive as comfortably as he did. I have searched books and other resources about the French Resistance. Curators and archivists at the National Holocaust Museum have been helpful in steering me toward possible answers to my questions. But to learn more about who these "guardian angels" were and why they did what they did, would be, I think, a whole other project. It might involve spending serious time in archives in France. It would certainly involve a good measure of luck, since I lack anything resembling the credentials of an archival scholar.

My daughter-in-law, Mo Healy, a real historian who has written a fine book about World War I Vienna, has demonstrated to me some of the serendipity of tracking down information. When I visited her and our son Will in Vienna a few years ago, she helped me locate the former Cottage Sanatorium, the place where my grandmother Elza Fürth jumped to her death in 1931. The building still stands, but is now a residence. I took a lot of pictures, but did not try to go inside. I could tell from the outside that the second and especially the third-floor balconies were high enough off the ground that anyone jumping would succeed in her goal.

Then, a few weeks after my return, I received an e-mail from Will, saying that Mo was sending me something. Indeed she did. It was a photocopy of a beautiful booklet, printed in 1909, extolling the aesthetic, therapeutic and culinary benefits of the newly opened Cottage Sanatorium in the treatment of all sorts of illnesses, including "nervous" ones. The booklet, with its color lithographs, had, as Mo said, "fallen out of a box" of unrelated items she was looking at in Vienna's police archives. It was a wonderful gift, an utterly surprising and unlooked-for discovery, one that no effort of mine could have duplicated.

Still, in smaller and larger ways, my search continues. In the summer of 1999, Bill and I spent a week in France visiting Arcachon and Angers, two of the places that my grandfather and his wife lived during their French exile. Both of these are perfectly reasonable places for a tourist to visit: Arcachon is a quiet resort town on the Atlantic coast. And Angers, situated on the western edge of the Loire's chateau country, has a spectacular fortress and fine displays of tapestries. We rented a car and stopped in a few other towns on the Loire, then drove down the coast. I did not add significantly to my knowledge in either place, but I wanted to have a chance to walk the ground, look up the addresses where my grandfather lived, look at the front doors, look out at the views, try to see something of what they saw, imagine how they might have lived. I found those houses, but I did not find any missing pieces of the puzzle. I gathered impressions, took photographs, kept a journal and picked up a few stones and shells to bring home.

Simon Schama, in his book *Dead Certainties (Unwarranted Speculations)*, ponders the "habitually insoluble quandary of the historian: how to live in two worlds at once; how to take the broken, mutilated remains of something or someone from the 'enemy lines' of the documented past and restore it to life or give it a decent interment in our own time and place." Historians, says Schama, are "doomed to be forever hailing someone who has just gone around the corner and out of earshot." I make no claim to be a historian, and would not presume to provide explanations about the past. What I seek is understanding, mainly the private sort that can be gained from revisiting family stories, from combing through my own and others' recollections, from studying the written word and from visiting places.

Why do I visit? Why does anyone? Location, location, location. The measure of real estate's value, the pilgrim's justification. This is the very spot where General Wolfe died. In this room William James lectured on pragmatism. Here, at this zebra crossing on Abbey Road, the Beatles marched across the street. Here is where the Allies landed in France. And this is the house where my grandfather spent his last months before being imprisoned in Drancy. The pilgrimage is a way of offering homage to the past. The pilgrim hopes to absorb some of the aura of the saint, to assuage suffering, to gain a blessing, perhaps even to find a cure for her own mortal ills.

PHOTOGRAPH BY HANS AND NICK TEENSMA

18

Postlude

BUT MORTAL ILLS HAVE NO CURES, it turns out. All flesh is as the grass. The only treatments are palliative—the lessening of pain, the calming of fears. And although the ghosts of the past can seem fearsome to those of us in the midst of life, the hallucinations that precede death are not always frightening. In the bedroom of her condo in Amherst a few weeks before she died, Mother asked me to pick some cherries from a nearby tree. There were no cherries, no trees, except for the maples outside her window, but of course I said I would do my best. She seemed satisfied with my words. The imagined scene must have been from some happy moment in her life, and it was more vivid to her than the hospital bed in which she was spending her days. She was still wearing her pretty white flannel Lanz nightgown with the small flowered pattern that my sister had given her, but now that she was bedridden, it had been cut open in the back so that she could be turned and bathed more easily.

Mostly she was lucid and had recently recounted to me a dream she'd had in which she was going to the bathroom in the dining room of the Hotel Baur au Lac in Zurich, an elegant hotel she and my father had often stayed in. She laughed playfully at the implausible waywardness of this situation, then quizzed me about her current physical capacities: Why did she have a catheter? Because she was not able to urinate on her own. Could she eat and drink? Yes. Move her bowels? (*Stuhl machen?* she asked in German.) Yes, I said. Was she dying? I gasped inwardly at this addition to her mundane catalogue, but the hospice nurses had reassured me about giving honest answers to such questions. Yes, I said, she was dying. She accepted this peacefully. I was the one who wept.

Appendix

CAST OF CHARACTERS

MY FAMILY: PERLS

My father, George Perl, born Budapest 1895, died Amherst, Mass., 1988.

My mother, Eva (Fürth) Perl, born Vienna 1907, died Amherst, Mass, 2003.

My sister, Doris (Perl) Ablard, born Budapest 1932, living in Alexandria, Va., married to Charles Ablard.

Me, Marietta (Perl) Pritchard, born Budapest 1936, living in Amherst, Mass., married to Bill Pritchard.

The Perl family came to the U.S. in April 1939; spent a year in Evanston, Ill., settled in Scarsdale, N.Y., in 1941.

MY MOTHER'S FAMILY: FÜRTHS

My maternal grandfather, Ernst Fürth, born Bohemia 1865, died Paris 1943; head of Solo Corporation, match manufacturing founded by his grandfather Bernard in 1843.

My maternal grandmother, Elza (Roheim) Fürth, born Budapest 1877, committed suicide Vienna 1931.

Ernst Fürth's second wife, Ella (Pollak) Siebert Fürth, whom he married in 1936, and who came with him to France during the war. Died in Vienna 1967.

My mother's sister, Gretl (Fürth) Strasser (1899–1979); her husband, Paul; their children Erna (1924–2002) and Fredi (Alfred) (b. 1927); came to this country in 1939 (Paul in 1941).

Ernst Fürth's sister-in-law, Cecile Fürth, his brother's widow, who came with Ernst and Ella to France during the war, died in Angers August 1942.

Cecile's children, Mädy Redlich, who came to the U.S., and Paul Fürth, who went to England during the war.

MY FATHER'S FAMILY: PERLS AND GUTTMANNS

My father's siblings:
His sister, Klári, later Clary (Perl) Svéd, who spent the war in Budapest, came to the U.S. with her son, Paul, after the war.

His half brother Imre, later Eric, Guttmann, who, with his wife, Lilly, came to this country about the same time as my parents. Imre joined my father in various agricultural enterprises.

His half brother Robert "Berti" Guttmann, who spent the war in Budapest, then lived in Switzerland, England, and eventually, the U.S.

OTHER IMPORTANT CHARACTERS

Frederic and Angèle Reyfer, French citizens living in Switzerland, working for the Allies, part of the Resistance, we believe, who made it possible for my grandfather keep in touch with his family after the German occupation of France, and who helped him in countless other ways.

Pierre and Marguerite Lelièvre, Parisians, friends of the Reyfers, who kept an eye on Grandfather after he and Ella moved to Angers, trying to keep him safe, who helped release him from Drancy, and who cared for him after he was freed.

Frank C. Wright, American friend of my parents, businessman, part of FDR's Brain Trust; had met Grandfather and my mother when visiting Czechoslovakia in the '20s; sponsored my parents' immigration, then helped them in many ways after they came to this country, especially in the effort to bring Grandfather out of France, then later when there were problems about sending him money.

Family Photographs

1.) Eva Perl with granddaughters Cecilia (left) and Elisabeth Hoff 2.) Eva Perl 3.) Klári, later Clary, (Perl) Svéd 4.) Robert "Berti" Guttmann 5.) Soma Perl with his children, Klári and George, about 1900 6.) Lenke (Lederer) Perl, later Guttmann, George, Klári, Imre and Robert's mother 7.) Paul Strasser with his children, Fredi and Erna.

1.) *From left, George Perl, Doris Perl, Ernst Fürth, Ella (Pollak) Siebert Fürth 2.) Gretl Strasser and Eva Perl 3.) Imre, later Eric, Guttmann with daughter Tilly 4.) Doris Perl, Fredi Strasser, Erna Strasser, Eva Perl, Gretl Strasser 5.) Eva and George Perl 6.) Eva and George Perl.*

1.) Bill Pritchard and Marietta Perl 2.) Standing, Doris Ablard, George Perl, Marietta Pritchard; seated, Bill Pritchard, Eva Perl, Charles Ablard 3.) Doris Perl, Budapest, 1937 4.) Paul Svéd and Erna (Strasser) Neumann de Vegvar 5.) Charles Guttmann 6.) Charles and Doris Ablard 7.) Fredi Strasser 8.) Doris Ablard, Marietta Pritchard 9.) Marietta Pritchard 10.) Doris Ablard

1

2

3

1.) Top row: Jennifer Ablard, Cecilia Hoff, Lisa Nicholas, Elisabeth Hoff, Jonathan Ablard, Charles Ablard, Doris Ablard, Marci LeFevre; front row: Alan Hoff, Delia Ablard, Katie Ablard, Evan LeFevre 2.) Charles, Katie, Doris, Jennifer and Jonathan Ablard 3.) David Pritchard, Will Pritchard, Katie Ablard, Jonathan Ablard, Jennifer Ablard, Michael Pritchard.

1.) Lisa Nicholas, Jonathan Ablard, Delia Ablard 2.) Elisabeth Hoff, Jennifer Ablard, Cecilia Hoff, Alan Hoff 3.) Delia Ablard, Jonathan Ablard 4.) Evan LeFevre 5.) Marci LeFevre, Evan LeFevre, Katie Ablard.

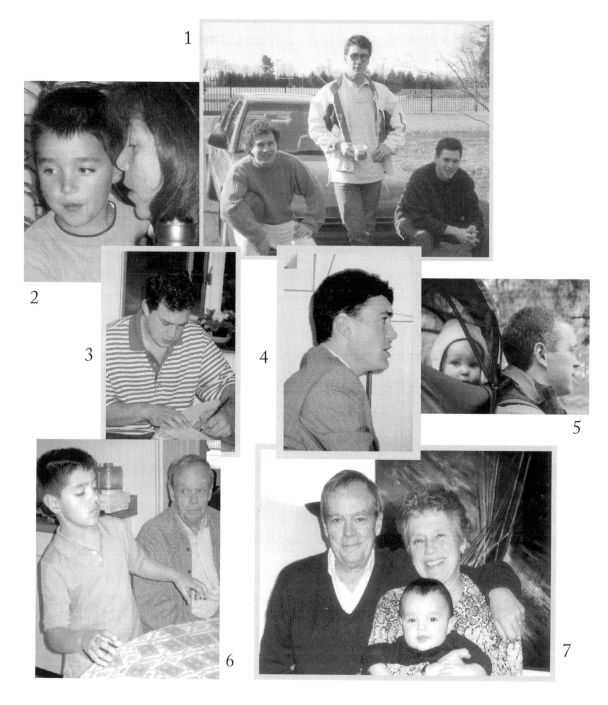

1.) Michael, David and Will Pritchard 2.) David O. and Maria Pritchard 3.) Michael Pritchard 4.) David Pritchard 5.) Ava and Will Pritchard 6.) David O. and Bill Pritchard 7.) Bill, Marietta and David O. Pritchard.

1.) *Ava Pritchard* 2.) *Michael Pritchard with Kirby and Lulu* 3.) *Mo Healy and George Pritchard*
4.) *George, Ava and David O. Pritchard* 5.) *David O., Maria and David Pritchard* 6.) *George,*
Will and Ava Pritchard, Mo Healy 7.) *Marietta, David, Will, Mike, Bill Pritchard* 8.) *George Pritchard*

Text set in Adobe Caslon Pro 11.5/16

Designed by James McDonald,

JAMESMCDONALDBOOKS.COM

Published by The Impress Group, Northampton, Massachusetts.

First paperback edition

ISBN 978-1-4507-1040-4

PRINTED IN U.S.A.